Not One Sparrow

Estelle

with affectionate greetings

& warmest good wishes

Ronald Smythe

April 04

Not One Sparrow

Ronald Smythe

Pentland Books
Edinburgh • Cambridge • Durham • USA

For Wynn, my wife
unique partner in leisure and work
an unfailing friend and joy

First published in 2001 by
Pentland Books
1 Hutton Close
South Church
Bishop Auckland
Durham

British Library Cataloguing in Publication Data.
A Catalogue record for this book is available
from the British Library.

ISBN 1 85821 875 6

Typeset by CBS, Martlesham Heath, Ipswich, Suffolk
Printed and bound by Antony Rowe Ltd., Chippenham

CONTENTS

LIST OF ILLUSTRATIONS

FOREWORD

This is an important book; it is the autobiography of a very gifted priest who, having faced considerable personal and professional challenges, went on to master the craft of psychotherapy and create a counselling service in the context of a busy parish life.

Canon Ronald Smythe has had a most illuminating life, punctuated by work in the Middle East, especially the Holy Land, and shorter stays in South Africa, other African countries, India, Sri Lanka, New Guinea and the Antipodes. This is no mere account of travel excursions but a keen analysis of regional attitudes to life and relationships with neighbouring countries, seen through the eyes of a compassionate, intelligent Anglican priest. The chapters describing his pastoral ministry show the round of parish work in parts of Essex, and the gradual transition to counselling practice is fascinating to behold. Ronald Smythe's life has been one of unremitting service in an ecumenical setting – laced with humour. May what he has achieved be augmented by other Christian ministers who are able to combine skilled counselling with running a parish.

MARTIN ISRAEL

DR MARTIN ISRAEL
Well-known pathologist, co-author of the classic work *General Pathology*, speaker on the frontiers of medicine and spirituality, writer on mysticism and contemplative prayer, Anglican Priest and spiritual director.

In a dissolving
world what certainties
for the self, whose identity
is its performance?
You have no address,
says life, and your destination
is where you began.
But love answers it
in its turn: I am old now and have died
many times, but my rebirth is surer
than the truth embalming itself
in the second law of your Thermo-Dynamics.

R. S. Thomas The Echoes Return Slow p. 33 (Papermac)

It's marvellous to have the possibility of being a real person; not bits
and pieces of other people

(Remark made by a male client aged about 29)

Not one sparrow shall fall to the ground without your Father's knowledge

(Matthew 10:29)

PREAMBLE

'Books are a mighty bloodless substitute for life' says Thomas Carlyle, so why add to their number? My excuse is that an inner pressure of words and pictures from the past has built up, and is crying out to be understood. I need to write for my own comfort and would be sad if at the end it must be said: 'We had the experience but missed the meaning.'[1] Moreover, the practice of psychotherapy over the last thirty years has led me to believe that 're-owning' past feeling and experience is both liberating and healing. Once you reach the seventies there's a desire for greater clarity about the past and the hope of some final healing. Looking back may not promote peace of mind: it is risky but could be creative.

Recently I learnt from the American classicist Bernard Knox[2] that the Greeks did not 'face the future'; they believed you should go backwards into it. According to George Steiner[3] a similar attitude is embedded in the languages of Latin-American aboriginals: 'what is yet to happen is set at the back of the speaker. The past which he can see, because it has already happened lies before him'. The Oxford Companion to the Bible has an almost identical point: 'The past is what lies ahead (Hebrew *quedem*) and is therefore known: the future is unknown and is behind.'[4]

Thomas Curran, whose article in the Oct. '98 issue of *Modern Believing* opened my eyes to this early mindset neatly sums it up: 'Our future lies in the more certain recovery of what we have been and what we are.' Could I have a better reason for undertaking memoirs? So, recovering something of what I have been in order to know better what I am and could yet be, is hardly a bloodless substitute for living. I hope it will be a flesh and blood re-entry into the warm-blooded, and at times 'bloody', reality from which I have emerged.

---

[1] T S Eliot
[2] *Backing into the Future* (London WW Norton '94) p. 11
[3] *Language & Silence – Essays 1958-60* (Faber '67) p.85
[4] *Oxford Companion* (OUP '93) p. 743

PART I

CHAPTER I

FAMILIES

The baby that arrives seeming to be all future and no past, is already a creature of history. Whatever its parents have been and are, immediately shapes a child as strongly as its genes. I arrived when my hole-in-heart brother was terminally ill, my parents anxious and already half bereft, my mother barely out of her teens. Another son had to be welcomed and family resources stretched to meet the cost of the extra nursing. Years later I recovered a strong recollection of longing for, indeed vociferously demanding, a beautiful little mother who could not be at hand. I had already heard how often 'pramming' out in the garden was my fate and my father said: 'However thoroughly I tightened up the screws attaching the hood to the body of the pram; you always managed to work them loose, so it collapsed.' The satisfying crunch must have expressed a powerful protest.

My dad, Eric Smythe (born 1887) was the second son, and followed the profession of his father, Arthur, as a consultant engineer. They came from the younger branch of Smythes who had left Rosedale, a Yorkshire valley below the magenta stretches of heather near Lastingham[5] for the emerald acres of Co. Antrim, NE Ireland where the first Smyth (*sic*) died in Ballymacash. There his son Ralph became a well-known and successful tanner, dying at Lisburn in 1689, and from him Dame Ethel Smyth, composer of operas and orchestral works, and my own forebears were descended. His eldest boy, William, became Bishop of Kilmore and Ardagh, married the daughter of a Chief Justice of the King's bench and bought land round the attractive Lough Lene in County West Meath. There at Colinstown, near Mullingar, his son, William, built a fine Georgian house,[6] named Barbavilla after his

---

[5] Beautiful Yorkshire Wolds village with ancient Saxon church. Originally the home of St Cedd

[6] Ingoldsby Lyster Smythe sold it in 1955.

wife Barbara Ingoldsby, sister of another Chief Justice. His grandson, though a layman, was known in his time as Billy the Saint, particularly respected for his refusal to treat Irish people in the rough and tyrannical manner that was then all too common, and for his just and lovable nature. In a letter to his father he complains of the King's and the government's failure to address the real grievances of the people. His third son, Henry, was my father's grandfather and my mother's great-grandfather.

'No wonder you're odd,' commented a candid school friend. I'd been attempting to explain my family. It was odd enough that my parents were first cousins once removed (who ever grasps the 'once removed' bit?), and therefore my paternal great-grandfather was also my maternal great-great-grandfather, colourfully known as Tiger Smythe[7]. What provoked the comment was that I added for good measure that my mother's parents both had the same step-mother. This doesn't in fact make them blood relations, though it explains how they were initially thrown together. (After losing his first wife Ingoldsby Smythe remarried, a widow who already had a son. That son eventually married Ingoldsby's daughter by his first wife.)

However, in seeking to recover the feeling of the Smythe family I sense a whiff of in-breeding, common, I believe, in Irish Protestant 'gentry'. It may account for my almost obsessional interest in genealogy. Our nursery was plastered with extensive charts of the royal families of Europe – arising in part from the history I was reading, and perhaps in part from a refined snobbery that hung around the family – refined, because it wasn't tastelessly intrusive; just taken for granted that we knew distinguished people (very few in fact); that we were descended from the Plantagenets (as half the population of England), and were 'gentry' (barely). Add to this our classy form of the name 'Smith' and my being saddled with two ponderous family names, Ingoldsby and Meade,[8] it all illustrates the classic principle that 'families muck you up'. Those names hung like an albatross about my neck from the time I revealed them unguardedly at school.

My first name too was initially a source of family controversy. Dad had registered me as Graham. Why he chose this name in preference to the family

---

[7] He was mauled by a tiger while serving in India (at first under Arthur Wellesley, later Duke of Wellington). He bore deep claw marks on his shoulder and back for the rest of his life. (S. Penny. *Smythe of Barbavilla*. priv. pub. p.127). He married his first cousin once removed, Frances Cooke, when she was 18 and he was 49, and had 12 children.

[8] Meade – from a forebear who lost a lot of money racing horses.

names William, Ralph, Henry and Richard I have no idea: but in the event it was found to be unsatisfactory. Ronald was put forward for the christening, but even on the way to church discussion was lively, my prospective godmother, great aunt Nell, going so far as to venture a total novelty, Bonaventura (her favourite Franciscan saint). At this, I suspect, the family closed ranks and settled for Ronald unaware of the strange significance attached to the name Bonaventura to be revealed at a later date. All of which goes to confirm Marshall McLuhan's dictum: 'The name of a man is a numbing blow from which he never recovers.'

Eric's father, Arthur, and his family, had very nearly failed to recover from a life-threatening blow. When he was a comparatively young man Arthur contracted lung TB and was not expected to live. His wife Alice refused to accept the death sentence and promptly transported the whole family to Davos believing that the Swiss air would cure him. After eighteen months in bed it did. Settling in the mountains by Davos' icy blue lake, Eric and Gordon skiied to school from the Platz to the Dorf and back each day while their father slowly recovered his full health. He became known as the 'Davos Miracle' and lived to the good age of sixty-eight. The enterprising and courageous Alice saw the boys into their careers, Gordon in the Burma Rifles of which he became Colonel, and my father via Lausanne Gymnase and Heidelberg University, to qualify as a Civil Engineer, and later achieving the equivalent in Mechanical and Electrical Engineering[9]. I remember Alice's lively, petite figure dripping with beads, necklaces and bangles. She died when I was five.

Mother was the daughter of a Cotswold vicar, William Frank Curtoys, and the youngest of four, with three lively brothers. She partly avoided their mild oppression by horse riding and boarding school where she did well enough to be considered for university. However, while out a-hunting, her dashing cousin claimed her: they both loved horses and by the age of three I was in the saddle on large and mainly docile hacks. At six I was given my own pony Bubbles, and rode him in the Richmond Horse Show in 1933. (The family horse-riding saga led to my sister Pat's international fame.) Marrying at nineteen a man of thirty-seven, mother was nearly as junior to her husband as she was senior to me, and the death of her firstborn made me an object of exceptional affection. As I grew older my arthritic father aged more rapidly,

---

[9] i.e. he acquired membership of the Associations of Civil, Electrical & Mechanical Engineering.

throwing into relief Monica's equality with her children, much of her lively behaviour having a brightly adolescent quality, perhaps arising from an unconscious desire to retain the youthful carefree-ness of the years she had mortgaged to early marriage. Maddeningly erratic, unpunctual and impulsive, she nonetheless possessed my heart.

My father, though also warm-hearted, was meticulous, well organized, emotionally restrained and practical. He once confessed to me that he had spent hours of tongue-biting frustration either waiting for Monica or adapting to her unpredictable ways; but he loved her very much. His wary attitude to life was summed up by the name he gave our first home: Quien Sabe, the Spanish for Who Knows? As a child I think I loved and admired him dearly, but I recollect his somewhat closed-up feeling. Now I attribute this to four years' painful wartime experience followed a few years later by the shattering loss of his eldest son, Richard, whose character was similar to his own. He was left with a younger son whose character and interests were different, and I sense that this was a disappointment too.

Richard, usually referred to as 'Little Dick', was born with a chronic heart weakness. Early photographs show a sensitive, thoughtful little person viewing the world reflectively. I am 15 months younger but look a lot stronger and more lively. My father once referred with some poignancy to the remembered contrast between the immobile Dick and the almost hyperactive younger baby. My mother kept a diary of Dick's last weeks: in early November 1926 she wrote:

> I had them both in the warm nursery, Dick quite bright but looked very tired. Got cross with them as they both shouted at me for food – the first time they'd had a meal together for a whole fortnight.

inserted later:

> The last meal my two dear little men had together.

The diary continues:

> Eric came in after squash and I showed him Dick – temperature up. R full of beans, of course . . . Up all night with D and comforted him. He loves me holding him – my last night alone in charge of my darling.

4th. Dr thought him very bad and had a 'serious talk' with me, quite unnecessary and most upsetting . . . D very swollen eyes and bad pneumonia. Dr pleased with Ronald who shook hands and made friends. Eric fetched oxygen cylinders . . . where will it end? D has given so many frights and always pulled round in such a marvellous way. 5th. Fireworks all around, but he didn't seem to mind them . . . Little blue-backed Mason Pearson baby brush came for Dick and he loved it . . . soothed him when restless . . . Sunday 7th. Nurse went to early service, I to Matins . . . Dick a little better. We went to theatre as guests of G.A.

The next few days Dick was

very washed out . . . I longed to hug him . . . Little Ronald just saw him, but Dick did not feel up to him so took him out again. Armistice Day . . . so thankful Dick has so far been spared. Bought poppies – rather sad . . . while nurse rested I looked after the little man . . . he loved me to jump up and down, I played with ping pong ball and he laughed.

Monica's mother arrived out of the blue having sensed something wrong; but she had bronchitis and had to be nursed and returned to a hotel. Then the diary records:

Black figure by the cotside, I had a <u>feeling</u>, I could not bear it. That night really <u>terrible</u> . . . Dickie choking attack . . . Nov 21st. Dr came . . . I heard conversation with E, said he'd never had any hope . . . I felt very frightened, tho' one had known . . . made me realize how afraid of a shock one is . . . sweet little man was so good.

Next day:

Mother arrived . . . still very seedy, came and sat in the sick room with me.

Later:

altho' so weak D is wonderfully bright and quite on the spot, but his heart not working properly.

9

Digitalis was prescribed and the doctor thought Dick was fighting hard, but his temperature crept up from 102° to over 104° and leeches were prescribed to relieve the lungs.

> E hopped into the car in search of these horrid things, and returned with two . . . had to find three more. Eric and I feeling pretty blue; went for a walk along Beverley Brook as I did the day he was born [*sic*] . . . and into Richmond Park to help blow away the clouds. Returned and little Dick took 2oz of Bengers from me, I was so pleased . . . then I said to Nurse 'his breathing is all wrong,' it was so laboured . . . then I saw his eyes turn up . . . E dashed for more oxygen, I took the horrid leech off my sweet little man . . . I told Nurse to go for her bath, and then saw the end was coming . . . I held my little man's hand and called hopelessly for her. She came rushing back and moistened his lips with brandy but it was no use. I felt I just wanted him to go peacefully and untroubled. He was so plucky . . . It was just 5.00 p.m and the little man, my darling little Dick, shut his eyes and gradually, gradually ceased to breathe, lying there so still, but with a look of heavenly calm on his sweet face – no hint of pain or care was there on that little angel face . . . but I knew that little Dick himself had gone away . . . the spirit left that little body only a yard or so from the spot where 2½ years ago he was born. Now he was born again into happiness, but what a helpless feeling, left behind, with a great gap . . . he'd been such a loveable and affectionate little charge to care for . . . such patience and pluck in suffering . . . we went and hugged Ronald who had been sent to be a comfort to us, we felt sure . . . so cheerful and unconscious of it all – a ray of sunshine.

So my earliest vocation was 'to be a comfort': but the assumption that I was 'unconscious of it all' received a striking challenge forty or so years later. The Clinical Theology Centre was trying to help with my chronic headaches and migraine and had set up some group therapy: I was lying on the floor surrounded by group members when I suddenly heard myself saying very bitterly: 'They are all grieving him, and have their backs to me, they think I am not dreadfully sad he has gone. They think I have no feeling!' Then I wept for the infant who had left me; anger and loneliness surged up. How can people say that 'babies are too young to know grief'? Later, a clear and conscious memory is of playing chords on the piano – I had begun lessons when about six. I am making up a tune and intoning words of a story about the death of a little boy. My sister (aged three or four perhaps) is with me and has been reduced to tears. I am impressed by the effect this musical drama has upon her and upon myself. Throughout childhood music would continue to express the pain and drama of life.

Music had come through Monica, who played piano, violin and flute: my father had tried the cello for a time. Monica sang beautifully, a very true, boy-like tone, and as we grew up, songs round the piano were fun. Her father was a pianist but had ceased to practise and usually strummed. Even young children must have some taste, for I disliked the banal strumming and 'breaking' of chords whenever he played. Unfortunately I became a strummer too, though I called it 'improvisation' and perhaps it was harmonic exploration too. This grandfather, Frank Curtoys, and his wife Charlotte, having retired from a Cotswold parish came to live in a pleasant Georgian house opposite Henrietta Park in Bath. He read widely and listened to symphony concerts on his crystal wireless. He showed interest in my music and my use of words: we enjoyed chatting together, but he was not pleased when I disturbed a 'wireless concert' by detaching an external wire from his set to the garden railings and burying it in the flower bed – I'd been told it was the 'earth'. My grandmother did the scolding, but I loved her 'matriarchal' qualities and was distressed by my grandparents' frequent disagreements. He became quite depressed, and I recall his strangely despairing repetition of 'Oh, dear!' which punctuated our meals together.

Early memories of depressed people linger quite strongly. My father and I were walking on Barnes Common opposite our second home. I loved the bracken and the wild spaces, using as temporary homes and fortresses the great spreading, umbrella-like trees. I wanted to show him a special stronghold where I 'reigned over' my younger friends, and walked through the hanging branches to find a plump woman sitting on a small wooden crate, disconsolate and bedraggled, in a sea of discarded fruit and vegetables, orange peel, tomatoes, bits of bread and other debris as though she had thrown them away in a frenzy of life-rejecting despair. Instantly I felt aware of the heavy misery of her humped-up posture and hopeless gaze.

My grandfather's wretchedness was all the harder to understand when compared with my mother's warm, almost radiant, joyful and very active Christian faith, which I assumed had come from him. Her courage in the face of bereavement all arose from a resolute trust. She frequently spoke of Dick as safe in God's hands and later we used to discuss how he would be growing up as a person in some special heavenly way. I used sometimes to get irritated by these references to someone of immense importance to her to whom I did not really know how to relate and who had 'got in before me'. . . . You cannot compete with the dead; and it was important to me that I stood high in mother's favour. It reminded me that I was ineluctably and immutably my parents' second, and not their oldest son. Perhaps too there was guilt that I had supplanted him. From early days I was seeking a replacement for him, and the search for a close friend was dominant throughout childhood. Indeed the emotional urgency of the search could frighten off its objects and the strength of the need and desire was too often self-defeating.

The drama of Dick's death may also have been behind an early fascination with the past. Before I was aged seven I had asked for a 'proper history book' and been given Arthur Ransome's *History of England.* It became well-read and was followed by historical tales and novels. I think in this I was encouraged by Grandfather Curtoys, with his penchant for study, and his book-lined home was a favourite resort. Evidently I wanted to travel into the future with a lively appreciation of the historical past. I loved Bath and within a few years mother was sending me down to stay with them, despatched by Great Western Railway with an addressed label round my neck 'In the care of the guard'. (Who would dare to do this today?) It was immensely exciting and I recall the guard demonstrating the function of immense levers in his cab at the back of the train. Revisiting Bath many years later, the experience of the train's arrival, snaking into the platform raised high above the surrounding houses, terraces of Georgian crescents rising layer upon layer on Lansdown, had so vivid an impact that I might have been a six or seven year old again. As a boy I was enchanted by the stately squares and buildings around the Pump Room, the Roman Baths (real history), Milsom Street and supremely Bath Abbey, which was the subject of an earliest attempt at verse. When in hospital at an unhappy time, occupational therapy consisted of an attempt to model the abbey in clay.

My grandmother took me to her very High Church eucharist at Bathwick, but I decided quite soon that this was not the religion for me. Early on I seem to have had the rudiments of a practical theology. I was sure about God: it might be said that for me the answer to my father's question, Who knows? was firmly, He knows, for (whether as a convenient cop-out or an expression of conviction) when I was adjured before one of our motoring expeditions to give notice of feeling unwell I retorted, 'Only God knows when I'm going to be sick'. My mother's Jesus attracted more ambivalent feelings, because she would respond to my bad behaviour by the reproof, 'Jesus wouldn't have done/said that'; and I came heartily to resent this paragon. Unfortunately, the name has continued to elicit 'negative vibes' and I tend to prefer 'Christ' without in any way depreciating his thorough-going humanity.

To review: facing the remote and early years, what becomes clear as I back into the future? The original closeness of a loving foursome shattered by death? Finding myself wounded through loss, yet designated a helper and comforter? The resulting strength of love between mother and son? Turning to music, history and in time, to my parents' Christian faith as resources for personal growth and reinforcement? The emotional search for whole-hearted friendship? Reviewing a child's response to the challenges of *school* will perhaps make clearer the springs of personality as they begin to break out and flow.

CHAPTER II

SCHOOLS

'It has a beautiful chapel,' said mother in a comforting voice. Just eight years old and on my way to the unknown challenge of boarding school, I was uncertain how reassuring this sounded. However, there was something God-given about our arrival. Motoring through the deep-banked lanes in the hills by the Lea Valley, my father had got lost. About to lapse into confusion, we saw a recognizably uniformed boy wave to us from a passing car, signalling that we should follow his parents. This was Arthur; promptly and for five years he became my hero and friend. Luckily he had a phlegmatic and kind-hearted temperament, able to endure my expectations, though being a year senior he was not one of the everyday mob. These engulfed me in a bewildering succession of tests and traps – routine and ritual law had to be learnt, the shame of sheer ignorance, eg, not knowing how to handle herrings at breakfast, having to respond only to surnames, and being subject to fearsomely large boys called Prefects: not to mention the hazards of bullying, and the chanting of the heavy family names in deafening mockery.

Later aggravation arose from my mother Monica, 'looking far too young and girlish', an accusation I levelled at her on an early visit to school. This had become more grist to the teasing. (The issue resurfaced when I took her to Italy in 1949, and was mistaken for her husband. 'Will the signor wait for the signora?') But she did appreciate the young schoolboy's need for a fairly matriarchal mother, and behaved tactfully when visiting school. The only hiccup occurred when she became a VAD nurse a year or two before the war and wrote 'Shall I come in my uniform or in mufti?' to which I replied, 'Come in neither! For heaven's sake wear your ordinary clothes.' To my young ears, mufti sounded dangerously exotic.

The Headmaster of Bengeo School was a large man called Captain Lyon, who was given to beating his boys. Scruples, of which I for one was quite unaware, compelled him once to write to my parents apologizing for whacking me without good cause. Reluctant perhaps to undermine the establishment, my father did not tell me until much later. I gave Captain Lyon no credit, and when his school went bankrupt two years later, my unconscious devised a strangely effective revenge. In the school with which we had amalgamated (Fonthill in the Ashdown Forest region) my taste for drama was developing. I had written and produced a play entitled 'The Ghost of the Earl of Rutland'. The school was invited to see it performed in the gym-hall, staff and pupils alike. Captain Lyon lived outside the school building and by an oversight received no invitation. The following day he arrived in the staffroom to hear all about 'Smythe's play'. He was hurt and indignant.

Singing in the 'beautiful chapel' was an agreeable alternative to the schoolroom jungle, but friendship was the chief sweetener. Arthur was a protector in the wings, only once seriously appealed to after a severe 'going over'. Then he sensibly encouraged me to explain that I hated hitting back to defend myself physically. I realized my tendency to passive resistance rather than the use of fists seemed only to encourage more baiting. Surprisingly the tormentors came to appreciate my dislike of violence. The friendships themselves were quite intense and attracted ribald comment; a strong focus of affection was somehow compulsive whether it was Harry, Derek or the plump Whitsun-Jones brothers, the younger of whom gently enlightened me about the facts of life. Some years later it was a delight to see his older brother as the beadle in the London production of *Oliver*. The chapel too made me think: visiting speakers could be quite arresting and I was profoundly moved by Kennedy Cox when he came to speak about the Dockland Settlement and conditions in the East End.

The same year I began boarding school we had moved home from the fairly box-like rows of East Sheen housing to a charming detached house at the end of a cul-de-sac near Barnes Common. My father used an imaginative garden designer to develop an attractive quarter-acre walled garden; an idyllic playground for Pat and myself – she usually making the dogs jump over obstacle courses; I attempting to engage her in some elaborate and often dramatic game. A loggia was built in front of the sitting room from which my parents could watch our games, and upon which the latest play would be produced. One day a new bicycle was placed upon it for my birthday, and led to long excursions over the Common lanes and up to Putney Heath – safe enough in those days. In the playroom upstairs I constructed vast genealogical tables or sat at the desk control panel I had made in school carpentry, linked to lights and bells and buzzers all over the place. In the sitting room I was often seated at the Steck Baby Grand my mother had bought with a £100 family bequest, practising, improvising and trying to write music. Sometimes mother played and we sang Irish songs like 'Kathleen Mavourneen', or the latest Noel Coward hits like 'I'll see you again'. I relished the sentiment. During the holidays I found a young neighbour called Joy. Her company was blessedly tranquil, but she had to be caught up in drama too – together we arranged a wedding ceremony in elaborate costume. Less tranquil, but more immediate feminine company was provided in the family next door, most particularly the girl called June, who is now Jill Freud, and a 'dramatic neighbour' each year in the Southwold Summer Theatre. Last year I learnt from Jill that she had asked Pat to teach her netball (climbing over the wall for lessons) and was charged 6d a lesson!

The most acute experience of the first school was a master's reading of John Keats' 'Ode to a Nightingale'. I cannot have been more than nine years old when this reading transported me into another land of heightened and entranced perception. All was light and beauty, my surroundings mysteriously fell away giving place to a sense of total bliss, peace and delight; in a shimmering world of profound meaning the words are a gateway into an eternal present until they 'toll me back . . . to my sole self . . . Was it a vision or a waking dream? . . . Do I wake or sleep?' Awareness of the experience never departed, and could be secretly recovered as a consolation or inspiration all through my young days. Half consciously it raised the question in my mind: Is this what heaven is really about, in contrast to the relative tedium of church and the severe moral demands of adults in the name of religion? How reassuring if it were. The poem also expressed the poignant, bitter-sweet quality of human relationships, heightened by the experience of boarding school; a sense of life as gift and loss, with its roots perhaps in the experience of Little Dick. Did this find echoes in the poet who is 'half in love with easeful death', and ready 'to cease upon the midnight without pain'? Feeling crushed by a bullying prep school and deprived of loving and adored parents, my heart certainly ached, and some 'dull opiate' would have been welcome.

Some years later I read Paul Horgan's *Things As They Are* and found this passage: 'When [little] children love, they do not give, they only receive. It is a love that creates a self. The aching desire to give, to create life beyond the self, calls boy into man. Gratified, this love creates an analogue of heaven on earth. Denied or betrayed, it sets forth the terms of hell in the stuff of life, unless it can be resolved by sanctity.' I have yet to work out fully its significance for me.

Normal boisterous boyness nonetheless prevailed; larking around and finding friendship became an acute pleasure, though also an excruciating hurt when it failed. One evening in the Seniors Common Room I found a copy of the *Apocrypha* and was gripped by the beauty of verses in parts in the Wisdom of Solomon and Ecclesiasticus. When I came to verse fourteen in the sixth chapter of the latter my heart burned with joy. 'A faithful friend is a strong defence and he that hath found such a one hath found a treasure.' Sometimes I turned to a protecting deity and before a boxing match was discovered on my knees in a dormitory. I promptly denied that I was praying; thankful that no one referred to it again. I did enjoy the chapel music at Bengeo; the response, 'There is none other that fightest for us but only thou, O God,' had special resonance. At Fonthill I was in the choir singing solos like Attwood's 'Come Holy Ghost' and Mendelsohn's 'Come to the Waters' and became a leader, but my piano teacher, Miss Wright, tended to rap my knuckles with a ruler and disapproved of my cockiness. 'You stand there looking round the congregation and thinking how marvellous you are.' Regrettably I burst into tears – as much hurt vanity as wounded musical éclat, I suspect. Friendship remained my chief consolation: Arthur had also come to Fonthill, attracting affection and admiration which I expressed in two long poems. These he was kind about; not the normal currency of twelve-year-olds. However, he matured more rapidly, and I found everyday companionship with two others, John Severne and Richard Lamb in a troika. Richard provided the fantasy technical interest in spacecraft and the galaxies, modelling a rocket launch pad, and John such practical initiations as his father's motorbike on visits to his home. He later became a distinguished air ace.

Neither shared my interest in acting, though Richard was expert on stage lighting and effects, and John took a minor part in the second play. In retrospect the first to be performed is the more interesting because I wrote it and am still intrigued by the fascination of this story to an eleven-year-old. It came from my reading about the Wars of the Roses when the young Earl of Rutland had been slaughtered ruthlessly, as a Yorkist heir, by several Lancastrians after the Battle of Wakefield. In the play, responsibility for the atrocity was placed firmly on the shoulders of the Queen, Margaret of Anjou, and the chief assassin, Lord Clifford. Fate pursued them in the form of the young Earl's ghost till the denouement at Tewkesbury when Edward, Margaret's son, was felled, being about the age of young Rutland at his death. Curiously, I set the first appearance of the ghost in the humble cottage of a villein and his wife. Only recently I discovered a story that Rutland had been cut down while battering on the door of a poor serf. But why the ghost? Did I bring in a spiritual *deus ex machina* to redress the injustices of life and the loss of a young boy?

Viewing the 8-13 schools period, the complexity of human relations appears a paramount concern, controllable perhaps in genealogy and the already existing and immutible panorama of history. Looking at the past is a compensation, safe compared with the uncertain future, but experience of the present is deepened and enriched by words, music and drama, all of which help to make it tolerable.

Some emotional and intellectual stability must have been achieved because I was made a prefect and then the Head of a School House. John thought I became rather solemn and heavy! Too often I was top of everything in work and, of course, expected to do well when I sat a scholarship for Greshams School, Holt. Unfortunately the school had overlooked Greshams' requirement of biology as a subject, and though my performance in other subjects was up to the mark, I failed the natural science totally. My parents were very understanding, but with my father now declining into severe osteo-arthritis and his income dwindling through inability to work and medical expenses, they would have been glad of the money. Later Greshams kindly awarded an Exhibition when the situation became clearer and my performance was adequate, but the transition to a public school was accompanied by a sense of partial failure and some trepidation.

At Greshams I found myself in a study with three strikingly handsome boys, whose urbanity inspired awe, admiration and a promise that I might become like them. Hawkins, Perkins and Foster were icons of godlike youth, companionable in a lordly way, witty, athletic but not particularly bright. Of the new boys with myself, Peter Brook, ugly, self-contained and clever, was the most impressive and in time became a powerful influence on me – though viewed with mixed feelings. Later he became an internationally acclaimed producer of plays and films.

The staff were not impressive. The Headmaster, an unattractive mathematician unsuited to the job, later became a successful Civil Servant; my housemaster, Max, a bachelor attracted to boys, could show compassion but excited little respect, and only one memorable pastor and mentor stands out, the second music master, Hoult Taylor. To him I owe a second parenting in which vicarious fathering gradually became profound friendship. He taught me the piano and he produced the annual Shakespeare play: out of my limited dramatic gifts he drew a shy Curio, a declamatory Chorus in *Henry V* and finally quite a powerful, if not very subtle, Mark Antony.

Hoult had a fund of delicious stories arising from his musical career, about Beecham, Britten – who had also been his pupil[10] – Henry Wood and others, all told with an inimitable sparkle. He was a listener too, a consoler and an encourager. I came to love him dearly in a platonic friendship of complete openness, which kept me sane in a time of tumultuous change and frequent isolation, helping to mature my mind and sensibility. Hoult encouraged me to compose, but more usefully got me to learn Bach, Mozart, Beethoven, Chopin, McDowell and Debussy; to listen to broadcast music and to develop a more accurate ear. Gradually he formed and improved my taste, introducing me also to literature far beyond my limited reading: so did Peter Brook, already more widely read than most boys of his age. My mother contributed by taking me to plays: Leslie Banks in *Clive of India* and *Henry V*, the memory of which is so overlaid by later performances by Olivier and Branaghan that I remember only the impact of stirring prologues declaimed by Leslie Banks as Chorus. Banks' Clive suffered from headaches (a blight on my own health), and the sight of his wife's tender hands upon his forehead moved me deeply. So did the dramatic events in India. Mother's *coup de grâce* was to introduce me to opera – Verdi's *Il Trovatore*, no less, and we sang duets together; 'Home to our mountains', a nostalgic reminiscence by the hero and his ill-fated mother, my poor sister being pressed into the part of Leonora in the Miserere scene to accompany my Manrico. But for the outbreak of war I would have devoured more opera: instead I tried writing one – as wildly dramatic as any from Italy. The hero was named after one of my admired sporting heroes at the school. Before the final curtain the stage was littered with corpses.

Normally you did not expect hero-worship to issue in a relationship, but this handsome Scandinavian engineered a brief contact, heightened by the drama of a meeting on Kelling Heath. He stirred my young heart by expressing approval but dashed it by saying there was no future because he was leaving. I am grateful for his integrity for, a relative innocent at fourteen, I had no idea what he had in mind. It did, however, confirm my conviction that personal love was unpredictably compounded of joy and pain, with the scales tipping towards loss.

---

[10] Britten wrote a poignant Elegy for Viola shortly after leaving Greshams.

A romantic view of friendship continued to permeate all my relationships: acute delight in moments of candour, humour, enlightenment and warmth; sharp disappointment, dismay and dudgeon when affection was rebuffed, teased or rubbished. It took a long time to find wisdom: it all mattered too much. Peter Brook counselled the cultivation of 'a sense of proportion'. However, this sensitivity did open doors to musical ecstasy and a wealth of new meaning in words. Denis Thompson (co-author with F Leavis, the Cambridge Literature Professor) taught English and introduced me to such classics as Arabia Deserta, Religio Medici, as well as the romantics, Wordsworth, Shelley and more Keats, not to mention a number of Shakespeare plays. My grandmother had already given me Jane Austen to enjoy and Hoult started me on the Brontes. Brook read me the poetry of T S Eliot to my initial bemusement, and encouraged a taste for Mozart, regretting my preference for Brahms. Max tried to interest me in Studdert Kennedy and Lowes Dickenson, failing in the first but sharpening a taste for Greek philosophy in L D. Though I have since appreciated the power of Studdert Kennedy's faith, the Greeks seemed nearer to what I was seeking.

The only personal answer to the conflicts of joy and pain I found in rather frantic or agonized prayer, which occasionally subsided into tranquillity. Every evening a five-minute silence was compulsory and we repaired to our bedside, easily policed in dormitory, but rather optimistically continued in the collection of small rooms in the hotels to which we were later evacuated. I shared a room with Peter and another Brooke, the son of a University Professor of History. Peter certainly did not believe conventionally, but he was drawn to mysticism. He rather disapproved of *The Four Quartets*, considering that Eliot had betrayed his original agnosticism.

For a time Peter launched a powerful attack on what he considered my superstitious beliefs. I had recently chosen to be confirmed, though I doubt whether personal conviction was as strong in that decision as parental influence. With Hoult gently encouraging me to read Bertrand Russell and Aldous Huxley, under such assault my religion proved to be a frail plant. I soon ceased to attend Communion, though prayer remained, and a sort of yearning for what the church stood for. My parents, soon to be swallowed up in ill health and war, were too far off to influence my practice, and in May 1940 breakdown in the ordered dance of class and chapel attendance was precipitated by evacuation.

My religion was second-hand, self-centred and narcissistic (at confirmation

I had hoped that the shaft of sunlight falling upon me at the Bishop's feet was somehow significant!) and Peter's scepticism burrowed into my certainties. Dear Hoult had no answers; he gave his musical best in Chapel but neither of us was impressed by the Chaplains, one of whom told me he had had an analysis and went from time to time for what he described as 'a de-coke', meaning analytical psychotherapy – quite a novelty for clergymen in the 1930s. However, the Freud whose writings Peter had introduced me to seemed to regard the Chaplain's religion as an illusion and, being ignorant of C G Jung, I thought psychoanalysis was another nail in the traditional coffin. A process of increasing reductionism led to painful disagreements at home, with my mother over religion and with my father over my adolescent socialism. We also differed in our attitude to 'nature'; for me there was something sacred about its beauty, to him, as an engineer, it was something to be conquered or at least mastered.

At this point my academic future came into unexpected focus when the staff decided that, although I was but fourteen and a half, I should drop physics and chemistry, in which my knowledge was elementary, and aim for the heights in history and english – a decision in which I had no part whatsoever, though I managed to salvage that fascinating subject, biology. A shy and good-natured biology master called Ramage generously offered extra tuition so that I would be ready for an arts-weighted performance in the School Certificate, July 1940.

The fall of France intervened and, two months before School Certificate, the school, suddenly thought to be in danger from an invasion of East Anglia, was spirited off to Cornwall and jammed into two jerry-built hotels in Newquay. Two hundred and fifty boys were let loose on the Atlantic shore and expected to study in makeshift classrooms ('biology in the bar'), traipsing up and down the cliff between the Bay Hotel by the foam-swept rocks to the upper hotel on the heather-strewn Pentire Headland. In winter windows were blown out by the ocean gales, and in summer the beach gleamed invitingly, but for the rolls of barbed wire overlooked by sandbagged pill boxes. Luckily surfing was possible on other beaches.

A domestic bouleversement had accompanied the preparations for evacuation. With his brother's financial help, my sick father had tried as a last resort two cures, one in Biskra on the edge of the Sahara, the other at Aix-les-Bains where he was when France fell. Mother with remarkable courage used her 'pull' as a VAD nurse to obtain an air passage to Aix;

reached my father's hotel in an air raid, cycled to another town in a thunderstorm to obtain an exit visa and got him on to a train to Bordeaux, where she commandeered a reluctant taxi driver to take them to the last ship to leave for England. On this private vessel built for about 500, she was welcomed as the only nurse for some 1,200 passengers. They spent three days dodging U-boats to arrive in Falmouth, my lame father very much the worse for wear. Pat and I had no idea what had happened to them, but I remember chiefly the halcyon early summer with my Uncle Gordon and Aunt Dorothy at their retirement home, Swindon Manor near Cheltenham, awaiting evacuation to Cornwall. My sister, used to her parents' company, was a lot more anxious. In the circumstances, my School Certificate results were surprisingly satisfactory.

Preparation for Higher Certificate in September 1940 introduced me to the quiet competence of the Senior History Master, Eric Kelly. His 'department' was sited over our hotel boiler room, so the dictation of notes was accompanied by the subterranean stirring of the heating system which worked up to an orgasmic pitch before subsiding into contented gurgling. Somehow on this background the persistent flow of historical information in Eric's connected and limpid style effected impregnation or osmosis. His notes took what I came to see were the main essay subjects of the examination to be fleshed out with our own reading. Effortlessly I learnt to swim in the wide pools of historical information and opinion. Of pedagogy there was none, and I suspect that anyone without a natural attrait to the subject might easily have sunk. In other spheres like literature and music Peter Brook continued to enlarge my comprehension; he also revealed more of the mystical streak in his nature, notably I think through an interest in St John of the Cross, but it was curiously combined with the philosophy of Huxley's *Ends and Means*. Through reading Huxley I eventually came to his remarkable tour de force *Grey Eminence*, which contained large tracts of mystical theology – a brightly illuminating journey to a rich feast – a marriage of philosophy and mysticism in the context of political history.

Since his Fall of France drama my crippled father (and ever-active little mother) had been living with Gordon and Dorothy in their charming Queen Anne manor. Gordon was Master of Foxhounds (The Cotswold Vale) so his stables were available for mother and Pat. Dorothy had literary and other interests I could share and we occasionally walked the countryside together. Though I was fond of them, Gordon was not too keen on an aesthete of a nephew and Dorothy was a strangely rigid person who found it difficult to accommodate mother's rather unpredictable ways. Her critical attitude would make mother weep quietly. However, they found me a pianola so my vacations could be spent in wild piano playing or rolling off the pianola's nineteenth century operatic repertoire in the billiard room, well away from the main house. It was here too I conceived the idea of my own opera and began to write it.

From Swindon Manor mother brought off a major coup: she found us a home (being let virtually for a song) – Crickley Lodge, superbly sited overlooking one of the finest views in the Cotswolds. It stood at the end of the companion spur to Birdlip Hill, part of the dramatic edge of the north Cotswolds as they drop into the Severn Valley. Standing on its terraced lawn you could see the camel-humped Malverns cavorting away to the west; on clear days the Abergavenny Sugar Loaf stood nobly in the distance, the foreground some eight hundred feet below being the extensive Gloucester valley with the River Severn winding its course through hillocks, copses and a jigsaw of little stone-walled fields. On fine days one exulted in a coloured kaleidoscope, now bright, now subdued, as clouds sailed gently by. Some mornings you woke to an utterly still panorama of crystal blue sky and a white, woolly mist below through which the hills protruded, pretending to be islands in a surrounding sea.

The house itself was built so close to the hillside that it seemed one with the granite of the escarpment. This climbed steeply up the banks to a Stone Age fort[11]. From there the view broadened to the west to include the tall hills above Cheltenham. To the east the rolling plateau stretched away to Cirencester. Caves in the rocky face behind the house called to be climbed to and pretty, deciduous woods spread across the summit of the escarpment to be explored. One of these, mixed with fir trees, rushed steeply from the highest drop – we called it 'Little Switzerland'. From these heights the valley glowed and withdrew, and returned again in brilliant panoply. I would scramble up to a high point to gaze in stillness and feel strangely at one with the vibrating beauty.

In such an aesthetic nursery, poems and music, of no great worth, gently flowed, amongst them two songs written for my mother to sing in her true and boyish mezzo-soprano: Yeats' 'Down by the Salley Gardens' and 'The

---

[11] The area now designated as the Crickley Hill Country Park.

Cloths of Heaven'. Though artless and undeveloped, they nonetheless expressed accurately the poignancy of our relationship, against the backcloth of my father's pain and disappointment.

All this was, however, shot through with the discontent and moodiness of adolescence, focused partly on the rival claims of animals, especially the horse. We rented land bounded by a ha-ha, stone walls and a hedge. Farmers grazed their sheep which frequently broke through and ravaged the garden: my task when at home being emergency expulsion duty. It was a joy to mother that she had grazing too not only for horses but also for a charming little Jersey cow (called Delphine) – to supplement the butter ration and make our own cream and cheese. Pat and mother were milkmaids and also hunted the horses (I confess to having enjoyed one remarkable run over a mile or so of exciting walls and springing turf, but preferred to hack over the hills, as quite the most attractive way of exploring the countryside). My sister was soon up to the hilt in gymkhanas and jumping competitions. Later we ran an 'equestrian event' in aid of the Red Cross – our contribution to the war effort – in which I found myself muddily replacing bits that riders knocked off jumps as they hurtled round the course. I was supposed to be studying during the holidays, but found life at home far too seductive and disturbing.

The need for study was intensified by a school decision in the autumn of '41 that I should have a shot at an university scholarship in History, since the requirements appeared to be much the same as those for the Higher Certificate (A level today). I inspected the list and found that Queen's College at Oxford offered the best return (£100 p.a.). I had no chance of affording a university otherwise. Moreover, Oxford was the nearest to home. Eric Kelly said it was a trial run for the following year; I would be unlikely to get it at the age of sixteen.

Two episodes linked with rugby, the only team game I cared for, unwittingly encouraged at school the study I seldom achieved at home. After a fierce game I went down with appendicitis – during convalescence my school timetable was deliciously flexible. I was given *carte blanche* to read throughout the day and, as the weather was unusually fine, did so amongst the heather and rocks on the Pentire Headland. Once recovered, I began to prepare to play for the School XV, but had a fall, putting my legs partly out of commission, so once again had long afternoons free of sport and available for work – though I don't recall being very conscientious about it, and certainly continued to give time to music and drama. I do, however, remember (as part of the eighteenth century studies required by the syllabus), Edmund Burke's speeches on North America and Reflections on the French Revolution. His sonorous and stately style of writing entered my soul and enormously improved my own presentation style. At times his influence almost 'took over', producing a remarkable clarity of thought and facile flow of expression. Later I felt that he had had a hand in my performance in March 1942.

That month mother took me to sit the scholarship exam. I had a splendid room in the mediaeval part of Queen's and at once felt embraced by Oxford's embodiment of historical atmosphere, cloistered aristocracy and sempiternal calm. It was impressive to have the services of a college scout and the comfort of my own sitting room. If this was university life, I could do with it. The exam papers were somehow geared to my expectations and Edmund Burke's inspiration appeared to flow: the interview with dons was surprisingly cheerful, though I recall nothing of what I wrote in the lofty hall, or what was said by them in the more intimate Georgian panelled room. I returned to school regarding the excursion as an agreeable adventure that had little practical significance.

School assembly a week or two later suddenly became electric when the HM stepped forward after prayers and proclaimed rather dramatically: 'Smythe has won a top scholarship at Oxford'. The cheers that followed almost reconciled me to public school education. The news had in fact come an hour earlier to my Housemaster via a telegram from mother, but I had felt too dazed to digest it. The reality was quite hard to assimilate. What did I have to live up to? Could this let me off Higher Certificate? No, that feather had to be plucked for my cap – the possible County Grant was essential to finance a university. Anyway it would keep me out of mischief in my final term, and perhaps with the same idea in mind Max made me a Sub-Prefect: I appreciated the privileges and more or less fulfilled the duties. Responsibility, and joining the Home Guard at sixteen to patrol the barbed-wired beaches in the early morning, gave rise to new and solemn thoughts. I had learnt that I could study for a year only at Oxford and then be called up, on condition that I joined one of the university cadet forces. What was my attitude to all this? The OTC had been an abomination of boring drill, unintelligible field days, bullying leaders and time-consuming cleaning of kit.

For a time I'd been placed in the so-called commando section, but blotted my copy book by forgetting to un-khaki-blanco my buttons for an inspection which followed a field day. Our immediate CO was a junior master full of army guff: he ordered me to report to him duly polished up between breakfast and school assembly. This would have involved walking the gauntlet of the entire House and up the cliff path leading to the other Houses, exposed to the ribald comments of all. Thinking it through at night I decided this was not an appropriate punishment for a Sub-Prefect, resolved to disobey, and got him out of bed before breakfast to report my insubordination. He was almost speechless with fury so I made a quick getaway. Luckily the Corps CO, a Housemaster, saw my point, perhaps assisted by Max, and I was let off with reporting to himself in the lunch break while the House was eating. The prospect of increased OTC vying with Oxford studies was not attractive, but I disagreed with my contemporaries who wanted to be conscientious objectors.

The real failure of the school during the three months of schooling that remained to me was that no-one made any attempt to prepare me for university life. I would be seventeen in the month before leaving: I had no idea what it meant to have to combine two full days a week military service and the weekly requirement of a scholarship undergraduate: only when I reached Oxford did I realise how ill-equipped I was to work methodically under these conditions, and neither the school nor Queen's suggested how I might usefully engage myself in the two and a half months of vacation before the eagerly awaited October 8th – when the Michaelmas term began.

However I did receive a memorable letter from the Chairman of the Governors. Written on Royal Automobile Club paper, it reads:

3.3.42

Dear Smythe,

Very heartiest congratulations from all the Governors, and not least from myself, on your splendid success at Oxford. You may remember that at the age of four Macaulay observed 'Industry shall be my bread, and attention my butter.' That you, while still under seventeen, should have won this fine scholarship proves that, without his sententious precocity, you must have followed his example, with the result that Greshams is proud of what you have done, and her exile sweetened by so notable a feat.

I am yours sincerely
Edward W. Fordham

The last school term had a hectic brilliance about it. I was Mark Antony in
Julius Caesar and we were booked to present it over three July days at
Newquay Theatre. A scene or two were also entered for the Truro Festival of
the Arts in June, when at the last minute Hoult found a leopardskin which he
insisted on my wearing at making the first entrance from The Games. We got
so hooked on this magnificent bit of fauna that he overlooked my need for an
accompanying undergarment. Consequently quite as much of my own skin
as the leopard's was on display when I made this dramatic appearance: I had
to live down at least one wolf-whistle before the famous funeral speech.
However, the performance was awarded First Prize at Truro; the Newquay
performances were attended by contingents from other evacuated schools,
whose reactions might have been critical, but who in the event treated us
kindly. Reward came a month later when, leaving from the National Gallery
after a Myra Hess lunch time concert, I was accosted on the terrace above
Trafalgar Square by an attractive Benenden girl. 'Excuse me. Aren't you
Mark Antony?' Fame at last. Alas, she had an escort.

A few weeks before the end of term a wayward impulse took me in the
early hours of the morning to a room from which I could climb out on to a
low roof and down a drain pipe to the cliff path leading up to the Houses on
the headland. The moon shone with blatant splendour, the sea whispered
below, not a soul was around. I climbed the fire escape on the upper hotel,
and negotiating a few windowsills reached the sash window to the dormitory
in which I thought I would find a friend. The window moved up silently and
'Fish' (he looked like one) sat up, hardly believing his eyes. We chatted
quietly. It was an entirely innocent relationship, and I returned the way I'd
come, mildly elated and conscious that somehow I had fulfilled an item on
the schoolboy agenda before moving on.

CHAPTER III

OXFORD

At Queen's I was housed in Drawda, the mediaeval part of the college where I'd put up for the scholarship exams. The sitting room had a raised window seat giving a grandstand view of the High. You could sit, drink coffee and carve slices of Hovis with an unending vista of activity – and relatively little traffic. The timbered and whitewashed homeliness of the room contrasted with the elegant grandeur of the front quad and the baroque beauty of the upper Library with its dazzling Charles Roberts ceiling. I relished the intimacy of my sitting room with its sofa, desk, chairs and gas fire with ring for the coffee kettle – to which I soon added a rented piano – a major temptation. One received little guidance on how to handle the new freedom, and perhaps if offered I should not have listened to it. I was allocated a Moral Tutor but our first solo meeting was to receive a rebuke for playing my piano 'out of hours' when others wished to work. Mr Jones was a kindly Welsh don in the Law schools whose warning I didn't heed, so I found myself banished in the third term. It felt like ejection from the Garden of Eden.

Military service took a large hunk of my week: the remainder was spent in attempting to satisfy two tutors, each of whom required a substantial essay. To my disappointment I was obliged to go over the same period of history as the Higher Certificate when my instinct was to make a start on the Middle Ages. Nonetheless the Revd Professor Norman Sykes[12], my chief tutor, was kindly disposed and was heard to comment that 'Smythe was the most Georgian of all his undergraduates', implying, I suspect, not so much an understanding of the period as a propensity to a rather grandiose lifestyle. Soon there was a never-ending stream of fascinating people; profound conversation into the small hours and less profound merry-making. Peter

---

[12] Later Dean of Winchester.

Brook was at Magdalen and roped me in to transcribe *L'Enfant Prodigue* for a production in 1943; he mobilized a small orchestra for me to conduct but it came to nothing in the end – apart from a gratifying comment on my orchestration.

Technically 'in the Army', I elected to join the Signals but very soon found I could not concentrate on 'dots and dashes'. There seemed to be a hiccup in my vision. Then my health deteriorated: this was partly helped by a tonsillectomy in the Christmas holiday, but headache was the chief enemy. Having become friendly with a man in the Naval Division, I decided to transfer and with Philip became a rating in bellbottoms, spending two days a week at the Naval Division on the Isis by Christ Church Meadows. Philip was a very good companion: he had a fine tenor voice so together we joined the college chapel choir and the Eglesfield Choir to sing Bach's Christmas Oratorio, and together we explored the city and its surrounding countryside. Friendship took over from work, and delight in finding a kindred spirit with whom everything could be discussed or enjoyed was the priority. We found mutual friends too: a RAF undergraduate also at Queen's, Kenneth Jones, an immensely charming musician and composer; John Heath-Stubbs the poet, one of whose poems (unpublished) I set to music for Philip to sing. The only blot was the naval service and the prospect, rarely acknowledged, that this delight would come to an end in July – with call-up.

Like many who grew up in wartime I accepted this as part of life's routine, with little patriotic feeling; only some distaste for anticipated discomforts. Oxford was a final diversion, a charming irrelevance to be savoured before the serious business began. Because the future (in the form of military service) made such inroads upon the present, the diversions of undergraduate life were even more precious. One night, protecting the Science Laboratories while firewatching, I encountered the thrilling intensity of Mahler's Ninth Symphony, on records brought by a colleague.

After Easter, Philip and I found digs in Wellington Square about half a mile from the college, near the Playhouse and the Randolph Hotel – bright, cheerful lodgings, ideally spacious and happy. Our relationship had become rather intense, unhealthily so, partly through my increasing dependency. This arose from the headaches and the alarming development of quite serious and continuous double-vision (without the benefit of alcohol). We spent more time studying and listening to music, one memorable and bright evening, the first performance of Vaughan Williams' Fifth Symphony; somewhere in it is inscribed 'In his will is our peace'.

However, in spite of halcyon moments I began to feel agitated; I had sought reassurance, going to a gypsy at a fair by the river at Abingdon to 'know' my future – viewing my hand she was worryingly reluctant, though money had first 'crossed her palm' as required. Philip suggested we try for guidance with a glass and an alphabetical circle: it raised my spirits with fascinating messages, until Philip had to admit he'd been pushing! However, his imagination produced a strange spin-off. One of the messages had purported to come from a Bonaventura who had proceeded to give valuable spiritual advice. Neither of us knew about my godmother's proposal of this name at my christening but it impelled me to purchase, or maybe Philip bought for me, Etienne Gilson's *Philosophy of St Bonaventura*. I began to devour hungrily his exposition of the Christian faith.

Not seeing clearly or accurately rendered me almost useless as a sailor, and after a medical I was ordered to rest – not very practicable as I had to take the Part One exam: but with Philip's patient support this hurdle was overcome. I returned home to my sick father and overburdened mother; but a few weeks later made a flying visit to my digs and also (for no reason I can recall) to the distinguished historian J M Thompson, who had tutored me on the French Revolution/Napoleonic Era. This impulse elicited the following letter from Norman Sykes, so typical that I must include it to remember his kindness and his character:

25th July 1943   The Queen's College Oxford

Dear Smythe

I write to tell you the good news that you got a 2nd in Part I of the History school; and to offer my cordial congratulations. In view of the very unsatisfactory state of your health last term I am much relieved that you have done so well. Unfortunately no details of marks in Part I are given; so that I know nothing beyond your class. I am sure you and your mother will be equally gratified and pleased. [He had met her earlier.]

Thank you for your letter of the 14th. I am sorry you did not find time to let me know of your visit to Oxford so that we might have met. I can hardly suppose it to have been due to 'disinclination to social pleasures', since Mr Thompson told me you had been to visit him; because this would mean either that your seeing him was not a pleasure or else that seeing me would have been no pleasure. But I quite understand that you had not time to visit both of us.

I am very sorry to learn that your doctors have commanded three months' rest, which will be very trying to a person of your active character. I hope very much that this rest will put you right and that the wretched malaise which has dogged you all this year will at last be utterly banished and driven away.

I look forward after the war to seeing a Nelson in miniature and to welcoming back not only a future Fortescue in slashing verdicts on British statesmen of the Great War but also a completely whole and well scholar apt and fit for a good 1st in the schools.

With all good wishes,
Yours sincerely,
Norman Sykes

Letters were at a premium in this period of depression and hypochondria. I wrote at length to my godmother Nell and received this reply:

You must not think me insensitive to your letter; it moved me deeply. I have turned it over in my mind and turned its sentences over in prayers for your comfort and strength of soul. You are come, more young that most come, to the pain and frustrations of life seemingly unreasonable and wholly unjustifiable: great gifts given and thwarted for no apparent reason and for causes entirely out of one's power to influence. Those gifted . . . have greater capacity for feeling, for grief and disappointment as well as for exquisite joy and delight, which serves to make the dead wall one comes up against all the more desperate and hopelessly crushing . . . These are matters for mind and soul . . . which engage and deeply affect the spiritual man.

Here, darling godson, is the healing remedy. Take these devastating disturbances and distresses where King Hezekiah took them [she referred to II Kings chapter 19] and spread them out before the Lord: 'in the secret of his pavilion' we may safely lay out and leave our problems. [then she took up a reference to Dante in my letter] In its fundamental

32

thought your version of Canto 29 is the true one – his fatherhood revealing itself in perfect wisdom; perfect love remains unshakeable, unalterable 'Nella sua volontade e la nostra pace': acquaint now thyself with Him and be at peace. [Echoes of Vaughan Williams!]

All this is dreadfully religious! But darling, that is the part of man that survives to eternity, hence its reality and potency; so my prayer for you is that of Elisha (taught in a life of hard discipline) for his young disciple (II Kings 6.v.17) 'Open his eyes Lord that he may see' . . . [the angelic chariots of fire that invisibly protected the prophet from a great host of enemies.] May you also see what lies around you and is so much more than the sinus pain, the defective eyes, the heavy limbs, the sense of isolation and all the hindrance to your aspirations. Goodbye dear, dear child.

I wonder how many godchildren have received such a letter: surely very few today? It impressed me. I looked up and have never forgotten the stories in the second book of Kings. I am not sure what I made of the letter at the time, being somewhat ambivalent towards religion and almost certain that much of my trouble had been of my own making. However, the reference to angels was strangely prophetic.

One evening the situation in its utter meaninglessness, together with a sense of my own folly, quite overwhelmed me. I left the room where my emaciated and crippled father was sitting; my mother seldom sat with us, being busy in kitchen or stables; my sister was at school. I climbed the stairs to my bedroom and opened the door. As I entered I felt strongly that I must not switch on the light. An intense awareness of other presences seized me. I fell to my knees murmuring with utter conviction the word, 'Love'. I had a sense of something infinitely real which was wholly other than my self. I stretched out a hand and felt as though it were held. I do not know how long I remained there. I could not speak about this experience to anyone, but in the following days I felt as though I were being refashioned. Later I read about 'rebirth' in others, but at the time had no knowledge of such things. I felt that I was a child, but not to be childish any more, sensing dependence on something beyond my own being, but aware that I must make some response, and that an utterly authentic one. Yet the moment I desired to make this, it was as though the response were given. Although it was a gift, it was still my own. I had no clear idea of what was happening and did not associate it with any orthodox religion. I guessed that somehow a training was being undergone, but what for or by whom was unclear. Nonetheless there was a definite sense of something vaguely 'angelic' taking place.

I was writing a sort of epic poem at the time, somewhat Miltonesque, which began with a knight demanding admission to a castle – the massive gateways opened to him of their own accord and he rode into deserted court-yards. There he prepared himself for a contest, both physically in equipping himself and his horse, and spiritually by entering the Chapel, kneeling before a rather modern-styled altar, standing away from the wall: the sun streamed through the plain glass windows. On the altar was a flame: the only line – a rather hammy one – that I now remember occurred at this point:

'. . . and blended his yearning essence with the flame.'

He then left the castle and entered a dark wood. A lake lay beyond, and the threat of some monster. But I never got any further.

In a remote way I wanted to believe that Christ was behind the experience of re-birth, though I had no devotion to him, only a sort of conventional respect. Once I was doodling when my pen firmly and unaccountably wrote the words, 'Jesus Christ'. I was very intrigued and tried more automatic writing but was eventually discouraged from doing so, and later it would only write 'Fool'. Another time as I sat at my desk my eyes were suddenly held and my head turned in a gentle grip to scan my bookshelves to the left of the desk. My gaze became fixed on Thomas à Kempis' *Imitation of Christ*. This book had only come into my possession a few weeks before as a gift from my grandmother; I had thought little of it. I took it down and as I read, my heart glowed with a palpable warmth.

From that day I seemed to walk with a lighter tread, entering a new world in which the most ordinary things, objects and events, were surrounded by a halo. Was this the bright world I'd entered while hearing Keats' ode? I began to realize how emotionally dependent I was on my mother, and to desire to be free from this and from other juvenile habits and attitudes. Most of my old weaknesses and faults were still there but no longer did they seem insuperable: all would be well if only I could wait in trust. Above all I must be absolutely honest. Day after day in a strange indescribable way it was brought home to me that I must not 'induce' feelings but wait for the authentic response, which I would then find to be more genuinely my own than any other I might have desired to make. Once it came strongly to me, 'Speak only when charity demands an answer'; advice later, in my incorrigible talkativeness, I have signally failed to observe except perhaps in the counselling session.

All this took place in the context of a companionship the like of which I have never known before or since. I cannot begin to convey the incredible joy that would sweep over me quite unexpectedly during the day and night. I remember one night entirely spent reposing in this state: although I appeared to remain in semi-conscious awareness throughout I awoke with an inexpressible sense of refreshment. At moments working in the garden (my only constructive activity during the five months of rest) and about ordinary jobs in the house, I would feel myself inwardly visited, an experience which I later found paralleled in *The Practice of the Presence of God* by Brother Lawrence. Yet I did not associate any of this with church Christianity. I felt more at home with the poems and writings of William Blake and much of what I was being taught was summed up in such phrases as:

> He who bends to himself a joy
> Doth the winged life destroy;
> He who kisses the joy as it flies
> Lives in eternity's sunrise.

I loved Blake's paintings, especially those in the *Book of Urizen*, which I possessed in coloured reproduction, and I devoured *The Marriage of Heaven and Hell*. My poor mother had to read me a learned book on Blake because my eyes were still bad: I think she felt he was crazy and possibly feared that I was. She certainly found me difficult and hard to understand.

An important part of my training seemed to be that I must face the meaning, or the fact of, Death. There was one inward journey at night as though in the fire of hell to abysmal darkness, or rather nothingness, which convinced me that myself, thought of simply as a separate unrelated being, did not exist. It was terrifying and yet cleared my mind and feelings: was my existence to be found only in God?

Meantime I was, as it were, given an external task: to write a Requiem for which I was shown the material mainly in Blake's writings and in the Bible, the whole to culminate in Dante's description of the Vision of God. I say 'shown' because I had only to take up a book and either my gaze would fall on astonishingly apt passages or else I would know just where to turn to them. I knew the Bible very imperfectly and both Blake and Dante were entirely new to me. Yet I remember turning straight to this passage from the Wisdom of Solomon:

The souls of the just are in the hand of God
And there shall no torment touch them.
In the sight of the unwise they seem to die
And their departure is taken for misery
And their going from us to be utter destruction:
But they are at peace.

For though they be punished in the sight of men
Yet is their hope full of immortality.
Having been a little chastised they shall be greatly rewarded:
For God proved them and found them worthy for himself.
As gold in the fire hath he tried them
And received them as a burnt offering.

In the time of their visitation shall they shine
And run to and fro like sparks among the stubble . . .
And their Lord shall reign for ever.

I took the words to mean that suffering and death could be keys to a new life: accepted, even embraced here, the new life could begin now. Oddly enough the relevance of this passage to my father's patient suffering and decline did not occur to me: we never thought that he, a relatively young man, would die yet. I learnt it as new truth, together with much else that turned my previous standards and values upside-down.

In spite of difficulties with reading, the texts grew so voluminous that I realised that they could not all be used, but I never succeeded in reducing them to manageable form. Some of the studies I wrote in preparation for the music were far better than anything I had written before, but frequent headache made it difficult to concentrate and as my health did not improve I was sent to the Radcliffe Hospital for investigation. There, the distinguished neurologist, Professor L Witts, thought that the muscle paralysis had been caused by a diptheritic germ, though it could be that a congenital weakness of the muscles had worsened as a result of strain (burning the candle at both ends?). 'You will feel a lot better in five years' time,' he said. It sounded like a judicial sentence. No remedy was available at the time, so my discharge from the RNVR was recommended and I was advised to return to Oxford.

But I did not feel ready to resume study, and as a cousin kindly offered to subsidize treatment of the type which had improved Aldous Huxley's sight, I obtained my parents' permission to live in London and undergo the course.

The treatment and my efforts to cope with a temporary teaching job were not successful, but I was able to spend some time trying to understand what had happened to me. The writings of Nietzsche evoked an echo, but there was something repulsive there, too. William Blake still 'spoke to my condition' better than any other, and I began to study his writings more carefully. Finding a room in a charming house (formerly Whistler's) on Cheyne Walk in the company of intelligent young people in their early twenties, under their influence I began to wonder whether in fact something was psychologically wrong with me. One of them advised me to see Dr Gillespie of Guy's Hospital, which I did. He recommended that I went back to Oxford and undertook psychotherapy while studying. I recall leaving him with a glow of gratitude, reflecting how delightful it must be to help people in this way.

Shortly before this, my spirits had been given a lift by a series of chance experiences. Gordon and Dorothy kindly invited me to join them on a brief winter holiday in a beautiful part of Wales, Lake Vyrnwy. Hotel comforts were an unfamiliar luxury enhanced by bright frosty weather: the lake and hills were entrancing. Moreover, among the guests was the pianist Moura Lympany and her concert manager. By happy chance we got talking music together, she played for me and asked to hear compositions of mine. I was dazzled – and even more so when she suggested that I came behind stage to see her during the interval at her next concert. By then I was in London so took myself to the Cambridge Theatre (scene of many superb performances during the war) imagining with adolescent naiveté that I had only to turn up at the box office to obtain a ticket. The concert was sold out: I was appalled! but standing nearby observing my dismay was a distinguished figure. He came forward to explain that a friend had not turned up. 'Would I like the ticket? Nothing to pay, of course.'

In our seats together and finding him ready to talk I couldn't resist telling him about my tryst with Moura and also about my 'works'. Either on my return from behind the scenes or at the end of the concert he said: 'I am Ralph Hawkes of Boosey and Hawkes. May I arrange an interview for you with one of my staff?' Amazed, I gave him my address and, sure enough, a smart envelope arrived with a letter – from Irwin Stein, offering an appointment.

It was not my first visit to B & H because at the age of thirteen when I was taking a few lessons from the organist at our church on Barnes Common, I had responded to their advertisement offering a chance to try out the new Hammond Organ. Mother came with me to Regent Street, and later dined out on the story – especially the expression on the demonstrator's face when the expected well-heeled would-be purchaser turned out to be a brash lad.

Walking through the same doors some six years later brought back cheerful memories, and I was ushered into an elegant room to meet Irwin Stein - a small man, reminding me a little of Peter Brook, with a fine cranium and kindly intelligent manner. He looked at my 'oeuvres' and then showed me a copy of Britten's Hymn to St Cecilia, saying, 'This is the sort of music we are interested in.' He went on to talk of Britten very warmly. Philip and I had seen both Britten and Michael Tippett at the Quaker Hall performance of the Serenade for Tenor and Horn and Tippett's Double Concerto. They were both heroes of mine but I was sure I could not write music to match theirs. I tried – setting those words I had chosen for the Requiem, 'The souls of the faithful are in the hands of God', but when I next saw Stein he was perplexed: I had not fulfilled his hopes. By then, however, I was finishing a job as companion to a crippled boy and due to return to Oxford.

Queen's College was ready to renew my scholarship, but in the Oxford summer term it was extremely difficult to settle, and most of my friends were now in the Forces. I visited the psychotherapist, Dr Rolf Kosterlitz, regularly for about eight months. As a Jungian he was sympathetic to my 'religious' symptoms but was so sphinx-like that I had no idea what he really thought about anything, least of all myself. However, he was musical and invited me to hear his quartet playing twelve-tone and similar esoteric music, such as Egon Wellesz's (who may have been a member of the quartet). One day I felt so sure I should study music rather than history I took a train to London and headed for the Royal College of Music. *En route* an odd sense of being restrained overtook me: I sat down on a low wall near Kensington Gardens and acknowledged defeat – or (in retrospect) accepted reality. On return I continued to compose, but found it a struggle – I could not express the cosmic proportions of what I wanted to say. I visited Dr Andrews, the organist at New College, for some lessons, but after a while he commented dourly: 'I'm afraid you will have to work out your own salvation.' That is what I feared.

Meantime I had begun to attend church. A friend, Ronnie Bright, later Fr. Lawrence of the RC Benedictines, kindly accompanied me to St Paul's Walton

Street. Sung Mass I found too emotionally overwhelming, but felt at home in the tractarian type early Communion at Holywell Parish Church. It was an easy walk from new digs in Holywell Street, and reminded me of the country churches I had known. However, I allowed the parish priest of St Paul's, Fr. Billy Favell, to prepare me for a first confession at Christmas 1944 – and that has remained a useful discipline, which I dislike, but suppose one should.

Psychotherapy began to make me less ambitious and more inclined to accept things as they were. I made a few new friends in college, and got down to opening the oyster of mediaeval history. It became increasingly absorbing, and for the first time I was a fairly exact and painstaking student. Under dream analysis and related techniques many of the more eccentric features of my experiences disappeared, though I was occasionally visited by interior instructions. One came in the summer of 1944 while I was walking on Boars Hill after a composition instruction with Dr Karl Rankl. 'Your father will die soon,' I was told. Nothing could have been further from my thoughts at the time: in any case, as I have said earlier, it was axiomatic, an unshaken conviction of the whole family that he would eventually recover. By then I was inclined to feel slightly ashamed of interior instructions, and gave it no further thought. A few months later my father contracted pleurisy, but seemed to recover: I returned to College after Christmas and a week later he died, bravely and stoically as he had lived. Mother was left, just in her forties, with practically no capital, as our savings had been exhausted by his long illness, and Pat and I had still to complete our education. At my father's cremation I read 'The souls of the just are in the hand of God . . .'

After the funeral it was a comfort to return to safe lodging in Holywell, and to learn that Queen's would raise the value of my scholarship; but there were no funds for more therapy so Dr K and I had to part company. I settled to an academic routine, but also allowed myself to be drawn into the College Drama Society, responded to an invitation to help at a Youth Club in East Oxford and found a girl friend: the latter was a gentle and rather tentative companionship which did not last. Nor did I persevere with the Youth Club. The leisure activity I valued most arose from election as Secretary and later President of the University History Club, the Stubbs Society (named after the historian Bishop of Oxford whose mediaeval constitutional papers I was having to study.) This brought pleasant relationships with other history undergraduates, including Basil Hume and other residents at the RC Hostel, St Benet's. It involved meeting a host of distinguished and sometimes eccentric 'speakers', and the gentle charm of Professor Maurice Powicke, our Patron.

History felt a very live and relevant subject in 1945/6 as we were caught up in the events leading to the invasion of Europe. The high drama permeated everything as the world's colossi battled it out to the finish. On V E day, Oxford streets were crammed with a good-humoured crowd, at one point harangued by a Queen's man from the college steps claiming that he brought fraternal greetings from the Soviet republic of Uzbekistan. His colourful improvised 'Uzbeki' aroused gales of cheering laughter. A group appeared with a ladder and for no obvious reason we grabbed it and careered madly up to Carfax, where Roger Green (later author and poet) scaled the tower and dislodged the vast savings indicator: the crowds cheered yet more loudly as it clattered to the ground. I suppose it stood for wartime austerity.

I was engaged on a vacation job in North Oxford when the A-bomb was detonated and Japan surrendered; but celebration was overshadowed by mixed feelings about the advent of nuclear warfare, doubts which intensified with the seemingly gratuitous blotting out of a second city. Few of us fully registered the ethical or long term implications; mostly we were relieved by the ending of hostilities, as it had looked to be a long haul in the Far East. Thankfulness was uppermost and quite a few went to church to express it.

Christian worship was becoming a growing interest to me. An ordinand, Roy Porter[13], took me to Sung Mass at St Mary Magdalene's but again I found it too high-powered, eventually settling for lone attendance at the 8.00a.m. Communion at Holywell my nearest parish church. Here I experienced fairly muted joy and peace, a renewal of spirit – the new-born life I had experienced ignorantly in '43: its giver I could now acknowledge personally and gladly. Sometimes this new sense of devotion would be enhanced by a visit to Sung Evensong in Magdalen or New College, or sonorous stately Matins at Christ Church. The superb singing especially of seventeenth century settings, and new music from composers recently discovered, fell on thirsty ears, and an occasional thoughtful sermon was manna in a dry land (though Blake continued to be nourishing, joined by the poetry of W B Yeats). Towards the end of 1945 I was prevailed upon to attend Holy Communion in the College chapel followed by breakfast in the Hall – reluctantly at first, fearing to lose something precious, but the company of other young Christians gave communion fresh meaning, and friendship became less self-concerned.

---

[13] Later Professor of Theology, Exeter University.

Roy introduced me to a fascinatingly bizarre character, of great kindness to undergraduates, an erstwhile don in the Modern Languages (Portuguese) School, Kolkhorst by name. He owned the fine seventeenth century manor house at Yarnton and had invested much of his wealth, arising I believe from the tramway system in Lisbon, in a superb collection of carpets. Priceless Turkish, Persian and Far Eastern rugs festooned the house giving an almost sensuous heaviness to the elegant proportions of Jacobean spaciousness. There I met his lively and gifted lodger, John Betjeman, then working with the British Council at Blenheim Palace. Kolkhorst affected the style of an English country gentleman, besporting a field of rather smelly dogs whom he exercised daily. His friends had christened him 'The Colonel' – he was of quite magnificent proportions (larger than my Colonel Squire of an uncle) and an amusing conversationalist. Betjeman (like many of us who visited) teased and provoked him, and learning that I wrote music, produced 'The Colonel's Hunting Song' ('The Colonel comes riding from Froggledown Goose. His clothes are too loud and his language is coarse') and the 'Yarnton Boating Song', both of which I set to ribald tunes. Once I stayed at the Manor overnight and then had to catch a train. Betjeman's wife offered to run me to Oxford station. *En route* the rear of the car began to wobble; in St Giles the car shuddered and we saw a wheel bowling along, outstripping us as we drove down the broad highway. With a thud we came to a halt and I resigned myself to a lost train: as we got out a crowd of undergraduates and others suddenly descended on us from nowhere and, directed by an imperious Mrs Betjeman, jacked up the car, re-attached the wheel and got us to the rails in time. Something bizarre usually happened on visits to Yarnton.

By contrast, out of the blue came Dave Farnell, who had been slightly my junior at Greshams. David was a cheerful, fair, curly-headed youngster with considerable artistic gifts, always rather solitary. His paintings were striking, but the school did little for him. I recall a beautiful but immensely elaborate tree he painted, convoluted branches like great twisted arms, parts gleaming a brilliant yellow, the leaves prolific and olive-grey, full of amazing power and pathos. Later he did a woodcut of a man behind prison bars, head in hands: below were the words 'Lord, why do men suffer?' David was not overtly philosophical or religious but highly sensitive and thoughtful. He had a shy, staccato way of speaking, his small, quite fleshy mouth slightly twisted in a gentle, querulous smile, head on one side. I forget which of us left school first, vaguely I recall he had trouble at home, an unfeeling step-mother who made him work on her smallholding and look after hens. I felt sympathy, being myself a holiday stable-boy and garden odd jobber.

He turned up at Oxford on an RAF Short Course and got in touch with me. He seemed glad of an old acquaintance and I was more attracted to him than at Greshams. He was at New College so we had a better garden to walk in than that at Queen's, and we biked around the countryside, once as far as Kingston Bagpuize on the road to Swindon. There we discovered a pleasant pub and planned an expedition in the long vac, to stay overnight and explore the countryside. With bicycles in good nick we set out on a bright, leafy summer's day: David gave me encouragement as on a bike I was the weaker brother, and we made it in time for a good pub meal, an exploration of the village and surrounding woods, concluding with a fairly comfortable night (fraternally innocent) in an ancient double bed. The episode is invested with quite an idyllic quality but I recall little about the next day or the trip home, and a few weeks later his course ended and he returned to his RAF station. I think, before or after the expedition, he invited me to dine in College and I met his tutor, David Cecil, whom he admired. So did I, having just read and been moved by Cecil's life of William Cowper, *The Stricken Deer.*

That strickenness was around when a few months later I received a heart-searing letter. Dave wrote that he had had a breakdown and was in a psychiatric hospital: he would like to see me. Feeling rather daunted by the prospect of such a scenario, I took a train and found him in quite a comfortable and cheerful hospital. He was glad to see me but very anxious. I don't know why we didn't stay in touch – probably the approach of Final exams; but about eighteen months later I heard from his father, whom I'd never met, that David had taken his life by opening the veins in his wrists. The father insisted on my dining with him at his club: I was working then in London as a junior Civil Servant. It was one of the most painful meals I've known, partly because the father was so distraught and I wanted to comfort him: yet I also felt he and his wife could have been responsible for David's unhappiness. At least I could talk about David, which pleased his father, but I did a poor job as a comforter and wished I could learn how to do it better. 'O Lord, why do men suffer' and how can we respond to the other's pain?

Mother and Pat were standing up pluckily to their share of trouble. My sister puts the situation so clearly and simply that I cannot do better than quote from her first book *Jump for Joy* (Cassell 1954), a tale for anyone who enjoys a saga of triumph over adversity and the only one that I helped her to write. She says:

> After my father's death it was a choice between the comforts of family life at Crickley Lodge and the cost of keeping horses in the belief that I would make a show-jumper. What I owe to my mother can be seen from the fact that she did not hesitate to give up Crickley and move first to her mother's in Bath and then to various temporary quarters ending with a single room in the Blathwayt Arms on Lansdowne, to begin a riding school, by means of which she could support herself and maintain the horses for me. She even did without the help I might have given her; for, when some kind relations offered to finance my further schooling, she gladly sent me off to Talbot Heath, Bournemouth, to study for the Higher Certificate. Much though I would have preferred to stay and help her, I could see the value of continuing my education, and as I was more than ever determined to learn about farming, I was soon absorbed in science and biology.
>
> On the windswept heights of Lansdowne above the tranquil dignity of the lovely city of Bath, Mother's riding school gradually took root and blossomed. She was never very comfortable. At one temporary lodging the rain dripped down the walls incessantly, cooking was done on a primus, water had to be fetched from a pump, and the horses had to be content with a cowshed. It was so cold that we would resort to all sorts of devices to keep ourselves and our clothes warm and dry. At the Blathwayt, where we rose to the height of an electric hotplate, the result on one occasion was a pair of well-grilled underwear! There were many discouragements, the most familiar being well-intentioned people who let you down, but the first big shock came from Finality.[14]
>
> I was at Bournemouth, Mother had gone up to London, but Ronald was in Bath visiting his grandmother, when he received a telephone call from Lansdowne saying that one of the horses had broken out and damaged itself. When he arrived he found that the greedy Finality had used her skill to jump into a cornfield. Having gorged herself and made a mess of the farmer's corn, she had tried to get back: but who can rise

---

[14] Pat's first international show jumping horse.

to the occasion after a heavy meal? In attempting to return she had torn herself badly on wire and now shivered with terrible gashes on all four legs, bleeding profusely. Ronald called the vet and under his instruction bathed the wounds for the rest of the day. On her return Mother took over, but the vet's comment was, 'If she does recover she will probably be useful only as a brood mare. I cannot imagine that she will ever be able to jump again.'

Happily he underestimated Final's powers for, with the coming of summer her recovery was complete and she was ready to be ridden and jumped again. But for nearly four months my dreams had been agonized pictures in which endless miles of torturing wire had torn at my own limbs as well as Final's.

Our childhood pony, Pixie, was also at Lansdowne [Pat continues] but in honourable retirement as the most popular children's pony. She was now very sober and matronly. Our great hope had been that she would consummate her career in marriage, but we brought her to stallions that were aristocrats, to stallions that were strong and silent, to stallions sleek and handsome and all that an equine female could or should desire. But she did not love them. At length to our joy, however, she fell in love unmistakably and absurdly with a small carefree boy of the Welsh hills.On the very day of victory in Europe, just before we left Crickley, Pixie had her foal – a skewbald filly, dubbed Victoria, of course. The victory of the allies had been capped by her own personal achievement.

Victory in Europe also released on to the University campus cohorts of demobbed warriors, by and large older and more mature than us who had remained, and remarkably hardworking, determined to get jobs and set up their own homes. I remained at Oxford much of the time, but went now and again to help with the stables, the most memorable task being my attempt to teach a middle-aged Colonial Office administrator how to ride. He was going to be a District Officer in a part of East Africa where only a horse could take him from place to place. He never actually fell off, but we had some narrow escapes: he departed a few weeks later with some confidence in his equestrian prospects.

However, as the year gathered momentum, it was I who was becoming unseated. Anxiety about Finals began to seep in and a devastating sense that I had failed to tackle the wide range of work in a sufficiently organized manner to be able to recover it for revision before the exam. A lot happened between 53BC and AD1914! How could I be fully briefed, let alone cover as well all the Latin texts of mediaeval constitutional history in Stubbs' Charters and the voluminous original documents (some in French) required for the other special subject, The Commonwealth and Restoration 1649-62? Panic-struck at times, I was also undermined by an obsession. During therapy my handwriting had improved, from an untidy slope to a clearer upright style. Rolf had welcomed this as a good sign. Under pressure from increased note-taking it had reverted to the shapeless slope. I became convinced this must indicate deterioration. So I became hyper-conscious of my handwriting and almost paralysed by anxiety.

Ironically, a group who were planning to make a film about wartime Oxford invited me to take the part of an undergraduate who had struggled to reconcile the conflicting demands of scholarship work and military service – and had failed. His tragedy was a little too near the knuckle: the producer and his casting committee auditioned me and thought I would do, but I turned it down. Other anxieties loomed up. While staying at the Colonel's a few days before Christmas 1945, enjoying Betjeman's antics, mother phoned in great agitation because her brother had suffered major injuries from a road accident whilst serving in Italy. He was being invalided home: would I meet his ship at Bristol? This threw me; extremely worried and conscious of letting her down, I eventually said No. In practice, she herself was able to cope and we all met up later in Bath, farmed out on various friends: but it was a tense time.

When I returned to my Oxford haven I found the elderly landlady seriously ill. On the anniversary of my father's death she died, and I had to find new digs. Dennis Nineham, our College Chaplain, could find no place in Queen's; several friends suggested alternatives, but January is not the easiest time to find student accommodation. Eventually Alan, one of the returned warriors, told me about an upper room at his digs in Walton Street. Although a mile further away and no comparison with my separate study and bedroom at Holywell it would do, and Alan's kindness enabled me to effect a transfer. I felt homeless and dislocated: the 1943 symptoms of acute headache, sore eyes and grinding anxiety returned to plague both day and night. I believe the sense of failure was also fed by an awareness of not having contributed anything much to the 'war effort'. Fire-watching was not enough!

One afternoon I knelt at the diminutive bed in my claustrophobic top floor room, looking for some comfort and reassurance, but there was none. The joy of prayer had gone; the joy of worship was shortly to go too, but guided by a wise priest I tried hard not to despair. He showed me how foolish it was to love God only when it was pleasant to do so – 'cupboard love,' he would say. My insecurity was increased by the defection of some friends to the Church of Rome. I wondered whether I should not regain peace and security by doing the same; but one day while walking to Queen's I stopped at the Martyrs Memorial (always on my route from Walton Street) and had a sort of vision of the parish churches of England and the Anglican worship that had continued in them for four hundred years since the burning of our bishops. Could I repudiate that?

The answer was, No: but at the time it was hard to retain any religion at all. Since the joy of prayer and worship had gone it was simply a case of clinging to God with the will. Perhaps I learnt what faith really means, but it was extremely unpleasant. The pain in my head and eyes was almost incessant and deprived me of sleep. Ordinary personal relations became almost impossible, though Alan continued to be kind. I dared not rely on him too much – fearing it was the same temptation to dependency as the attraction to Rome. Work was excruciating, but I could do nothing else; all forms of entertainment seemed dangerous. My new landlady was briskly perceptive; 'Mr Smythe, you are letting yourself go to pieces'.

Several college men were supportive: and my RC friends were kindly; but perhaps sensed a potential convert. Invited to tea at St Benets, I was asked: 'Do you think the influence of Cardinal Newman is still strong?' Later Basil Hume came to my new digs and tried a direct approach. Softly bombarded with Roman arguments, I was forced to fight back: foiled by my response, Basil kindly remarked, 'Well, Ronald, you put up a good case for your faith and your church' and departed. Writing these words in the very week of his death, I am struck by the unwitting service he did in fortifying my wavering confidence. Rather more hurtful was an RC convert Michael's ingenious plan. I was fond of him and accepted his invitation to meet friends. I had no idea at the time, but these turned out to be two psychiatrists: a day or two later Michael informed me that I had been diagnosed an obsessional paranoid schizophrenic and should seek hospital treatment. Basil remained a friend and later in 1952 invited me to Ampleforth.

Meantime the dreaded exams approached with heavy step: on the day I was astonished to find myself dressed correctly for entrance to the Examination. I walked out of several papers unable to concentrate or write;

in two subjects I forgot myself for a moment and obtained borderline first-class marks, but probably it was chiefly the intercession of Maurice Powicke that obtained for me the cold comfort of a Third Class Degree. 'Well, Ronald, now you have suffered like this, you will be able to help others all the more', he remarked with his gentle almost inaudible voice. The remark meant little to me at the time and I almost resented it: a strange epitaph to a University career.

A dozen friends valiantly ignored my protests of ill health and staged a twenty-first birthday dinner at The Randolph. I am ashamed to say that I remember the names of only two of them. The next day I went into the Warneford Hospital, as arranged by my GP, feeling a total failure.

Looking back with an ear tuned to messages of the later Oxford days for the future, I realize now that they spelt radical disillusion with the motivation and preoccupation of my early adolescence. The powerful driving force of achieving success through examinations, the reliance on intellectual prowess combined with dependence on rather juvenile close 'friendships' had failed. A valuable insight surfaced: I had been pressured and hustled through childhood; the school had deprived me of most of the sciences, the opportunities of university had been compromised through war service, and ill-health had undermined my self-confidence. In future I would not let myself be rushed into someone else's programme or succumb to their expectations. Forced plants are less sturdy than those given time for natural growth. I doubt whether I saw this clearly at the time. Meantime, ill-health was slowing me down whether I liked it or not. I was in no hurry to leave hospital.

CHAPTER IV

LONDON

In most illnesses there are, I suppose, moments when the patient doubts whether genuine health will ever return: is it possible that the languid limbs and floating brain will ever collect themselves again and respond effectively to the stimuli of normal existence? I felt I had no coherent attitude to everyday affairs, only an inward oscillation between fearful anxiety and total lack of feeling: much of the time I had to contend with headaches and trouble with my vision. Could I recover, hold down a job and share the usual experiences of other people (who seemed to feel so differently about everything)? I tried to understand why all this had happened, in such contradiction to the joyful promise of the previous three years, and I concluded that a statement of Christ's applied to me. 'To whom much is given, of him shall much be required.' (Luke 12:48). I had been given 'the seed' but I had kept it for myself; I had not sown it in life so that it might bear fruit. 'He who would gain his life must lose it.' Because I had failed in this way even what I had must be taken away. It was a bitter, humiliating and all but desperate conclusion: I must confess to a desire to end my life, only repudiated by awareness of the effect it would have on my family and the belief that this would be the ultimate failure. From some verse I wrote in June 1947 come these lines:

> Nothing that I can recollect in past
> Nor present understanding
> Nothing that I can yet retain at heart
> (Some comfort lending)
> Nothing of this remains to give me strength
> Or indwelling confidence and joy:

Except the hope that in some quiet hour
His arm will support me:
Except the life that flows unceasingly
With lost meaning about me:
Only these two constants to assure me
That I exist and He considers me.

Though I had failed God I trusted that he would not fail me. I would try to live a normal life, to learn what such living was like, not to expect or even to desire unusual experiences and above all to follow the practice of prayer and worship which I had begun, however unattractive I might find it. I was frequently tempted to abandon this resolve, to return to psychiatrists, to join the Church of Rome, to revert to a nebulous mysticism, but though I feared I would give way on numberless occasions, an almost imperceptible strengthening of will would save me. This would often come in Communion, though I always approached the sacrament with a wretchedly distracted mind and felt as though I should not be receiving. When I did receive, I could not tell at what point there occurred an infinitesimal moment of light, so brief that it was attested by no more than a bright memory. It was enough. Perhaps I was beginning to love God for himself rather than for the pleasure he gave me. A few months later than the first lines of verse, I wrote briefly under the heading

A Friend Tells Me to Think More
The learned man has counselled me to think.
No more reflection need I! But to move
In soothing practice, understanding men;
Not puzzling the mind with abstract thought and meaning
But learning significance in simple acts
Which train the good will to discriminate.

I sought an area of humdrum practical activity I might be able to manage. A month or two before Finals it had seemed the Administrative Branch of the Civil Service might serve. After Finals I was not fit enough to sit the examinations but was accepted on a temporary basis after interview as a trainee Administrative Officer in the Board of Trade, Statistics Department, then stationed on Millbank in IC House. However, after a month or so the headaches and de-personalized feelings returned with such force that I accepted medical advice and admission to hospital again. Being thoroughly unmathematical my concentration may have been challenged too greatly in wrestling with figures, graphs and projections in the department to which I was assigned.

In November 1946 the hospital consultant, Dr White, undertook a thorough investigation into the causes of the headache and diplopia concluding that I should have an eye operation and this took place a year later. Meantime, they kept me in, believing that the de-personalized feelings would slowly disperse. Life turned over to the rhythm of a large male ward, where I found two attractive Cockneys, John Gold (early 20s) with lively mind, quick wit, smart repartee, and a gift for writing, and Charlie Philips, in his forties, severely crippled with spondylitis. Later, a tall man from Rhodesia, Guy C-B, provided the stimulus of a university mind and experience of original, demanding enterprise. Two youngsters arrived on the ward and I was detailed off to give them lessons. Tommy, a sturdy likeable lad of about fourteen, tested my maths to the limit; Richard was interested in religion so after some explanation I took him to a service. Later I was asked to teach a pretty, dark-haired girl (about 11) to play the piano. She had a turned-in right foot and it was thought she might come to use it on the pedal. I was sceptical about the therapy but we got along well. Both the parochial curate and the local rabbi visited, the latter being a doughty disputer. Anna, the wife of Kenneth Jones, my first year friend at Oxford, charmingly called too – and mother came at least twice for brief visits in spite of the exigencies of earning a living at the Blathwayt stables.

After one visit she wrote:

What I shame I didn't have long with you; next time we will know the ropes and I shan't have to be helpful about myself, Daddy and forebears, our gifts and mode of living . . . a large part of the quiz was directed . . . to find how I am off financially and whether depending on you as breadwinner . . . He seemed very interested in my movements and is anxious that you shouldn't feel obliged to work until you feel fit. Of course you know you needn't . . . Dr White is young and very painstaking and has your interests at heart. You must not take too seriously his studied manner of making the person he's speaking to into a heavy case. I felt a terrific case myself while being cross-examined but got my own back whenever we came to the subject of riding! [deliciously typical]

During the summer holiday I had found her a handy little Singer van for about £50 and she wrote in her next letter:

I love the van, she's like a nippy polo pony . . . Pat is mad to drive [it] copying you! And has bought herself a driving licence! I'm glad to hear that the Dr is not heavy with you, and that you are giving pleasure to others through your music though I would not think the Maths coaching was a good thing . . .

Mother's feeling about my illness was that I just needed to do next to nothing, to stop worrying and have more faith. Sadly, religious people don't realize how such a view only increases the patient's sense of failure. If you *could* stop worrying you would. The good Christian fears what appears to be dangerous introspection as the disturbed person tries to understand what has gone wrong. Nonetheless, the love and the good cheer, even at a distance, were a comfort.

Dr White thought I needed creative activity, and arranged for the use of the hospital hall to stage his prescription, namely 'the production of a hospital pantomime'. John enthusiastically volunteered to help me write and produce it, with half a dozen of our men, some with good voices, and patients on loan from the women's ward. Well-known tunes were pressed into service: 'Jealousy' became 'Therapy, occupational therapy': Gilbert and Sullivan resurfaced as 'Two Little Doctors Round are We, Tweedledum and Tweedledee' (the rotund pair who actually did the rounds each day) and 'Tit Willow' in the form of 'The therapist sat on the patient's bed saying, I'll fix your pillow, your pillow'. A love affair was 'fostered' between two good-looking young patients, who sang a sentimental duet I wrote for them and we got the audience to sing it too. The show contained some rather wicked references to staff and procedures, but ended happily with an adapted form of the popular song 'Bless 'em all'. I was the band as well as the producer. It beats me how I managed to ignore the physical discomfort, the relentless boring-away of anxiety and sense of debility. Wild appreciation on The Night was a tonic, but the success was a bitter-sweet reminder of failure in more significant spheres.

The severest winter for years (1946/47) had seized the land: the hospital gave us a warm haven but when I heard that mother was trying to get back to Crickley Lodge, I got myself discharged and went to Gloucester, finding her quite ill in a cold snowbound house. Like the phoenix, Crickley Lodge rose from the ashes and for a time became a holiday home for guests who wanted to ride. Mother worked hard – and Pat when she returned from school – but it was an uphill task. I returned there at Easter – amongst our guests was a boy who developed chickenpox: mother and I both went down with it rather severely . Eventually she decided to relinquish the lease, move the horses to better stables at The Royal George, Birdlip, and to find local digs for herself and Pat.

I had found a room in a Toc H hostel near the hospital in Denmark Hill, Camberwell (other residents also working in London), a noisy and congested district – trams ceaselessly charging past up and down the hill; one of them took me to a point from which I could walk to IC House. I shared my room with a young man who suffered violent dreams arising from his sojourn in a Japanese camp for civilians: only later did I realise how traumatized and truly plucky Jim had been. Several others in the hostel had had a rough time, and one committed suicide in the cellar: but the hostel's atmosphere, largely thanks to the shy but dedicated Warden, was warm-hearted and helpful. Though I was reluctant to undertake it, the Warden appointed me his Sacristan, with charge of the chapel equipment and vestments, to serve the priest who came for a weekday celebration.

Being in the parish of St Giles, Camberwell, I found my way to their Sung Eucharist and became both a server and a Sunday School teacher: behind this was the assiduous visiting of the curate, Norman Waring. He had come to the hospital, he called at the hostel and for his pains I gave him chicken-pox too. Norman got me to write and play music for his parish pantomime; I began to coach a woman for History Higher Certificate; and the hostel recruited me for their annual play, *A Midsummer Night's Dream*, as both Egeus and Quince the carpenter, an outdoor production in the large garden. When transferred to the grounds of the local hospital we got slightly lost on unfamiliar terrain and I was heard to utter an unShakespearean 'OK' in the heat of confusion. Hermia was a particularly charming girl with whom I found brief companionship until she apologized for 'leading me on' when she already had a boyfriend.

This felt like a re-run of an experience after the eye operation. One of the hospital staff was a dark-haired, lively and intelligent nurse called Tipsy by her colleagues. Her gentle, but brisk humour brightened the blindfold fortnight; restored sight confirmed my awareness of her attractiveness. I boldly invited her out and we met in Richmond Park, near her home and of course a home-from-home to me. The Park was brilliantly sunny and evoked childhood memories as well as the hope of future charms. Alas, towards the end of the day Tipsy confessed that a regular boyfriend existed and would return from working elsewhere – she warned that he was rather jealous. When this occurred a second time I began to wonder if it was the standard 'turn-off' when one hadn't come up to scratch on the first meeting! In both cases I decided that discretion was the better part of valour. Instead of amorous adventures I left the hostel and moved to digs in Half Moon Lane, not far from Dulwich Park and Sydenham Hill, whose superb view over the wide vistas of the Thames provided a final destination for summer bike rides. I also managed to bicycle to see Alan and his family in Wimbledon when I could, the especial attraction being Rodger, their second son and my first godson.

At the Board of Trade my job as a trainee admin officer had survived the stay in hospital but I was spared statistics and returned to work in the Raw Materials department not long after an outstanding chief Oliver Franks had ceased to head it; later he became the Provost of Queen's and then Ambassador to the USA. His leadership was legendary, and wind of it still hovered in the Timber section where I worked to an able but curiously moody Principal called Cruikshank. Apart from assisting him, I had responsibility for the charcoal industry. This summons up a picture of grime-laden factors encamped in dense thickets of the forest but in fact mainly involved regulating the import of Swedish produced charcoal for case-hardening in the manufacture of steel. I also worked for a rather grandly flamboyant American called Toby, who amongst other colourful tasks was secretary to a prestigious committee assessing the country's timber needs, resources and overseas supplies. When I became his assistant, memos and minutes from me were unwarily signed over the description 'Assistant Secretary', the proper name for a senior Civil Servant, so it was rumoured that this newcomer had rocketed from the lowliest place to giddy heights. However I did hobnob with 'timber giants' like the Latham Brothers and Sir Herman Lebus, whose Utility Furniture factory I visited as his guest. Since our committee met in the President's room at the top of IC House the *coup de grace* was to encounter Stafford Cripps himself.

In 1948 I was 're-scheduled' as an Assistant Principal and transferred to 'Cotton': but by this time I had lost interest in trade and petitioned to be transferred to the Ministry of Education where Alan worked and I felt I would be more at home. Education was attractive and anyway the Board of Trade itself was rocking with the Belcher scandal at the time. Harold Wilson was appointed to steady the ship, but after the glorious reign of Cripps we had mixed feelings about the whizzkid in his thirties.

I arrived at the Ministry's spacious and genteel quarters in Belgrave Square to be the humblest of administrators in the Emergency Teacher Training Scheme. It was rather splendid to have three Higher Executive officers 'below' me, HMIs to consult, and a cohort of Clerical Officers; I worked to a Principal, Colonel Tanner (who was also Mayor of Aldershot and quite often found himself detained there) under the authority of a former Fellow of All Souls called Denis Routh, who took a kindly interest in me. Mostly I was kept on the straight and narrow by an experienced Chief Clerical Officer called Mott, who had known the ropes from the beginning. Selecting potential teachers from demobbed men and women for a thirteen months' crash course leading to Qualified Teacher status, setting up, staffing and overseeing the admin of colleges, relating to their Principals and tutors, assisting students (and at times interviewing those in dead lumber) overseeing programmes – all this was a lot more congenial than entanglement in the cotton industry. Visits to colleges made for agreeable contacts and helped to earth decision-making. The department had more the feel of a family business than Government intervention in a complex and competitive world. Being an autonomous initiative the Training Scheme was also mostly independent of the Local Education Authorities.

A highlight that summer was an inter-departmental conference at Horace Walpole's mansion, Strawberry Hill, where I discovered the subtle charms of eighteenth century Gothic. Our major achievement, however, was suddenly to be confronted with the consequences of 'the Bulge' i.e. the enormous post war increase in the birth rate which meant that far more female than male teachers were required, and to turn round, at short notice, and re-equip largely male colleges for the hundreds of women teachers now required for our infant and junior schools.

A particular advantage of the move to Belgravia was that I could travel a lot more comfortably by Southern railway to Victoria and walk to work; but even better was the discovery that Alan, having been the Minister Ellen Wilkinson's Private Secretary, was to be promoted to the job of Principal in charge of our UNESCO relations and to work in an office near mine. We frequently lunched together in the inexpensive canteen the other side of the Square and occasionally walked briefly in Hyde Park. By inviting me to Wimbledon, he and his wife, Joyce, helped me to recover emotional sanity in the equilibrium of their home, generously to share their family life, and to experience their gradual and unsensational growth in religious belief and practice. With a brilliant first in Philosophy after only a year at Oxford on his return from the RAF, Alan had a far better grasp than I of modern thought. Starting from a gradual conviction in the primacy of metaphysics he was moving from a thoughtful agnosticism towards Christian belief. He taught me that genuine religion has, and indeed must have, an intellectual content as validly cogent as any scientific demonstration or philosophical argument, and to find roots of authentic reason in the ground of faith.

The idea of taking orders in the Church had occurred to me speculatively once or twice but I suspected it was a 'way out' or else that I was uncalled and unsuited. I strongly disliked the idea of being a parson. But conversation with Alan often brought to my mind the thought; for instance as we walked home one night he remarked, 'There are so many people today in search of guidance and support, and so few to give it.' A spontaneous query arose in my mind: How could I help such people? and at once came the inward answer, as a priest. It sounds pious and presumptuous, but the idea recurred, insistently and rather disagreeably, sometimes making me frightened. I wrote and talked to various friends, including priests, finding no definite view within myself and strongly suspecting that I was trying to recover the old comfortable relationship with God by this means.

At length, advised to try an objective test, I chose two – to enter for the Civil Service Exam (though fairly certain that I did not want to be a permanent Civil Servant) and to submit myself to the Church Selection Board (known then as CACTM). After passing the Civil Service preliminaries I failed the famous Stoke D'Abernon country house weekend test of personal qualities; at Lichfield Selection Board in the shadow of that great rose-coloured cathedral they decided to accept me for training provided my health improved in the next two years: till then my entry to a Theological College would be postponed. It was clear that the operation on my eyes had been only partially successful. Health once again had proved a bar and the objective tests had produced another situation to be resolved. My days as a temporary Civil Servant were numbered, but I was not much nearer a decision about the priesthood. Assailed by doubts about my suitability, I feared that by taking

Orders I was simply trying to substitute an official role and authority over people for genuine human relations. I dreaded the dog-collar as a social barrier no less than as a restriction on my inward self. Above all I shuddered at the ghastly presumption of grasping at the priesthood without an inward sense of God's approval – and how was that to be acquired? My inward feelings were still quite numb when not agitated, and relationships demanded an effort.

Turning away from fruitless introspection, I wrote some piano music and planned a visit to Eire in which I might discover family roots, accepting a week's holiday invitation from two elderly Irish cousins. The Holyhead crossing was wildly uncomfortable, but their house on a hill above Killiney was a welcome sight approached along an unexpected palm-tree-lined coastal road like a bit of Riviera, blue waters lapping the Georgian balustrades with cascades of mediterranean flowers on the neat eighteenth century houses. Eoghan's beautiful garden stretched down to a beach: he and his wife Frances poured out family history for my fascinated ears: but the only other relative I remember meeting, Agnes I think, was a ninety-year old widow who charged around in an ancient clapped-out Ford and talked with bewildering speed. However, new ground was broken when I encountered a cheerful group linked with Trinity College, including John Gray, a very able young lecturer in Modern Languages. Frances invited them all to the house one evening and we swam from the beach in romantically moonlit warmth. I remember an attractive Irish girl, but it was John who followed up my later enquiries.

In the autumn he was appointed Lecturer in Sanskrit and other Indian languages at London University's School of Oriental and African Studies and eventually invited me to share a flat with him in Kensington. John was a compulsively brilliant linguist and learnt a new language practically every vacation. He was also a good cook, which boded well for our partnership, because I am not. We enjoyed living near Kensington Gardens but also took weekend expeditions into the country. From Kensington I could bike to work in 20 minutes. That summer mother and Pat came for a hilarious meal with us during Pat's 1949 debut at the White City. As Pat was to jump in Paris later, I invited mother to join me on a September holiday in Italy – an unopened oyster for both of us. She could return home via Paris to support Pat.

Unfortunately muscular pain struck my back, neck and right shoulder which brought about a visit to St George's Hospital, then at Hyde Park Corner. This established that my eyes were still sufficiently divergent to have caused a crooked neck: so a second operation was planned for the late autumn to get them better co-ordinated. Meantime, John's mother decided she would like now to come and live with him, so I found digs nearby in Tregunter Road. These provided an agreeable bonus in the form of a fellow resident, Eric Miller, a young solicitor from Tynemouth, learning the ropes in his father's firm's London office. He was very good value, and, since mother could only manage half the Italian holiday, Eric agreed to come for the second half.

Travelling by rail, somewhat economically, through the night, mother and I reached Lauzanne as the morning broke over the lake in a mysterious medley of pastel shades. The really dramatic moment came as we emerged from the Simplon tunnel at Domodossola, from Switzerland's subdued light, into the astonishing brilliance of Italy, a dazzling new world. Arriving in Florence's hot, shimmering dusk I could not resist taking mother to our albergo by the Arno in a horsedrawn cab.

After intensive exploration of the treasures in this immaculate city, we left for the coolness of the coast in the Gulf of Spezia. A Ministry of Education colleague (in charge of 'Teachers' Misconduct'!) had told me he took *his* mother in the pre-war days to a small town called Lerici, near the place where Shelley had drowned. I had booked in at the Pensione Shelley e Palme. In spite of sad associations, the poet and the palms sounded an attractive prospect. Reaching La Spezia by train via Pisa, we took a bus along the coast. At one point mother knelt on the seat to view the scene in sheer excitement: a brilliant moon illuminated the rocks and wove paths across the water. The pensione was clean and cool; the town not crowded but colourful and cheerful – I managed to find someone to iron clothes mother had washed. We discovered a kindly old fisherman, Innocenzo Medusei, who took us out to sandy and secluded coves, where we swam and sunbathed while he dozed amongst the rocks to which he had discreetly withdrawn. He seemed fond of us and to my surprise refused any payment for his excursions. Later, from Florence we sent him some cigarettes before meeting Eric at the station. We said farewell to mother after dinner on the roof garden of the Balleoni Hotel in full view of the floodlit dome of the Cathedral. Mother was radiantly happy and looking prettier than many a woman twenty years younger. Family photographs are evidence that she grew more, not less, beautiful as the years advanced.

While mother sped towards Pat's show jumping triumphs, Eric and I took a coach to Siena and on to Rome. We hardly did justice in three days to so much history and such incomparable *objets d'art*: for me the most memorable was the Michelangelo Pieta in St Peter's. As I contemplated it, words spontaneously formed in my mind and issued in this verse:

> La Pieta
> The Mother
> Looks on her Son,
> Full-grown, mature, along her lap again
> As a child,
> But dead.
>
> O Mother
> There is a secret,
> Once heard but voiceless, held half-known
> In your heart,
> Now waking.
>
> Only
> This half-perceived knowledge
> Consoles you for the loss of your child
> In the revelation
> Of God.
>
> O Living Son
> Look on the weeping Mother!
> Raise her in Heaven ever to tend
> Your eternal child
> The Church.[15]

Pressing on via Naples to a remarkably inexpensive pensione at Vico Equenze near Sorento we had a launching pad for Pompeii and Capri. Maria at the Pensione Aequa could not have been more hospitable. In Capri, a young oarsman sang lustily while rowing us into the Blue Grotto. Everywhere heat and colour bemused. How did I find the energy to climb from the Grotto to the heights of Anacapri to see the San Michele Villa and tread the rough road

---

[15] I was not aware then that it had much to it and I'm even less sure now, though the dead son is obviously significant. It expresses feelings I had about Mary's demanding vocation and my own mother's, and has something to do with ideas I later developed about Jesus' resurrection involving the resurrection of his community of friends at the same time.

down to the harbour – a kaleidoscope of views over the whole island? Two things became clear: my health was improving and I was discovering a taste for travel. A final bonus: the day we set out for England, Stafford Cripps devalued the pound and the remaining holiday money promptly appreciated.

Some weeks later, the next eye operation became due and I entered St George's Hospital. The surgery was done briskly and I had again to keep myself amused while blindfold for a fortnight. John and Alan came to visit, but a second Tipsy did not materialize. Instead mother invited me to convalesce at her new home, and it was a 'sight for sore eyes'; I could celebrate both her good fortune and an improvement in my optical divergence. The charm of this house reinforced a growing conviction that I should seek better health by exchanging the pressures of London life for a lighter programme in the country.

External developments had made this practicable. Mother and Pat had been offered the peppercorn tenancy of a fine old house with stables, not far from Birdlip, in which she could realize her Crickley plan of entertaining guests and providing horse riding, as a background to my sister's show jumping career. I asked if she would like me to come and stay for a while, help with redecoration and maintenance and handle the business side. She accepted the idea; which became a financial possibility when I heard of a new prep school opening about six miles away near Crickley, offered my services as a teacher and was taken on the staff by the two clergymen who were setting it up. It was a curious turn of events that the land on which we had organized fund-raising gymkhana events during the war should be about to witness my inexpert attempts to referee football and cricket. Meantime, a residential riding school was in the making.

London had done good things for me. The Civil Service taught me method and practical skills like writing an effective letter or an incisive memorandum. I learnt to work with experienced people in a team and gained both increased self-confidence and a down-to-earth awareness of my limitations. Since then, although I have too often forgotten the latter, basic organizing capability has remained and I can face the future even now with some hope that whatever practical challenges arise I shall be able to respond usefully – provided I 'retain my marbles'! The fear and feeling that I might not retain them at the time had also been faced and endured during this period. Only faith could cope with that: and my faith had increased with the confrontation. It was, however, a faith with little structure, if such be the right word.

CHAPTER V

MISERDEN AND ELY

Miserden is a neat little village of some fifty inhabitants within a Cotswold triangle of Cirencester, Stroud and Birdlip. The two roads into it go nowhere, except to a stately house and its woodlands. In the centre of the village stand the Carpenter's Arms, the old school building and Miserden House, its handsome Georgian front facing the rolling hills, capable of housing about a dozen people comfortably, and accommodating a number of horses in its stables.

On returning from Italy I had heard about the proposal to move there, so put my bicycle on a train one Saturday, got out at Kemble, and did the cross-country pull to the village. It was enchanting: autumn leaves glowed around the grey Cotswold stone: the garden side of the house was gently aflame with Virginia creeper. The hills skipped and danced like the psalmist hills of Hermon, steep banks plunged down to the two lakes, majestic shields of elm and oak mounting the ridges, intimate little lanes burrowing beneath interlocked branches; everywhere a profoundly restful stillness.

Early in January 1950 I came and settled with a paint brush, and also prepared my syllabus for teaching at Ullenwood Preparatory School. I was to undertake English, Geography, Religious Knowledge and French, mainly with the 11-12 year olds. It turned out to be mildly enjoyable, and the local bus services got me there and back in good time. Much work was needed to make the house habitable and ready for guests. With admiration I watched mother transform it week by week, returning from sales with almost incredible bargains, finding just the right piece of furniture or old carpeting, heavy curtains or a new idea for redecorating, all quite remarkably within our restricted means. It seemed as though things were given as we required them, and all the time mother worked hard to facilitate my sister's career. She invested everything with a particular grace and charm shot through with lively humour.

I had quite a struggle with the business side. No Income Tax return had been made for nearly five years as, like so many charming women, mother did not think the Tax Inspector served any useful purpose. One typical story of these days must be told. Our main difficulty was, of course, capital: there was nothing but an overdraft on which to raise more. So mother decided to interview the Bank Manager – which is exactly what she did. The bank was under reconstruction and his office temporarily reduced in size with casual furniture. He ushered her in with his usual courtesy, vaguely indicating a chair. She sat down and began to outline her problems and requirements; he was quite remarkably accommodating, looking in fact ill at ease and almost at a disadvantage, only too willing to oblige. When she left the office she suddenly realized which chair she had occupied – none other than his own at his desk, leaving him with the unusual experience of occupying the visitor's chair and being interviewed in his own bank. However a further overdraft had to be serviced and I found it exasperating that my efforts with the accounts and returns would be brushed aside as so much heavy weather. In her heart, I suspect, mother regarded such business paraphernalia as a male invention to justify the existence of people who were otherwise inferior in practical ability.

In moments of stress there were always the soothing green fields where I could take the dogs for a stroll, clambering over stone walls, heading perhaps for the Holy Brook which flows gently through the pastures below Sudgrove, a nearby hamlet, and on towards the beckoning spire of Bisley. I would return as the early evening light wrapped the hills in a garment of dove-like peace, past the little hamlet of Througham and over the brook again at Honeycombe farm, the cattle like as not stolidly swinging through the mud after milking. Soothing and refreshing, but I could not repress the question, what was I up to? This was an escape, and, try as I could, I was unable to find any certainty about the future. Nonetheless I wrote some music, completing a set of variations on an ancient nursery rhyme tune, which I had been mulling over for a year or more. It was gratifying too, that my teaching was approved when the school underwent a full Ministry of Education inspection. Should I perhaps remain a teacher? Mother was most indignant that I was considering burying my talent in a Cotswold village and a Preparatory School.

Our young Rector, John White, was an attractive man whose Family Communion sung to Merbecke's music I enjoyed. His excellent relations with the village school drew children and their families, and his preaching was clear and succinct. The life of the church was quite central to the community and he visited most of the elderly and sick, in spite of having three parishes to care for. He participated diplomatically in the civic functions of the village and was generally popular: his friendliness I valued. He gave me one of his surplices, the first I'd possessed, and he invited me to preach my first sermon. However, I didn't feel I could discuss my problems very fully with him. He suffered from 'nerves' of the sort that issued in feverish activity and high-speed 'amusing' conversation; entertaining but rather tiring, though he could use humour to defuse a situation. The PCC had been discussing *ad nauseum* whether to insure the Annual Bazaar against rain. Not very much income resulted from this event which was of social rather than financial significance. Everyone was getting rather cross and thoroughly bored with the wrangle. Suddenly John inquired how much was involved. Apparently the payment of a small premium ensured the princely return of over £100 if it was wet. 'Oh well, then,' he replied, 'let us pay the premium and pray for rain.' The meeting came to a final decision fairly smartly. He could deal with difficult parishioners too. Once he was being bullied by a wealthy lady in the congregation who tended to 'run' one of the churches and fancied herself as a High Churchwoman. Her criticism, followed by demands, culminated in the threat, 'and might I say I am thinking of going over to Rome.' 'Really,' responded the Rector, 'and when do you go?' Such episodes perhaps gave me a glimpse of the shadow side of the parson's job and, handled so lightly, made it seem not unmanageable.

However, the year drew to a close and some sort of decision had to be made. Making a Retreat after the summer term, three days of hard meditation under a most helpful director brought little clarity of purpose and ended in uncontrollable and unmanly tears. There was only one way forward – the external test again. I would go for another medical and if I passed this time, proceed to a Theological College. As I had made about fifty pounds translating a French book on show jumping, I had the cash to repay a term's training if the worst happened. It should be test enough! I passed the medical, and in January 1951 I went to Ely.

At Theological College, I soon found that simply to study the scriptures, to pray and worship and to learn theology, though it was absorbing, brings one no nearer to certainty about God's will for oneself. I hoped that Christ's message to Paul applied to me: 'My strength is made perfect in weakness'. Interestingly, Paul's physical weakness was almost certainly to do with his eyesight. One day I would feel that I had done the right thing: the next and often many others would be a nightmare of doubt and scruple. Nights were lost in gyrations of thought that would not be resolved and the early light of dawn breaking over the fens would find me wandering irresolutely round the room or lying down gripped in panic. In such moments I remembered Peter's rhetorical question when faced with doubt, 'To whom else, Lord, can we go?' Yet I learnt a practical theology which began to live in both thought and feelings; I learnt some discipline and the old ambition revived in the stimulus of competition. Once again it was enjoyable to beat the examiners in the way I had relished exam success at an earlier age – not that success in the General Ordination Examination is to be included in one's obituary notice. Perhaps that was all that was meant to happen, but it was a strange and unreal life preparing for something one hardly believed one should do.

It started quite attractively at the top of the Bishop's House. There was no room in the College, so I was parked out at the very handsome mainly seventeenth century residence of the Bishop (a bachelor). I wondered if this was significant of a 'non-starter' or of future elevation to the episcopal bench. Being outside the College I relished the few liberties it gave me, if not the early winter morning sprint to chapel. The house stands immediately beneath the Cathedral, whose massive lantern and rugged towers impressed me with a sense of awe, almost fear, embodying the soaring beauty of the faith I believed in and compounding it with a sense of the doom that hung over me, the fate of becoming a clergyman. I had been somewhat comforted by meeting on the first day a man who was as doubtful as myself. Climbing the hill from the station together I had ventured rather ashamedly to unburden myself: 'I suppose everybody who comes here is pretty sure about what they're doing?' I said. 'Well, I'm not' came the rather abrupt answer, 'they just about bullied me into it.'

We lived an intensely subjective and isolated life in a Victorian institutional building without the stimulus and distractions of a university: the murky gloom of the fens seemed at times to penetrate the dark passages of the College. The chapel was, however, fairly light and well-proportioned and the liturgy colourful. Companions were light-hearted at times and routine often issued in humour. The staff, though serious, were not over-solemn (the Principal expressed dismay at the ordination of a woman in Hong Kong, whereupon the Vice-Principal commented: 'They can't very well unfrock her.') and once again I found myself writing and producing a pantomime. I chose Snow White and the Seven Dwarves as we had each and every character amongst the students. Ostensibly it was for the entertainment of the local special school for handicapped children, but The King's School, a minor public school which provided boys for the cathedral choir, got wind of it and we were press-ganged into an additional hilarious performance there. For the Christmas Concert '51 I set the College prospectus to music in the form of a Handel oratorio concluding with the list of things you had to bring with you. 'Pillow cases and towels' made a rather good fugue. The singers put it over well and the audience enjoyed it enough to get the whole thing taped and recorded, under the title 'Cantata Eliensis'.

The King's School were not likely to be amused by that, but they invited the dwarf 'Sneezy' and myself to help coach the rugby. To return to the three-quarter line at twenty-six was quite exhilarating though I got scragged rather more often than I had bargained for. Getting to know school staff and boys was, however, a bonus, and in particular the Head of the Junior School, Rodney Saunders, who was excellent alternative company. He thought I was more suited to being a teacher than a clergyman!

By way of another practical test in the autumn of my first year at College, I offered to join a team on mission in one of the south coast dock areas, near Devonport, called North Keyham. A Franciscan priest led the team, which included a Franciscan brother and a young oblate, two Sisters of the Epiphany Community at Truro, a Church woman worker and myself. We were scattered in houses over the parish: the Missioner Fr. David and I stayed at the fine modern Vicarage with the incumbent and his wife, a charming and vivacious pair. David was thoroughly Franciscan in his irrepressible and somewhat impish humour, attractive humility and very human sympathies. I was apprehensive and excited in turns. Visiting little dockland houses in their long, sloping lines, and their canny, but friendly occupants gradually became less of an ordeal, though the great blocks of flats I hated for their impregnable indifference and innumerable steps. Publicity and visits had, of course, preceded the Mission for some months, but we spent the first week in intensive preparation, getting to know the people and letting ourselves be known before the Mission Week itself began.

The Bishop himself commissioned us at an impressive service and the work began. Mornings of prayer and discussion, afternoons 'following up', Children's Mission services as soon as school was over and a big adult service in the evening, were followed once or twice by a torch-light procession to one or other of the corners of the parish. A short time before one of the torch-light processions set out, David asked me to speak at the first stop. I assented but what on earth was I going to say? Panic-struck, I gazed at the small processing group straggling out of the church door and along the streets. A few idlers joined on and then a few more, younger people came running along to see what was up. It wasn't just a case of making a fool of myself: if I failed, I failed them. O Lord, what was I to say? The words came into my mind: 'The sword of the Lord and of Gideon'. Where had I heard them? Of course, Gideon and the Midianites! A tiny group of Israelites had overcome a mighty army by surrounding their camp at night, lighting torches, blowing trumpets and shouting these words (Judges 7:19). Had the torches or the darkness set off the idea? There was no time to speculate: we had arrived . . . doors were opening along the street we were 'attacking' . . . the Missioner announced the hymn . . . I must speak when it ended. I found I had already begun! The story of the small army faced by a vast host of adversaries – I had not thought of it for many years – unfolded before me. *There* a faithful few, a mere handful of ordinary people, set out to rout the heathen hordes – and they did it! – by faith and intelligence. Should we despair, a small band of faithful facing the ignorance, hostility and indifference of the vast multitude in our cities? I spoke for some ten minutes: it had been easier to start than it was to stop.

Afterwards the Vicar and others were complimentary; no one had been more surprised than I – feeling more at home with set drama I had not made a success of spontaneous public speaking at school[16], and had deliberately avoided debates at the varsity. Since that day I have never feared to speak and what to say has often been given, sometimes at a moment's notice. I suppose I should have taken seriously the promise in Luke 21 (verses 14–15), but once again I did not discover the reality of Christ until I had to. At question time after the mission services I enjoyed being given some knotty challenges to face. The Mission had been a maturing and affirmative experience.

There was, however, a greater test than that of college or mission life to be endured. Shortly after, the mission, finding the Gloucestershire-Ely train journeys expensive and time-consuming I purchased a motor bike, an ex-WD 350cc Royal Enfield. My mother and sister were furious; Pat, who risked her neck practically every time she entered a horseshow arena, was convinced

---

[16] The exception being when challenged during a Greshams debate with girls from our also evacuated neighbours, Benenden School, at Newquay. Someone protested: 'The Hon Proposer is reading his speech.' 'On the contrary,' I replied, 'although one eye may stray to my paper, the other is fixed on our fair visitors opposite.' I was allowed to continue.

that I would come to no good. I was rather surprised at my own dare-devil qualities in the saddle, I must admit. Motoring brings out the worst in some! but it not only shortened my journeys to and from Ely, it encouraged me to explore the countryside. I did several tours of the north and south-west at odd moments during vacations, and revisited the mission parish. The new taste for travel was reinforced.

My mother had always been a keen and skilled motorist so it was with unexpected and overwhelming shock that the news came one January morning in 1952, just as I was about to set out on the bike to visit the Thompsons *en route* for Ely. She had been taking two guests to the station. Her car had skidded on a very icy bend where the Stroud road had no guard rails and fell away on one side into a deep gully. Mother had been killed almost instantly. Mercifully our young guests had survived. It was unbelievable, contrary to the laws of existence that her vital, exuberant charm and grace could be extinguished in one blow, and when she was still so young, only forty-seven! How could such a thing happen just when financially we were coming out of the wood? The business was at last secure, mother less overwhelmed with problems, my sister just beginning to make her name. Pat and I were both dazed and bewildered, and for a time too we both felt what a wretched return we had made for all her goodness to us. I could not overcome my sense of failure as a son; how much happier I could have made her last years if only I had been less preoccupied with my own problems and less ponderous in my recent relations with her.

Yet in spite of the numbing sorrow and shock, she remained with us. The house was still warm with her gaiety and love; the rooms still spoke of her and smiled as she had: but then came the anguish. Only those who know it can understand the devastating sight of the clothes and possessions of one who has recently died; yet over and above this and penetrating our grief was a vital experience of her living nearness. My sister and I received Communion a day or two later and the experience was intensified. 'With angels and archangels and all the company of heaven . . .'; she was there as we offered the holy sacrifice, united with us in the communion of all God's people. It dawned on me even then that I might be able to convey this to others in the same trouble: but the sorrow at losing her was intense; and made me inwardly raw. Death was frightening in its finality. In all this, John White's successor as Rector, Tony Thorpe, was as steady as a rock and without him I could not have borne hammer-blow events, like identifying mother's body and attending the Coroner's Court. He said little, but he was wholly present with me.

When I returned to College I knew one thing at least: though not deciding against taking orders, I could not face the pastoral work of a parish priest just yet. I could not help others with their sorrows until I had properly mastered my own. I could not help them to work out the problems of evil and pain until I felt I had properly grappled with them myself. I thought I had, but her death was too near the bone: my 'answers' were too facile. What we laboriously work out in our minds is not always real and emotionally true enough to marry with the event. I would not, after all, be ready for ordination at the end of the year. What was I to do? Give up? As if in answer, two possibilities arose without my looking for a way out. My Principal urged me to apply for a Studentship at the Union Theological Seminary, New York. At the same time out of the blue, all Theological Colleges were circularized with an appeal by the Headmaster of St George's School, Jerusalem, for staff at the Senior School which they were trying to build up again on grammar school lines after the Israeli War. There was only a remote chance of obtaining the first: I was drawn to the second.

It seemed churlish and inconsiderate to leave my sister only nine months after our bereavement but she pluckily urged me to take the opportunity. She herself would often be away, frequently out of the country, show-jumping, and we had obtained the services of a reasonably competent resident housekeeper. Gordon and Dorothy lived nearby and had tried to be like second parents to us: Pat had a large number of good friends. Even so it was generous of her to part with me so gracefully; there was a big difference between having me in an English parish at the most a hundred miles away and there being four thousand miles of land and sea between us: in those days too, telephone communication was nothing like so reliable. (Even around Jerusalem, calls were frequently abortive: you thanked the telephonists for their efforts to which the current reply was always 'Afwan', 'For nothing'. Only too true in most cases). The Jerusalem Mission kindly made allowance for our situation and agreed to let me return to England the following June for two months, during the school vacation. So other things being equal I felt I should go to Jerusalem, and for the first time in many years it was something I really wanted to do.

CHAPTER VI

JERUSALEM AND GALILEE

Approaching Jerusalem by air from Beirut, the little plane climbed over wooded hills and the first range of the Lebanon mountains and then traversed the sharp shoulder of majestic snow-capped Hermon. Over the arid but neatly parcelled farm lands of Syria you swing to the south west and there, a bright green strip set in golden hills like beaten metal, stretches the Jordan valley with its mass of vegetation and curling river, the Dead Sea appended like a great irregular turquoise. Our plane hovered over diminutive Arab villages, collections of light brown boxes scattered loosely on the hillsides, and fell to meet the landing strip at Kalundia airport.

Geoffrey – from the British Consulate – was there to meet us and soon we were on the road to Jerusalem, revealed in golden beauty as we topped the crest beyond Ramullah. David, Geoffrey and I were all in much the same situation, for David had completed his theological training without being certain about ordination and Geoffrey was a prospective ordinand but had not yet decided to begin training.

David had passed adventurous war years in the Marines but peace had brought dissatisfaction. He did not wish to go on learning the art of war, but had only vague alternative plans. At first he had had a slight leaning to taking Orders, but forestry was a preferred alternative. It was not easy to resign his commission: he has a pleasant through probably apocryphal tale of an interview with the CO and his response to the idea. 'Sir, I am thinking of taking Orders.' 'Taking orders, huh? I should think so. I give 'em. You take 'em. Get out.' However when at last he was permitted to resign his commission he started to work in the forests of North Wales while awaiting training; but when offered a forestry course decided that people were more interesting than trees, and began to look for welfare work in the Social Services. A chance weekend at the Shrewsbury House Boys' Club in the Scotland Road district of Liverpool opened his eyes to possibilities in this sphere and eventually he found himself assisting full-time at the Club. Early one Christmas morning after setting the tables for the Club breakfast which followed Holy Communion, he sat listening to children singing carols in the street outside. Mingled with their voices came the coarse taunts and laughter of drunks, singing in crude mockery songs of a different character. It seemed a vivid parable; men who had lost the way, perhaps blind now to innocence and truth, on the one hand; on the other, children (perhaps their own) offering their voices to God but equally ignorant of what they were doing, equally in need of guidance and help before they became the drunks of the next generation. What could be done about them all? Came the answer unexpectedly, Why not the all-embracing ministry of the Church? Shortly afterwards David wrote two letters, one to HM Prison Commissioners offering his services, the other to CACTM. Both were addressed and sealed. He does not know why he sent the latter.

David did not enjoy his training at Theological College, and when exams were over and ordination due he was still undecided. Jerusalem offered a new opportunity of experience and service which, like me, he took in the hope that the question of the priesthood would get an answer.

Geoffrey had come out to Jordan some years before as a member of the Foreign Service, but at the back of his mind was the thought of a religious vocation. At first it was no more than the desire to cease being a bad Anglican and to recover the faith of his younger days. His work put him in touch with a great many interesting people in cosmopolitan Jerusalem society, and his natural charm brought him friends, particularly amongst the communities of the Eastern Churches. He became devoutly attached to one of the Patriarchs, a fine man of attractive character and wide culture; he was a second father to Geoffrey. Not long afterwards the Patriarch died and the emotional shock for Geoffrey had been very profound. His sympathies had undergone a great change and he found himself drawn towards the Eastern Church.

During the first half term break Geoffrey took me to Galilee. As a member of the Consulate staff it was easy for him to arrange the crossing and re-crossing of the Israeli frontier. From the Italian Hospice on the Mount of Beatitudes at the northern end of the lake, we looked out over the tranquil waters extending beyond Tiberias on the right, with its huddle of domes and minarets and to the left, the sandstone hills of the Syrian shore. The ruins of

Capernaum lay below to the east behind a shield of pines and cypresses, populated only by Franciscan monks and colourful birds like the hoopoo and golden aureole. Three neat stone jetties reposed under the shade of voluminous trees, on the land lay a few derelict mosaic floors and time-eroded stones exposed to the blue sky. The largest ruin is the synagogue where Jesus probably taught: Roman pillars stand surrounded by a collection of detached capitals, a number of Jewish symbols carved in the stones of a Roman-styled building – gift perhaps of the Centurion 'who loves our nation and has built us a synagogue.' (Luke 7:5)

In the all-pervading stillness one can forget how different it was at the time of Christ: it is easy to sentimentalize when everything is veiled in a delicate mantle of contemplative charm. In the days of Jesus it was packed with commerce, loud with sales, customs, bargaining, men jostling roughly in the noisy, narrow, dirty streets: probably over a million people resided in Galilee with all the hardness and cruelty of a flourishing business community.

The still beauty today is moving and refreshing; you feel that you breathe an essence distilled from the hills in nineteen centuries of meditation upon the events they had seen. We walked down to Tabgha where a German priest had constructed a fine garden, by a little chapel decorated with fourth century mosaics of loaves and fishes, and bathed in the transparent blue waters, watching little fishing boats setting out for a night's vigil in the deep. On my return to Galilee the following spring I saw them bringing in their nets about six o'clock in the morning, men calling to one another across the echoing waters, no doubt recounting the night's experience.

On our last morning Geoffrey and I rose early to watch the sun rising over the Syrian mountains, a single flicker of light becoming an opalescent glow until the hills were suffused with fine gold. Slowly the lake responded and iron grey ripples were transfigured into a blue-silver sheen. We went in to the quiet Mass that had begun in the chapel, which juts out over the lake as though reaching as far as it can into the waters. As the Holy Sacrament reached the height of oblation and communion, the sun was flooding sky, lake and hills with irresistible light.

Nazareth was our next call – the neat and compact charm of the Orthodox church at the Virgin's Well, the rather garish Latin Annunciation Church, the purer, clean lines of the Joseph Church built over the reputed dwelling of the Holy Family, a spacious cave with two or three alcoves and a raised table of stone in the centre. By a well in one corner and some deep holes in the stone

71

floor where grain was probably stored, a staple had been carved out for a rope and leather bucket. A blackened hole indicated the place for the oil lamp. The cave had a feeling of authenticity: it had not been hung about with lamps and draperies and converted into a chapel. The village carpenter may have lived here and his workshop would have been above at ground level.

We climbed to the fine modern orphanage and Church of the Adolescence on the road to Cana. There in the tower above the altar and cleverly illuminated by lateral windows, stands a beautiful figure of the boy-Christ. Few boys look so intelligent and poetic as the statue: at the time I was finding classes of thirty or so Arab adolescents fairly heavy going. We returned to them via Haifa, which is an attractive modern city, and Tel Aviv which is not. Geoffrey had helped with the problem in two ways: in trying to persuade him I had begun to persuade myself, and by seeing Galilee some of the sheer physical authenticity of Christ's life had begun to dawn on me. This impression gathered force in Jerusalem and Bethlehem.

We returned to the School via Geoffrey's lodgings. These were near the city's Damascus Gate, a fine example of mediaeval Turkish castellation, noble and decorative. I found it exciting from the first time I entered the city, and experienced fresh admiration whenever I passed through its wide portals into the Suq. Like Rome, the city is built on seven hills and much of its fascination arises from the narrow winding streets and stone-stepped alleys which climb all over them. Every night the Arab Legion cleaned them thoroughly. Cars were only allowed in at one or two points and the only competition a pedestrian met was from little, ill-nourished and heavily loaded donkeys and an occasional camel. There was endless delight in exploring the alleys and devious back streets, which were relatively clean and seldom smelly, with their over-hanging casement windows, their sudden openings on to irregular courtyards or diving under arches to emerge on different levels and in places quite other than you had expected. They assume a different character in varying light, a change in the slanting shadows alter their complexion, and by moonlight an entirely fresh and mysterious city springs into being. At odd turns these little streets run up to or alongside the wall, the sight of which from the inside is peculiarly beautiful and reassuring. Everything is in the same golden-brown stone as the surrounding hills, rough-hewn and mellow. The broader streets (room for three or four abreast) are festooned with wares and shaded with ancient and modern varieties of sunblind. The ragged children swarm round the stalls looking for jobs – 'Basket boy, sir.' 'Carry your bag, miss.' 'Shoe-shine, shoe-shine' – or pelt along the streets weaving in and out of the crowd in sheer high spirits.

Upon Mount Zion, with a rough gulley running between it and Mount Moriah, are ruins of the Jewish quarter and beyond them the rugged mass of the Armenian Patriarchate, Cathedral and Monastery. On Mount Moriah, where both Solomon and Herod built their temples, stands now the Moslem shrine of the Dome of the Rock, shining like a jewel in the dignified setting of trees and delicate stonework. Between these two hills rests the Church of the Holy Sepulchre, a sturdy Frankish exterior imposed on a much older medley of buildings which seem (like a venerable matriarch) to have lost shape in the course of time, surmounted by three domes of varying size, the middle one contriving to give the building some unity. To the right of the bastion-like frontage (now supported by girders) stands Calvary, reduced in size by the process of enclosure, reached by a dozen or so steep steps from within the Church and opening on to a broad low-ceilinged chapel. The floor stands upon solid rock, in one side is a fissure rent by earthquake.

Under the largest dome about fifty yards from Calvary, stands the Holy Sepulchre – what is left of it after centuries of indiscriminate decoration, devotion and destruction. The exterior is garish, but the interior mostly simple and convincing. A small cave, it is divided (as was then the custom) into outer and inner chambers; the latter being the smaller and containing the stone ledge on which the body is presumed to have been laid. The entrance is low and you have to bend down to go in. There is just room for two to kneel. I used to sense a rare and warm peace in the Sepulchre. The Garden Tomb, or Gordon's Calvary which lies outside the Damascus Gate (and which for various reasons General Gordon and others have thought to be the authentic tomb) gives a striking example of what the sepulchre probably looked like in Christ's day but the balance of evidence seems to favour the traditional site.

Though I loved the Holy Sepulchre, the Eastern Orthodox ceremonies there did not greatly engage me. The ordinary liturgy, though beautiful, is long and involved, its shape lost in interminable repetitions. The Maundy Thursday ceremony in the outer courtyard is impressive and colourful – David and I watched from the roof of the Sepulchre Church as the Patriarch solemnly washed the feet of his fellow bishops in a specially staged open air 'Upper Room'. Again it is extraordinarily prolonged for such a straightforward act and similar ceremonies in other churches, notably the Syrian (they used a tablet of Lifebuoy soap), were more effective for their simplicity. The Armenian services at the Cathedral of St James were particularly beautiful and the music usually energetic and forceful, an intense expression of the accumulated and deeply felt experience of a small nation which has suffered much.

Part of one night I spent alone in the Holy Sepulchre Church. It was an act of piety during the week of the anniversaries of my parents' deaths – January 14th and 19th; partly in hope, not of a great spiritual experience but rather that complete isolation and quietness might bring some inner clarity. The Church was normally locked from soon after 6 p.m. until the Midnight Liturgy. I had once been caught by this closure, lingering until too late in a lower chapel. Fortunately two or three monks were still in the Church before returning to their monastery which abuts upon it. I was not permitted to go through the monastery, but they fetched a ladder, indicated that I was to lie flat on it and with great dexterity pushed the ladder and myself through a small aperture halfway up the great door into the outer courtyard. I debouched gently head first on the flagstones.

This time I asked permission to remain; it was granted with some amused curiosity, and I waited in the Armenian Chapel while the doors were closed and barred, bolts clanged into position and retreating footsteps indicated that the attendants had gone. A few oil lamps cast a dim mellow light. I descended over the iron grille steps that lead down into the subterranean chapel where Helena is reputed to have found the remains of the True Cross. I doubted this story but the small grotto was nonetheless dear to me. It is cut out of the living rock, very crude with overhanging shelves of stone and a stone altar. There were no lights, but I could feel my way to the altar step, and spent some time there in preparation for the evening.

Remembering that I had shortly to introduce a study group to St Peter's First Epistle I had brought a notebook for intervals between prayer, and now repaired to Calvary for meditation. The epistle's constant reference to suffering was apt for this location, and also in tune with my own thoughts. Here candles as well as oil lamps were burning so I could see the text.

I found myself recalling 'the souls of the just are in the hands of God and there shall no torment touch them. In the sight of the unwise they seem to die.' Memories surfaced of the death of my mother and father. How fundamental are questions about pain and evil! People turn from the Church because they sense a failure to address them; but who today can feel convinced about an angelic 'fall' introducing evil to an otherwise perfect creation?[17]

Clearly three-dimensional existence is imperfect, painful and unjust from the start. Jesus attempted no explanation. He only contradicted the current notion that you get what you deserve (see Luke 13:1–5 and John 9:1–3). His answer to mankind's suffering was simply to suffer too – which, if nothing else, shows a high degree of concern and identification: Christ asserts 'He who has seen me has seen the Father,' and then goes on to crucifixion. The Father cares to the point of death, but with him, can death be the last word? The sparrow does fall to the ground, frequently, but not without the Father who exists eternally. Evil and death can be endured and overcome: life can be given or taken away and regained. Jesus expected suffering as a consequence of his work, but as any other human feared pain and went through the agony of physical and mental torment, as well as the temptation to evade it. He did so voluntarily: in no way was he obliged to. Here is no final explanation, but if the Creator himself suffers through his Son it is a divine response to evil, and the vision at the end of the Scriptures (Revelation 13:8) speaks of a lamb slain from the foundation of the universe, implying that the Creator knew from the start the cost of creation to himself. I stood in silence on Calvary, perhaps where the pagan centurion had stood before, gazing perplexed at the dying figure and yet compelled by the quality of Christ's death to utter words of faith.

I left Calvary and walked round to the Tomb. It glowed with candles inside and looked alive and welcoming. Did willing and creative acceptance of death bring resurrection? If so, how does that link up with our death? God in Christ had taken on darkness and death and wrenched life and light from them. Could evil always be experienced in such a way that goodness was forged in the fire of suffering? human suffering appeared so often to overwhelm and even destroy personality. Yet how could I say that there was a better solution? It was not difficult to conceive an easier way, a way more consonant with human ideas of health and well-being, but who could say that Christ's way

---

[17] The scriptures suggest that some amongst angelic beings made by God to live with him in eternity, having free will (without which genuine love is impossible) decided to rebel against him, and being cast out of heaven came to earth to create havoc. Their evil will is represented in the Eden myth by the serpent who tempts humanity likewise to reject God – to 'make themselves gods' instead of trusting the Father's way of giving us eternal life. As a parable the Eden story makes a lot of sense.

did not bring the greater healing? Was it the only way to resurrection or eternal life?[18]

Doors began to open and monks entered silently to light the candles for the early liturgy. Darkness was about to be overcome by the celebration of light. Dawn is born at the nadir of night. I was too tired to absorb more than the simple dignity of the liturgy, the recurring refrain of Lord have mercy on us, the glory and triumph of praise, Holy God, Holy and Strong, Holy and Immortal. God had been abundantly merciful to me in 'good measure, pressed down and running over'. Still surrounded by some of the light and peace of that celebration before the tomb, I trod the silent streets of the city; a slight morning breeze stirring the tarpaulins over the little shops and rattling the shutters, the trees of the Nablus Road, tall peppers, eucalyptus and cypress, gently sighing as I climbed the hill to St George's.

So much for spiritual experience: what about more earthly experiences? Shortly after arriving in Jerusalem, one early evening in the still transparent warmth after a hot day, David and I were on the way to shop in the Old City when I saw a very attractive fringe above intelligent bright eyes and a slightly upturned nose. She was with a small group, some of whom I already knew, chatting vivaciously in English. On such occasions I usually feel that I am unlikely to get introduced and give up from the start. Nobody bothered to greet us so it was just as I had expected: nonetheless I was determined to find out who she was. Geoffrey, I believe, vaguely enlightened me but the opportunity came a few days later at one of the inevitable consular cocktail parties, to which we had both been invited. She was a nurse – a sister – at the St John's Eye Hospital, in Jerusalem for a short period like ourselves: her name was Audrey Edwards, but everyone knew her as Teddy. I soon discovered she was musical and possessed a very pleasant mezzo-soprano voice. Altogether she was very charming indeed, with the wind-swept beauty of a cyclamen: I was astonished at my good fortune when she accepted my invitation to a meal in the Old City.

However the strongest day by day impressions were being made upon me

---

[18] Both the empty tomb and the resurrection are tougher facts than most people realize. Frank Morrison's book *Who moved the stone?* is impressive testimony by one who had completely doubted before he undertook a comprehensive study. The tomb and the existence of people who had known of it, even when buried under a Roman temple, ready itself to be resurrected, were solid facts that had survived, in the first instance, nearly three hundred years of deliberate suppression.

by our one hundred Arab and Armenian boys at the Senior School. The start of my new teaching job had been challenging. First, a heat wave on our September '52 arrival laid me low briefly. Then Denis Baly, the Headmaster, announced that the History master had decided to leave: could I swap English for history and teach O and A level syllabuses, Mediaeval Arab history for the lower sets, O level RK and some geography? I could hardly turn round and go home; so at once ordering books from England and beginning like some panic-struck spider to spin from academic innards a provisional set of notes, I embarked on Modern European history; and raided local libraries for Islamic sources. Denis had already planned to put the last year's O level history group through the November exams (a cooler time than the summer dates); and to offer them A level from January 1953 to keep them out of mischief for the rest of the school year. The Cambridge Exam Board obligingly agreed that they could take the papers for three parallel periods viz European history (which they had touched on for O level) English history and Colonial history for the same period 1714-1815. These would interact so that they had less raw material to learn: I had one term in which to prepare. An unexpected ally emerged, namely the Arab Memory.

From earliest days many of our boys had had to commit to mind yards of the Koran and to regurgitate them to parents and teachers. If I prepared detailed notes and diagrams they would memorize with remarkable accuracy: my job would be to teach them how to use this material to answer the examiners' often devious questions; so a large batch of previous exam papers was also ordered.

Classes in O level Religious Knowledge took on a special flavour because the biblical material often referred to places better known to my students than to me. They enabled me to track down the background to various episodes, as for instance, after walking over the barren hills north of the City to the village of Anathoth (now Anata). I discovered where Jeremiah had conducted his significant business and Abiathar the priest had lived (Jer. 32:6-15) and incidentally passed a pleasant Saturday morning with the village elders. [19]

However, tempers could get frayed. Teenage Arabs combine a fiery temperament with much charm and a sense of humour. Ours were basically

---

[19] Though the student body was fairly evenly split between Muslim and Christian families, there was no sense of conflict since both faiths drew on the bible, Jesus (Issa) being an honoured prophet in Islamic tradition. (He, they believed, would return to judge mankind).

thankful that the school provided an educational way out of their economic impasse: so when things threatened to get out of hand I would solemnly pronounce 'In these conditions I cannot teach: please come and inform me when you are ready to continue' and depart for the staff room. After five minutes or so a deputation would arrive. "Sir, we are now ready to be taught'; they had sorted out the cause of division and we could proceed peacefully.

Arab pupils were a lot more motivated to learn than their English counterparts: they had only to see the poverty of their families, their friends and the fate of youngsters without such opportunities, for whom the Israeli war had produced sheer hopelessness. Parents of some lived in caves outside and even sold wares at street corners in the Old City. It was exhilarating to work with the older ones, and the extent of their industry can be gauged by the fact that, though they had done no English history in their lives, and had only six months for the two year course, several reached the Advanced Level in 1953 and rather more in the following year when we took nine months. Some found their way to American Universities or into jobs with the oil companies.

The 'poetic English' of the King James Bible was at times a hurdle to be negotiated. We had to use it as the basic text and this produced a howler or two. During our study of King Saul, Jonathan and David, the serious sins and errors of Saul had to be recounted. They had read of his consulting the witch at Endor prior to the military disaster on Mount Gilboa and of course, David's moving lament over Jonathan's death. One lad, after listing Saul's mistakes wrote 'and finally he insulted a witch' (clearly the very nadir of error) and another, asked how David described Jonathan's affection for him, answered, 'It was better than the passing of women'. But mostly we got on well with Elizabethan English; I think the sonority and the long periods resonated with their own language. It was impressive to see them writing with me from left to right and reversing this direction so smoothly in the Arabic lesson that followed.

In addition to Denis, the Headmaster, our staff consisted of four English males; two Americans (a women teaching arts subjects, a male teaching science); an Arab and a Syrian mainly for the Arabic. Later a Greek joined the Science department. Denis was greatly committed to the people of the Middle East where he had already worked for at least twenty years: he spoke fluent Palestinian Arabic. It was not an easy time as anti-British feeling was strong, but the boys never introduced it into their personal relations with us and their friendliness was genuine and often appreciative. The Arab and

Armenian staff probably felt more strongly on political matters than the boys, but they too were courteous and agreeable in their relations with us. In truth I felt that both boys and staff tolerated the presence of foreign missions and educational facilities while they were without such resources of their own. Nationalism in the Middle East was quite uncompromising and it was painfully obvious how few in the West realized the strength and universality of these sentiments. Patronage by Western powers or people was profoundly resented and they saw through the 'benevolence' to the underlying economic concerns and political advantage which too often motivated it. I doubted whether our diplomats and representatives really listened to what Arabs believed to be their real interests.

David was concerned chiefly with sport but had also to teach general subjects to the younger boys who were a handful. Many of all ages had backgrounds that, through no fault of their own, were extremely unsatis-factory and the behaviour of some was almost incorrigible, but it was not long before David had won almost universal respect, and some genuine affection. He also ran the Scouts, mildly suspect in Jordan as a uniformed organization hailing from Britain – but they flourished in no time. He even took them camping near the Saracen Castle at Aijlun, no mean feat when all the kit, as well as the troop, had to be transported through rough terrain by an old bus through woods rife with scorpions and snakes.

At the Junior School, another ordinand, Roger Gaunt, had arrived to assist with the under-14s, some 250 of them. In contrast with David and myself he knew exactly what he wanted. He had not yet begun his theological training but as far as I could gauge had no doubts at all about being ordained. He was not presumptuous about it, nor inordinately convinced of his suitability, but to him it was quite clearly what he should do, his sense of vocation was distinct and unequivocal. I thought, was this how it should always be? Roger was also musical and rather more competent at it than myself. As the English community was relatively rich in musical talent he and the Cathedral Sub-Dean, Ronnie Brownrigg, organised a choir and orchestra, who later performed Handel's *Messiah*. I helped quite often with the organ at services and concerts.

Our Headmaster, a pianist, also organized musical evenings and introduced a weekly recital for the school after morning prayers, which was not unappreciated by them. Various talented visitors of all nationalities were invited to the musical evenings. I remember an elderly French monk joining us once. We had been led to expect something of a musical virtuoso though nobody knew much about him. The Headmaster played his usual ice-breaking piece, followed I think by some songs, when a pregnant pause indicated that the moment had come.

'And now Père, will you do us the honour?' asked Denis. The little man looked delighted and asked if he might fetch his music from outside. We waited in expectation as he returned with a battered leather case.

'I shall need an accompanist,' he remarked. This was to be a rare treat indeed: the Headmaster and I exchanged glances, both doubtful whether we could cope with the sight-reading. Out of the case came a much used copy of 'The Blue Birds of Happiness'. Needless to say, we all sang it with gusto.

It was not, however, either Roger, the Sub-Dean or Denis who provided the chief musical stimulus for me: it was Teddy with her 'Isobel Baillie' voice and charming nature. I wrote songs for her, as I had for my mother, the first being a setting of Blake's:

> How sweet I roamed from field to field
> And tasted all the summer's pride

But the most ambitious songs I had yet put to music were poems by Rabindranath Tagore, extracts from 'Gitanjali' which could be called the songs of a mother.

The sleep that flutters on the eyes of my child, does anybody know where it comes from? There is a rumour that it dwells in the shadow of the forest dimly lit by glow-worms – where hang two timid buds of enchantment: from there it comes to kiss his eyes.

The smile that flickers on baby's lips as he sleeps, does anybody know where it was born? There is a rumour that the young pale beam of a crescent moon touched the edge of a vanishing autumn cloud and then that smile was first born in the dream of a dew-washed morning.

When I bring you colour'd toys my child, I understand the play of colours on clouds – on water – and why flowers are painted.

When I sing to make you dance I know why there is music in leaves and waves send their chorus of voices to the heart of the listening earth.

When I give sweet things to your clasping hands I know why there is honey in the cup of the flower, and why fruits are secretly filled with sweet juice.

When I kiss your face to make you smile my darling, surely I know the pleasure that streams from the sky in morning light and the summer breeze.

The purity of her voice exactly suited the mood of these words, it did not overburden them with sentiment as a more fulsome soprano might, and her natural feeling for children invested them with a moving sincerity. My own love for children and for her were blended.

When Hoult Taylor, my music teacher at Greshams, heard the songs on my return to England he commented: 'These are written con amore.'

At Easter David and I, Roger and the American member of staff, decided to holiday in Cyprus. Teddy agreed to come too. Cyprus is beautiful in spring, especially on the north coast where we stayed. The mountains rise green and timbered (not unlike Capri) to limestone crags and mediaeval ruins. The coast is broken and rocky with little ports like Kyrenia strung along the coves, small terrace houses rising in narrow streets above the harbours and an English suburban skirt of villas and bungalows. The flowers were brilliant – red, yellow, blue and white – and March storms almost at once ceased to whip up a dark sea, giving way to a gentle sun and warmth. We received Communion on Easter Day at the little English Church to the east of the town and also visited our elder sister the Orthodox Church, ancient and colourful with a proud slender campanile rising above the harbour. We savoured the small church at Lambousa near by the sea surrounded by a mass of flowers, the fine rough porticoes of S. Appollinaris adorning a hollow in the coast range to the east, and massive monasteries like Apostolos Barnabas typical of the stolid endurance of the Eastern Orthodox Church through centuries of foreign rule. The finest monasteries, Stavrovouni, Kykko and S. John Chrysostomos were up in the mountains; the Latin Church (Roman Catholic) going with the Venetians, had left a picturesque ruin at the monastery of Bella Paise, just above Kyrenia.

On a backcloth of green and rocky antiquity, in the ruins of Castle Hilarion on the mountains above Kyrenia, rambling over the crags to giddy heights overlooking the sea, Teddy would sketch a view or a gothic arch (she was also an accomplished artist), flash a bright eye and a smile, speak with a gentle seriousness or laugh at one of David's inanities. Culture was not his line; he would rather go fishing and did, spending a whole night in the deep with one of the Kyrenia fishermen, Sekkides. Along the harbour the nets were laid out or strung over trestles, the fishermen either mending them or drinking at little tables in the shade, engaged in desultory conversation which flared into loud exchanges as some burning issue arose. David got to know several of these men and their families, and consequently while swimming in the harbour or sunbathing on the beach we would find ourselves surrounded by children. Christos and Andreou, the older sons of Sekkides the fisherman, amused us by diving from the pepper pot tower at the end of the jetty.

The night before I left Kyrenia I could not sleep. I got up at four a.m., dressed and walked out towards the harbour. No one was about; the castle towers and walls were still shrouded in semi-darkness as the dawn began to break. From one of the sleepy alleys of the town two slight figures emerged: I guessed who they were before we recognized one another. Christos and Andreou ran across to greet me, though we had few words in common. Sitting with them, legs dangling over the harbour wall watching the sunrise, I tried some New Testament Greek. It was not very successful, so I wrote a few words in a notebook, remembering that though modern Greek pronunciation is very different from ancient Greek the spelling and syntax is much the same. We managed to keep up an exchange and then went in for a swim. The boys were as lithe as fish, dived daringly and sported in the lagoon like young porpoises. They fetched a net and began to chase fish – and one another. Christos was twelve and his brother eleven: there were four or five more in the family. A strangely idyllic magic and immediacy hung over this unexpected meeting – somehow a fitting end to the holiday.

Mostly my thoughts and feelings were preoccupied with Teddy. I had seen her work at the St John's Eye Hospital and was astonished by the intrepidity with which she would take on far bigger responsibilities than an English Hospital Sister, including eye operations; and this involving Arabs who are not used to being treated by women. She managed everything with calm serenity – and humour, which appeals to Arabs. Now I saw her relaxed and charming with all nature springing into colourful life about us: I was proud of her, even showing-off a little to the others in the unaccustomed pleasure of possession. Her contract was, like mine, due to end in a year's time. What would happen afterwards? In a month or so I would be returning, as promised, to my sister in England and leave Teddy for a while; but I was hatching a plan which should appeal to her. I would use my return ticket to fly home now and motor out again. We would have a car in Jerusalem and could drive home together. The idea appealed to Teddy but she was reluctant to drive; so, learning in Cyprus that Denis had accepted an invitation to lecture in the USA and planned to leave Jerusalem the following summer, I invited him to share the driving – and David offered to join the party as a non-driving mate. We returned to the summer examinations in high expectation. My sister Pat completed it by writing to say she had found a Hillman Estate car that should meet requirements. In June I routed my homeward journey via Cyprus, spent a day with the Sekkides in Kyrenia, arranging some help for Christos' education and enjoyed a swim with the boys in Kyrenia harbour. There were seven weeks in England to plan the journey, learn to drive a car, pass the test, get the equipment and travel documents, and find companions for the journey back to Jerusalem. Teddy would be the lode-star in the firmament as we travelled.

CHAPTER VII

MEDITERRANEAN CAROUSEL (1)

Our journey began at Victoria Station, it was the rush hour and I hit a bus – gently: only a few days before I'd passed the driving test, probably because the Test Instructor being unfamiliar with Gloucester had directed me down a one-way street. Our party consisted of Eric, my solicitor friend who had holidayed with us in Italy and who was game to drive the whole way to Jerusalem; David's father Jimmy Street[20] who was hoping (unbeknown to David) to meet him in Venice; and, accompanied by Jimmy, a youngster called Roger from the King's School, Ely, a promising scrum half, with whose family I'd become friendly. Roger's father was keen for him to travel. David, Jimmy's son, was hoping to arrive in a 'banana boat' from Beirut, to join Eric and myself for the second half of the journey. The climax of the first half was to be David's astonishment at meeting his father in Venice.

Nothing stops in the rush hour, so in spite of tell-tale red paint on the front bumper we were borne along irresistibly to our first camp site on the Dover road near Charing, a farm where (in return for Pat's autograph) a magnificent high tea and comfortable barn awaited us. In the morning we were not allowed to make breakfast but brought in to the farmhouse for ham and eggs. Great kindness set us on the way and soon, hearts in our mouths, we saw the car swung up to a giddy height and hovering over the water before landing on the Channel ferry deck. The disembarkation was less alarming and soon miles of Belgian highway were devoured until dusk began to fall. Pleasant woods appeared in the middle distance, but could we reach them . . . ? Trying several narrow by-roads, suddenly one brought us out in front of a large and imposing chateau of baroque grandeur. We took our courage in both hands and drove in, looking rather a sorry and dishevelled

---

[20] J Street, Senior Master of Shrewsbury Public School.

sight to the grand gentleman who was coming down noble stone stairs. What did we want? My execrable French was soon exchanged for his superior English. He was Monsieur le Prince de Mérode: yes, we might camp – not in the Park because the trees were too valuable, but if we returned to the main road we would find a grassy track to the right where others were camping. We were intrigued at the thought of 'others', thanked Monsieur le Prince and set out for the grassy track.

It was not difficult to find, chiefly by reason of the caravan of gypsies already installed! We passed them with a cheery greeting and, happy in our common vagrancy, settled a little further along, very ready for a meal. It was nearly dark, so I experimented with a quick method of preparing by boiling the tin of beans in a saucepan full of soup. I still maintain that it would have been all right if I had remembered to remove the label.

Next day our 'kitchen' and other impedimenta aroused speculation at the German frontier and even more amusement to a group of German foresters who had to rescue us from a muddy road near Aachen: we had turned off in search of a picturesque lunch site in the woods. After a siesta we explored Charlemagne's Cathedral and found its dim mystery more interesting than the Kaiser's cathedral at Cologne – halved by needless British bombing.

That night we camped opposite the wooded heights of the Drakenfels and its illuminated castle ruin. The following day Roger swam in the Rhine, but the current was too strong for him, though it was warm and clear. The road which runs down the left bank of the river is very beautiful, though spoilt by its rival the railway, which seems continually to get in the way. Lunching at charming Bacharach, having heard Mass in a crowded church at Coblenz, (I was struck by the use of German in the liturgy, my first contact with the Continental Liturgical Movement) we found refuge in a forest near Heidelberg that evening, the buzz of mosquitoes accompanying the distant hum of traffic on the autobahn.

Ulm and its magnificent Cathedral were our main interest on the following day, approached through wide vistas of Bavarian hills and lakes, but the heat was telling on us and by the time we reached Ravenna, Roger was content to sleep solidly through our visit to the ravishing mosaics and marbles of San Vitale. However, Lake Garda had been a wonderfully refreshing experience. Approaching Malcesine we'd seen diamond lights flashing across the water and fishing boats bobbing lazily at their moorings, a warm white mist rising from a nearby lagoon. Some boys on bicycles pointed out a narrow track leading down to the water's edge and a row of barely visible little villas. A young woman emerged from one of them and greeted us easily: 'Of course you must camp here. You will be most welcome.' There was a flash of white teeth and in momentary light from the house long dark hair stirred on her shoulders: she went in and the door closed quietly. Jimmy was already pitching his small tent: Roger had settled down on his mattress in the back of the car, while Eric and I were setting out our camp beds under the stars.

I was entirely unprepared for the sublime beauty of awakening in the morning. A few feet from my bed stood three fishermen, silently winding in their nets: no word disturbed the rhythmic movement of their hands. Beyond lay a still lagoon, formed by an arc of land curving out into the lake: this sandy peninsular was covered with cypresses, and palm trees stood by the shore. A little jetty projected across a stony beach where a few boats lay. As the morning light increased the peaks of the mountains gathered a pink and gold aureole: the air was very still.

I sat up to watch the dim trees towards the summits of the mountain glistening and coming alive: the grey rock sparkled and stirred. As the mounting sun's rays struck the little harbours and villages they awoke until the whole extent of the shore was flashing with colour and life. The lake responded slowly, exchanging steely grey waters for a rich garment of dark blue.

'Coming in for a dip?' inquired Eric, already half-way there.

Jimmy had emerged from his tent and was gazing at the prospect: Roger did not stir early. I joined Eric, now plunging out into the lagoon. The water was clean, fresh and very mild. What an awakening! What a revelation! A lustration, a renewing of life and soul, an overwhelming sense of fitness, both of physical well-being and aptness of occasion.

Eric and I were ravenously hungry after swimming, and grateful that Jimmy had already begun to cook breakfast. A light breeze was now stirring and it was cool out of the water. Roger was awake and no sooner awake than dressed, eagerly discussing the lake. Jimmy gently teased him about his late rising; resolution was meantime gathering in his eye. He wanted to swim the lagoon; in fact he was determined to swim the lagoon. For a youngster he was a good swimmer, but this was a quarter mile of uncertain depth. Jimmy looked alarmed. I doubt whether any of us could have done much if he had got cramp on the way, but for no reason that I could think of I wanted him to try.

He set off plying a steady breaststroke, made good progress at first, but the further he went the slower he appeared to move, until right out in the middle he seemed quite stationary. Jimmy was worried and said so; I expressed unshaken confidence – Eric seemed little concerned – yet I began to fear. His parents had trusted me to look after him; they were a thousand miles away; I heard myself composing a telegram; 'Much regret . . .'

He was now just a bobbing dot in the water, indistinct as to arms or head. I began to run round the edge, not hurriedly because I found myself repeating, 'He'll do it'; but movement seemed the best outlet for my anxiety, and I gave myself a reason by taking his sandals for the walk back along the stony beach. It seemed to be miles away and I was making less progress on the rough edge of the lake than Roger himself in it. I had hardly turned the bend of the lagoon when I saw that he had arrived – and now the wretch had gone in again and was swimming back! I hastened back, determined that at least my effort with the sandals should be appreciated. He saw me and obligingly turned to swim towards me. He stumbled out and took the sandals.

'I didn't really need these. I was going to swim back,' he remarked casually, 'but thanks all the same.'

I felt rather foolish. Why had the crossing of the lagoon assumed such importance anyway? Roger and I strolled back to the others, now recumbent in the warmth. Time slipped away as the blue of the lake assumed the depth of a cloudless sky. However, Eric was alert, as ever.

'We must be off to Sirmio,' he cried.

'Yes, Catullus' villa,' remarked Jimmy reverently, 'is an absolute must.'

Roger wanted to swim again, but gave in when assured that swimming could be combined with Catullus, and after passing over the bridge and through the castellated walls and crowded narrow streets of Sirmione, we were soon diving into deep blue water from gold-brown rocky ledges in the shadow of classical ruins.

In Verona after visiting the amphitheatre I was briefly arrested for a parking offence outside the black Saint's elegant cathedral – I had no money to pay the fine (for letting my car stick out into the road). Luckily the Chief of Police agreed to accept a ten shilling note and we parted friends. That evening we picked on the River Adige for camping. However, our map did not indicate the many fens and ditches which crossed our chosen path. Finally with the help of the local priest we had to be content with a rather exposed position on one of the banks outside a village, soon becoming a source of local interest.

It did not last long that evening, but, when in the morning two young farmers carried Roger off to the vineyards, he returned loaded with grapes. Refreshed by a fruit breakfast we found the impressive cathedral at Padua and moved on to the even more remarkable mosaics and general atmosphere of Ravenna. The first and easiest half of our journey was completed as we stored the car in the vast multi-storey on the mainland by Venice: the world of automobiles was left behind as we crossed the causeway to the dream city on water.

Although it was August and not the best time for Venice, wandering along the canals and unpredictable alleys to our lodging at a Student Hostel was idyllic: and astonishingly when we repaired to the place where we were due to meet David, there he was; his 'banana boat' had docked on time, and his face on seeing his father was unforgettable. This was the climax of the journey for Jimmy: a superb meal crowned the occasion. Next day a French rail strike intervened and Jimmy had to take Roger home by air, Roger's appetite for experience rather more whetted by the prospect than by a visit to St Mark's. There, at the entrance to this immaculate cathedral, David, Eric and I faced the prospect of our next adventure – the Dalmatian coast of Yugoslavia.

When our Bishop-in-Jerusalem had observed my Hillman van (both of us were in London a week or so before my departure) he looked at the clearance with a practised eye and said 'You'll never do it.' His was not the only discouragement we received: stories abounded of broken axles, lacerated tyres, and cars stranded miles from human habitation on the 500 miles of dust and stone coast roads, up one of the stiffest passes in Europe, Mount Lovcen, then another 500 miles through Titograd and Skoplje over a 7,000 ft range.

Alternatively, there was a reasonably fast and straight metalled motor road inland covering the 500 miles from Zagreb to Belgrade, so fast and straight, and so utterly tedious, that one man had hit a cow which had strayed on to it. He simply hadn't noticed. However the inland route involved a detour to Lubliana and goodbye to the sea for over a thousand miles. Secondly, by good fortune we met in Trieste the son of Her Majesty's Ambassador to Yugoslavia, and his advice was quite simply 'The coast road is worth it.' All the risk was nothing compared with the experience. Thirdly, we felt adventurous. Now that Jimmy and Roger had left us we had only ourselves to worry about.

Hardly had the journey begun than the car came to a standstill on the road cutting across the Istrian peninsula. Eric who had driven lorries in the Army opened the bonnet and briskly examined various parts of the engine: bits of carburettor, the petrol pump, and lengths of piping soon littered the roadside. The fuel system was blocked. Few cars were using the road but one stopped; the driver turned out to be a garage proprietor in Rijeka. He fixed the engine, administering first aid until we reached his garage – and incidentally coping with a crisis at one of our stopping points when a child fell from a window. He was calm and very kind: one of the many who confirmed our trust in ordinary people throughout this carousel. We entered Rijeka with relief as the sun was setting over the Adriatic bays and promontories; once again greeted by the familiar breeze and smells.

Next morning our friend had cleaned out the tank and sent us off cheerfully; the rocky cliffs and crude little harbours were so enchanting that we hardly noticed when the asphalt ran out. A still yacht with white sail unruffled was anchored in the little bay of Bakarat; but car wheels ground harshly on the rough stones: the road began to throb with heat and the rocky crags all round reflected the blinding light. Mouths began to fill with dust, eyes to smart and lips became parched. There was little breeze to cool our hot bodies.

At length we pulled up for lunch; the sun was beating down and a steep hill had been almost too much for the loaded car.

Though the small clearing by the roadside had seemed deserted, soon girls and boys of all sizes were capering about, eyeing us with curiosity. The gas ring attached to the cylinder fascinated them; soon it became clear that they wanted a job.

'Water?' we inquired in our best Yugoslav.

A voluble reply accompanied by gestures indicated that water was to be found somewhere down the hill.

'Bread?'

Yes, there was some at home – up the hill in the village. Boys scattered in both directions, two bearing the jerry-can to the well. I wondered (not for the last time) whether we would see it again, but my suspicions were unfounded, and it was not long before they were staggering back – their zeal had not allowed for the labour of the return journey up hill.

The road now climbed away from the coast through a narrow wooded gorge, at some points more like a ravine, on to an undulating plateau strewn with large boulders. Stones rattled under the car and ricocheted off the mudguards, spitting in all directions like little bullets. Every few miles by the roadside a solemn and preoccupied figure, generally an elderly man, sat breaking up stones with a hammer. Small heaps of broken stones lay by his side, waiting to be scattered on the road surface. A wooden signpost marked 'Cester' recurred frequently on the way, and we surmised that it pointed to the roadmender's cottage. Perhaps we should need the help of this primitive AA, though what sort of assistance would be forthcoming from such benign and philosophic characters?

Although the following day began with a puncture in the early hours, it didn't blight our pleasure with attractively decorated horse carts bowling along the dust road and brightly costumed peasants driving to market. Later we stopped for breakfast by a wood and exchanged greetings with a wood-cutter. He had seven or eight children, and was earning the equivalent of £3 a week, but enjoyed a contented mind and characteristic light-heartedness: there was no country-bumpkin quality in these people; their poverty went with an alert intelligence and a good-humoured acceptance of the unfruitfulness of their land. You need to see such peasant-farmers terracing and ploughing their stony ground, little shelves of land that an English farmer would never bother to use, to know how false is the view of Mediterranean indolence.

A very uneven journey over wide, stony moorland had brought us down to a river valley and the town of Metkovic; along the river bank, small villages of very primitive dwellings, troglodyte in character, lined the rocky hillsides with wooden skiffs moored in clusters at their foot. The river was attractive after a dusty journey, but hardly had I bathed (this time the others were more interested in food) than we were surrounded by children again. A few adults came to inspect the car and gaze curiously at the baggage and gas cylinder. We were soon involved in conversation: Where had we come from? Where were we going? I wrote 'Jerusalem' in the dust of the car and the mileage we had done. Was there anything they could do? One group insisted on taking the breakfast dishes to the river. An attractive young girl wanted to wash my shirt! David hoisted a child or two on to his shoulders and was soon on good terms with a tall, strongly built labourer, who seemed to have fathered most of them. This man disappeared for a few minutes, returning with an enormous round basket of grapes: we must have all of them, he insisted – there were enough to supply at least two hospital wards for a week. David pleased them by taking photographs.

Yugoslavia was for me a land of hard driving and human kindness. Just as Lake Garda had brought new joy in life, so this Croat experience awoke a new wonder and joy in ordinary people. My affection arose quite simply from gratitude for their response to us as fellow humans. I began to see that in some respects I feared people, concealed it by conventional concern and interest, and that could be no ground for Christian work. True love, I think, arises not only from desire, but from a sense of the other's value and uniqueness. It probably helps to have had oneself the experience of being special, profoundly valued: and this I had known through father, mother, friends, animals too, all reinforced by the experience of God's love, especially in Communion.

Human kindness came to our rescue again the day after we left Dubrovnik, 'the pearl of the Adriatic', set in ilex and cypress and surrounded by mediaeval walls at the foot of terraced hills, golden in sunshine and gleaming in the blue of sky and water. The car had gallantly overcome Mount Lovcen, needing a whole morning to negotiate the seventy-two hairpin bends; the majestic prospects at every turn had helped. At the top we had passed into the barren and broken country of Montenegro, which can only be described in terms of a lunar landscape. Enormous light grey boulders were strewn around, forming crater-like circles, as if scattered haphazardly by some giant hand. In sharp steep curves the precipitous road descended to Cetinje, a shanty town with one tree-lined avenue, and a restaurant not unlike the 'saloon' of a western cow-punching town.

After Titograd, more modern but equally incomplete, the road took off into the mountains entering a narrow gorge as the sun was beginning to decline; the gloom was accentuated by the gorge's extremely steep sides and a torrential river ran below us with a subdued roar. I sensed the hostility of this canyon; the darkness grew as though a curtain were falling behind us preventing return and ending all association with the warm coast. Here we were arrogant intruders. Climbing out on to a broken and uneven plateau, where bright shafts of light pierced wreaths of yellow and orange cloud, while darker, purple clouds gathered over the small valleys that indented the plateau, we recalled that rain had fallen the previous night, obliging us to strike camp rather earlier than usual. (Jimmy had taken the tent.)

I was not keen on David's suggestion that we should seek shelter at the next farm. 'We can't afford to have our stuff pinched; in this area anything could happen.' 'We can't really afford to get everything wet,' retorted David, meaning all the baggage piled on top of the car. I reflected that a farm was not going to be conjured up in this alien land, but I was wrong. A little farmhouse appeared on the skyline and opposite stood a fine, low barn.

David assumed the task of negotiation, knocked at the farmhouse door and was soon engaged in his special 'dumb-crambo' with the young farmer. When the young man at length understood that we wished to sleep in the barn he protested indignantly and, fetching his wife and an older woman, insisted with them that we should come into his house and use their living room. Soon we were sitting round a table in their plain but spacious living room. They pressed food upon us and when they saw how tired we were they asked us to bring in our camp beds and set them up; they would leave us in peace until our early start.

David and Eric settled down; I decided to sleep in the car. There were strange noises in the night – rain on the metal roof, the barking and sniffing of dogs, the muffled pad of footsteps – my imagination? – a jerry-can I foolishly left outside had gone in the morning.

We rose at our usual 4.30 a.m. to be greeted by our host, who came to see us off. He was delightfully friendly and no doubt if we could have understood a quarter of what he said it would have warmed our hearts. I felt uncomfortably aware that we ought to make some recompense, but he emphatically refused any payment. I searched in the baggage and found some tins of spaghetti (rather too easily dispensable, I felt, as David loathed it); it was all we could spare, but he accepted it. Only later I wondered if he possessed a tin-opener. We had become used to being taken across fields, dried river beds and baked-mud tracks to avoid road works and broken bridges; we met a diversion (misleading word!) routed through muddy ditches and several water-courses, a sort of motorcar assault course – at length emerging triumphant on the main road again, when a military personage blocked the way. 'You are driving within ten miles of the Albanian frontier. It is not permitted. You must return the way you came.' There was no arguing; Yugoslavia and Albania were at war.

We had to do with 3-4 hours sleep which took its toll. On the bumpy road with deep ditches on either side of rough ground between Pecs and Salonika I fell asleep at the wheel – the midday sun was riper than ever, Eric was flat out on the back seat, David was nodding at my side. Suddenly there was a jolt and we were careering over the grassy dunes. Eric shouted, David held on grimly; dazed and without thought I steered the car in a gentle parabola towards the road, jumped the ditch and brought the car to a standstill. How on earth did the car get across that ditch, twice? However, one thing was certain – it was time for a change of drivers. I took the back seat.

Trouble at the frontier had also delayed us. At Skoplje a young and rather over-conscientious officer had wanted to check the engine number (stamped in a very inaccessible position) and put his head right in to the engine. David's job was to fill up the radiator: he did not think we were boiling but we were. The full force of this fact was received by the young officer on the back of his head. He extricated himself from the engine and boiling water with commendable skill, but he was not pleased. We were aghast, what would be the penalty for such treatment of an officer? Luckily his subordinate, standing at the ready for instructions, could not contain his amusement; he laughed and this saved the situation. Either the officer saw the funny side himself or he was unwilling to lose face, but the threatening moment passed and he made some joke (about getting into hot water?). Documents were handed over without further ado; so expeditiously in fact that we were tempted to stage a similar episode at the other frontiers, especially while waiting for two hours to enter Turkey. Sadly the Turks just weren't interested in the engine number!

David completed his humorous *tours de force* by setting Greece alight. We had dined on the front at Salonika at a colourful little restaurant near the White Tower. It was then too late to go far along the cost before nightfall so we took the steep road east out of Salonika and turned off into a large field of stubble, with a fine view over the Aegean. As befitted the Scoutmaster of the 1st Jerusalem Troop, David believed in tidiness and burned the rubbish. Suddenly a clump of brambles went up in flames which caught the dry grass on the banks around. Interrupted in my ablutions I seized the water jerry-can and ran towards the blaze, but by now the stubble had caught and a fine sheet of fire was advancing rapidly across the field at the height of some twenty feet. All Salonika must see it! I groaned: here undoubtedly was the end of the venture, our cash exhausted in compensation to some farmer, perhaps ourselves languishing in a Greek gaol. Eric and David were stamping the ground like dervishes, when the police arrived. There were shouts and a jeep tore across the field at breakneck speed loaded with uniforms – my heart sank. A moment later the wall of flame reached a path which ran across the field diagonally, and to my amazement sank to the ground as rapidly as it had arisen. I steeled myself for our arrest. The men approached, broad grins on their faces. What did we think we were doing? Staging a fire display? Had we thrown cigarette ends around? They scolded us like irresponsible children. It was all a huge joke to them, and piling back into the jeep they were soon rattling off down the road, no doubt looking forward to retailing the story with interest at the police station. We set out even earlier than usual the following morning, leaving the charred remains of British occupation.

Towards the end of the day the tarmac had deserted us once again and we were bumping along unmade road surfaces – the main road from Greece to Turkey, the responsibility of neither. It had already taken us laboriously through a number of baked river beds over precarious home-made bridges of wooden planks (with large holes and nails to welcome the unwary) and through fields where it had been difficult to distinguish the main road from the cart tracks (sometimes the same). Standing corn on either side brushed against the car and pot-holes were so deep and unexpected that the luggage on the roof rack was twice pitched on to the bonnet. It was worse the following day. Shortly before Didimotikon, built on twin hills, the road broadened (though still only gravel) enough to encourage my more predatory tendencies in traffic. The traffic consisted of an ancient bus, which had drawn up at the side of the road to receive fresh passengers. It looked as though it might have been plying the route since Philip of Macedon, the dust of innumerable journeys had turned it the colour of the surrounding country. Not that I had failed to notice it; in fact I had decided to pass it, when uttering deep and urgent groans it began to pull out into the road. I swerved to avoid it, too generously, and a front wheel slipped gently over the edge. A nose dive into the ditch would certainly have been followed by a somersault; too slight an angle would have put both adjacent wheels simultaneously into the ditch and we should have been over on our side. But once again the car took matters into its own hands and slid one wheel delicately after the other, settling into the ditch facing the right direction but firmly wedged.

Meanwhile the bus had halted, the passengers had enjoyed a grandstand view of this fine performance, and now tumbled out full of enthusiasm for the rescue. I retired in confusion; but fortunately Eric retained his usual presence of mind. Only a crane could have extracted the car; but could it be driven along the ditch and coaxed out at a point where the field was almost level with the ditch? (Helpful Greeks were collecting the scattered contents of the roof rack.) Eric found one of these points and skilfully surfaced the car. The passengers of the bus felt the occasion needed some celebration. With no alcohol to draw on, David's cigarettes came in useful, as well as his flair for international contacts. At length it was felt that the situation had been properly celebrated and the company returned to the bus, the driver resumed his seat and amidst general pleasantries and a cloud of dust the bus resumed its journey. Somehow we got the car out of the field and back on the road, soon to turn off amongst colourful heather for a night soothed by the tinkling of goat bells. (In Istanbul only a shock absorber had to be repaired.)

A white sun in a light blue sky was dispersing the mists of early morning as we went through a noble arch *eis ten polis*, 'into the city', founded by a British-born Roman, centre of Romano-Greek culture and empire for a thousand years after the fall of Rome, its Turkish name, Istanbul, simply a corruption of those three Greek words meaning 'to the city'. The mists drifted apart to disclose the line of a great wall distantly rising above the houses and stretching along the western extent of the old town, broken by ancient towers which held their dereliction with an air of majesty. The skyline was dotted with the heads of many minarets, which stand erect and defiant like new boys, parvenus, against the mellower remains of Byzantium. Within the walls, passing through a tall narrow gate into the packed streets, both Islam and Byzantium are swallowed up by the din of modern traffic and effaced by tram wires, shops and advertisements. Superior and impervious to all this, the Church of the Holy Wisdom stands in a sea of lesser domes. I sensed that Suleiman's Mosque and the Blue Mosque had an aggressive and over-elaborate beauty; only the 1400 year old original has the serene and lofty simplicity of perfection. We climbed a tower by the Golden Horn and viewed the city, from the Seraglio to the ships idling at anchor in the far end of the Horn. The domes shimmered in the light haze. Inside the Holy Wisdom, the screaming Arabic texts from the Koran, strung high along the walls, were subdued by the majestic dome. The eye is gently drawn from one level to a higher until it rests at the central height. Several times, fascinated, I tried this out by entering the main door and allowing my eyes to rise by sheer aesthetic necessity through these gradations to the dome's centre. I suspect that the Turks, when they conquered the city in 1455, felt compelled to build in the same style, for any other would have been overwhelmed by the Christian Cathedral. The charm of the Blue Mosque derives more from its wholly Islamic interior, the lovely stonework, the tiles and intimate courtyards. Exploring the rest of the city we found these more attractive still in the Topkapi and Seraglio, a frankly Islamic construction, overflowing with rich treasures.

Crossing the Bosphorus we eventually came to Ankara; hardly a city then, rather a shanty town bisected by a dual carriageway, less convincing than Titograd in its modernity, more crude and characterless than Amman. Its tall modern flats and department stores strung along the central boulevard rose contemptuously above the dark muddled and time-eroded dwellings of an old Anatolian country town. We stopped for lunch where the menu had been translated for foreigners, it proclaimed 'Soup of boiled hen's water.' Eric had to try it.

Pressing on we passed through lovely hills and woods; the road undulating across moor lands and wide cultivated downs, sown with flourishing crops of maize, sunflower and tobacco. Near the rivers, lazy herds of water buffalo were sunning themselves, and the little timbered houses, mud-daubed with bright curved red tiles, were hung with streamers of drying tobacco. After a stiff climb through wooded heights on to a plateau we found the bread-bin empty. David volunteered to go in search of 'ekmek' and discovered a farmer who sold it, so the shopping that evening at Gerade fell naturally to him while Eric and I filled the water jerry-cans at the town pump. The evening hummed with life and warmth after a very hot day.

Butter was the chief item on the list – in Turkish 'terayagi', as I shall not easily forget. I went in search of David, somewhat impatient to be out of the town and seeking a camping site before darkness. I met him coming out of the grocer's with a worried look.

'I took the large thermos as we are always running out of butter, and ordered a kilo. The old boy did not at first understand that the butter was to go into the thermos, but when he got it in I discovered the price was colossal! So I asked him to take some out.' However it is much easier to put butter into a thermos than to take it out again: and even less so when both staff and customers are insisting on giving a helping hand. David had begun to feel that it might be wiser, and perhaps more gentlemanly, to buy as much butter as we could afford. But– how much *could* we afford? He had been on his way to consult us.

When I entered the shop the counter was a focus of interest and excited speculation. A young assistant had his hands covered with butter; some had found its way to his nose and face. Butter smeared the counter and dabs of butter spattered the floor and the clothes of some of the customers. The proprietor had now resigned in favour of the assistant, and the young man was enjoying himself slapping butter right and left . David and I tried to tackle the business of apologetic explanations; it seemed to help a bit that there was another crazy foreigner who also wanted the butter taken out of the thermos, and seeing what money we had, the shopkeeper began to accept the fact that we could only afford a quarter of a kilo. At length the operation was complete; we had drawn quite a crowd. I felt that some appreciative gesture was called for but not being able to make a speech, could only think of purchasing half a dozen eggs and handsomely shook hands all round, conveying a final smear of butter to all and departing amid the plaudits of the crowd.

The journey's remainder now climbed between the alpine heights of the Taurus mountains and down through the rocky gorge of the Cilician Gates, scene of much ancient military history, to reach St Paul's home city, Tarsus. In its mud and wattle dwellings, trellised gardens, informal shops and unmade streets, it was a largely Islamic town: one could not imagine the Greek public buildings of Paul's time or the earnest study of Midrash and Talmud in this environment. Dinner al fresco might have been in Arab Jerusalem and after travelling through wide cotton fields towards the typical cosmopolitan Levantine port of Alexandretta, David and I began to feel back in the Middle East. By the time Damascus was on the skyline our route was familiar and eventually the only problem whether the Hillman would make the hairpin bends on the Jericho road without boiling.

Allowing her a prolonged rest while boiling a cup of tea for ourselves, we greeted Stewart Perowne, the Bishop's Secretary who was on his way to Jericho, and like the Good Samaritan stopped; we could have done with wine but fortunately there was no call for oil. His presence was encouraging and a spur to rejoin our friends at St George's.

With the Mount of Olives tower in sight and the air a little cooler we began the last climb to wind through Bethany on the round-breasted mount above us and take a final turn to face the Holy City, bright and welcoming, its castellated walls precipitous above the steep sides of the Kidron. And so the familiar sequence of city gates brought us to St George's.

Here our journey came to an end with a small party of greeting and farewell (Eric had to return) almost swallowed up in the preparation for the beginning of another term. One journey was over, but another loomed up; in less than a year I must decide whether to embark on the road to ordination.

CHAPTER VIII

CAROUSEL (2)

All through that return journey I had looked forward to seeing Teddy again. Having been preoccupied with the trip, I made the mistake of writing hardly at all. When I dashed up to see her soon after our arrival I sensed some restraint. It came out gradually that she had decided to marry a policeman from Kenya whom she had known at home, had admired and loved as a young girl. He had written out of the blue to ask her to marry him. He had an exciting life ahead of him and Teddy was thrilled at the prospect. I was sad and rather angry. Oddly the words of the last song I had written were Blake's Love Dirge:

> My silks and fine array,
> My smiles and languish'd air,
> By love are driv'n away
> And mournful lean despair
> Brings me yew to deck my grave:
> Such end true lovers have.
>
> Bring me my axe and spade,
> Bring me a winding sheet;
> When I my grave have made
> Let winds and tempests beat,
> Then down I'll lie, as cold as clay:
> True love doth pass away.

However I did not sink into a premature grave; we were neither of us in the throes of first passion and soon realized that we had a considerable depth of friendship to draw on. Moreover, living in a small community for another year, we needed one another. At first I did not think I could manage so equivocal a relationship, but her gentle kindness converted me: rightly or wrongly I felt she was not merely humouring me when she said that, if the other had not returned to the scene, there would have been no doubt in her choice. Our second Christmas, I was asked to conduct the Festival of Nine Lessons and Carols with a small but enthusiastic choir. In the graceful chancel of St George's we created a gift of melody for the Christ-child, the choicest offering being a rich little carol by Arnold Bax sung by Teddy. A new set of songs took shape – again from Tagore – and though they reflected my sombre mood I was glad she brought them to birth in her clear, boyish soprano. The words were about going through the night in order to wake refreshed to a new life:

If the day is done, if birds sing no more and the wind has died:
then draw the veil of darkness thick upon me.
As thou hast wrapped the earth in a coverlet of sleep
and tenderly closed the drooping petals,
for the traveller whose sack of provisions is empty,
whose garment is torn and dusty, whose strength is gone,
renew his life like a flower under the veil of thy kindly sleep.

In the night of weariness let me give myself to sleep without fear
resting my trust on thee;
let me not force my flagging spirit in a poor preparation for thy worship.
It is thou that drawest the veil of night on the tired eyes of day
to renew its life in the fresher gladness of awakening.

Our love mellowed during the final year at St George's, so that it felt natural that Teddy should after all accompany us on the return journey, David and I this time joined by Denis, the Headmaster, who would be *en route* to taking up his appointment as lecturer in an American University. He and I had some trial runs as co-drivers by exploring the Crusader castles in Syria. It was planned that, after A and O Level examinations in June '54, we would say farewell to Jerusalem and set out for England via North Africa. As the Israelis would not permit us to motor to Egypt through Beersheba and across the Sinai peninsula, the car had to travel by boat from Beirut to Alexandria (the cheapest way being fourth class without food) and be placed on deck so that we could camp round it. But first of all the car had to be overhauled for the long trip and the only adequate garage was at Beirut. I hoped to combine this with exploring Lebanon, especially the coast which is as beautiful as the best of the Mediterranean Riviera. Accordingly we set out, David and I, soon after the end of term, hoping to be back for Holy Week in Jerusalem.

The trip seemed fated from the start: almost at once we were in for fuel trouble – dirty petrol as usual, in spite of the special filter we had had made in Jerusalem. At length my first aid failed and there was nothing for it but to call at a garage. It was already afternoon and we had the second range of the Lebanon to climb before reaching Beirut. Two young Arabs wrestled with the carburettor: it proved intractable. We thought they had succeeded and set out again, but had to return. Not much more was needed but it was during this second visit that I made the fatal error of putting the travel documents on the roof of the car. (When you are standing by a car you imagine it is a naturally safe place; but your reflexes are so conditioned to the act of getting into the car again that the roof is the last place you observe.)

It was getting dark when I suddenly remembered the documents. We turned back for the second time to find garage hands in a great state from our driving off and jettisoning our passports at their feet. It was with relief that we recovered these, but there was no sign of the carnet (Customs permit). We searched in the dark as best we could, up and down the road until it seemed a mug's game. We would return the next day: but we had reckoned without the security arrangements in Beirut.

On the long descent through those lovely mountains we reached a check point. Where was our carnet? I told the story as best I could to an incredulous Arab gendarme. We were ordered to pull in to the police point. My heart sank, for we had had a similar experience in Syria when Denis was caught taking photographs too near a security area. Now it was night and we were already late for our appointment with the English chaplain with whom we were staying. Fortunately they agreed at once to take us to the main police station in Beirut where at least there would be someone who could speak English and who might check our bona fides with our Beirut friends. This they did, but we were very late; it was a bad start and, of course, if we did not find the carnet there was no knowing how the car could be driven out of Lebanon!

The next morning I had to take the car to be overhauled so David kindly went on the local bus (a hair-raising experience as usual) to look for the carnet. At our garage it became clear that neglect by my Jerusalem mechanics was going to involve me in heavy expenditure – far greater than I had anticipated. David returned in the evening without the carnet.

The carnet system of touring had so simplified exit and entry to and from countries that it was only when you were without one that you realized how desperately complicated it is to move in this modern world. The only thing was to wire the AA in London and this is what I did through the Lebanese AA. It would take some time, they assured me, so there was not much point in returning for a day or two. But the car was now in dock, so how were we to explore the Lebanon coast? I explained our sad case to a British doctor at the local Mental Hospital. I think we'd met after church. He invited us in for a drink.

'Well,' he said, 'I have just bought a new car. My old one is still here. It needs a bit of an overhaul before I sell it and the brakes are not too good. But you could borrow it if you liked.' I said I would like to try it first, especially the brakes. They certainly needed attention, but were not unmanageable, so I thought, and it seemed too good an opportunity to miss. We set off at once, aiming for an eating place once we were out of Beirut, where meals are rather costly. 'By the way', said the doctor before we left, 'I transferred the insurance from this car to the new one.'

The car jolted along merrily, and stopped quite obediently at lights, given sufficient notice. Emerging into the open country we found just the right little place by the roadside and set down to eggs, cheese and olives in the usual Arab style. Refreshed, we set off again, approaching the lovely bay of Djeune. Then I took a wrong turn, the old road into the town instead of the broader new one that bypassed it. We rattled over the cobbles, across a very uneven railway crossing and then at breakneck pace down a sudden incline which debouched on to the main street. By judicious use of the gears I had managed to keep our speed down to about thirty. As we turned a corner I saw some fifty yards ahead, one of the local buses with its great rounded behind protruding over the road. There was plenty of time to slow down and I jammed into third gear as I applied the brakes. But they had now given up the ghost, there was no contact – just the empty flexing of the pedal. Then occurred one of those ghastly slow-motion dreams. I dared not pull out for it was a narrow street with a slight kink in it: anything might be approaching at the customary pace and usual disregard and I should be sure to be hit by it. It was Hobson's choice; we slithered gently in to the back of the bus. Its behind was very much higher than our bumpers, in fact level with the top of the radiator, which slowly caved in, scattering glass from the headlamps all over the road; the bonnet rose to obscure the view.

At once we were the centre of one of those celebrated foreign occasions – and *what* scope! The bus driver was in full cry before we had had time to get out. David murmured philosophically but not helpfully, 'I knew we would never get there, somehow'. And at least twenty Arabs of all ages materialized from what had seemed a quiet street in the siesta. We had made quite a large dent in the back of the bus: all things considered that seemed to be the first item on the agenda. Fortunately I could not understand what pains and penalties the driver was invoking against me, but as I began to visualize another police situation aggravated by a borrowed car, no insurance and no carnet, an Arab who spoke English came through the crowd and proceeded to take charge of the situation. What did I want? I could not very well answer, 'To be spirited away to Jordan', but said something about coming to terms with the driver who was undoubtedly threatening me with the choice of a court case or a new bus. Negotiations began – I was thinking of the car's owner most of the time and exactly what I would say – but it was heartening to hear the English-speaking Arab arguing our case with a fervour and spirit that began to sway even some of the crowd in our favour. 'He wants £10, but it is too much,' our friend briefly reported and returned to the fray. I had thought that at least we should have to report to the police. However the naked bargain had many advantages for both parties. 'He has borrowed the bus;' reported our protagonist, 'it is not his.' That made two of us in the same boat – an alarming complication. The argument was now at fever pitch and all the passengers had alighted to join in, some very much annoyed at being delayed in the journey but not above making capital out of the situation. I felt that my case might be best argued *in absentia* for a while and asked for a telephone box. There was no such thing, but I might use one in the shop; shops were beginning to re-open now.

Returning from a somewhat uncomfortable phone conversation aggravated by a bad line and the owner's Scotch accent, I found virtual agreement on damages. I was to pay rather over £5 on the spot, in preference to a larger claim the driver now graciously waived. Fortunately we were able to put the money together, the driver was delighted, everybody returned to the bus and it disappeared down the street. We were left with the wreckage, and indeed the car was a sorry sight with the whole of her front smashed in and the bonnet erupting into a broken windscreen. Local inhabitants now stepped forward urging the claims of varying garages, but quite clearly the only thing was to get it back to Beirut to the garage already undertaking the repair of my own car. At least I should know what they were doing. It took some time to decline the hospitality of the local garages, and once more we found our English-speaking Arab a great help. He tactfully converted our refusal of a garage into a request for a tow and after further bargaining, the car was hitched to an even older machine and slowly returned along the way she had come – for another £5.

The Beirut garage accepted our arrival as a matter of course: driving being what it is in Lebanon it was a daily sight for them, but the manager would give no estimate. With no insurance to draw on I promised the doctor that I would pay: meantime he had his fine new Chevrolet.

We still had the problem of getting out of the country when my own car was ready. Perhaps the AA had replied? I enquired at the Lebanese office, but no. The sands of time were running out. David decided to return to Jerusalem by taxi (the usual and the cheapest method of travel) and left me with the chaplain's spare bed and a doubtful future. I now found myself involved in the affairs of another member of the staff who had come up to Beirut and met his destiny in the form of a young Greek. Each day I went to the Lebanese AA but always meeting those expressive hands held out in gestures of deprecating helplessness, 'Your Automobile Association has not replied. But,' he added as I began to get desperate, 'you can become a member of the Lebanese AA and I will issue you with the Lebanese carnet, if you like.' Of course . . . at a charge!

This eventually become the only solution: I paid for the wire to London and for my new membership and departed with relief at recovering my status as an international motorist to fetch my car. But it was not ready . . . very soon, of course; so much had had to be done. I looked at the account: it spoke for itself. It was late when we set off, the two love-birds and I, with the Lebanese mountains, two frontiers, Damascus, the desert road to Amman and the precipitous heights of the Jericho-Jerusalem road to negotiate. I was determined to get home by Good Friday, but it cost me a contretemps with an Arab legion lorry. This swung out coming round a dangerous corner and, in the small hours of morn, gashed a door of my car with its vicious bumper.

There was a scene, but I had ceased to care. In Jerusalem, blessed haven, it was soon put right . . . for about £5, of course.

In spite of these setbacks it was a thrilling Easter. The financial strain had been eased by a generous offer to contribute to repairs by the three who were coming on the return journey. As a back-cloth to the colourful Easter liturgies, spring had transformed the city: red and yellow anemones and the rare tender shoots of emerald green grass adorned the barren slopes.

Almost at once engulfed in preparation for O and A level exams, we had to combine fairly intensive teaching and getting ready for the journey. The youngsters said gracious and warm farewells: and most of St George's School and Cathedral staff were there to see us off, the car groaning with camping equipment, jerry-cans, spare parts and four passengers. So, on a placid June evening we glided down the Jericho road towards the Jordan for the last time, deliberately late in the day, having recently crossed the valley when a dry hot wind had practically blistered our faces.

Now it was still and mild, the Dead Sea the unfathomable molten blue I had loved to watch from the Mount of Olives or the Bethlehem road, the sky a wistful evening blue like a silk gown. The other side of the Jordan river the car began the tortuous climb through the Wadi Shiyeh, a torrent in winter, now lazily licking the stones and boulders in its course; shadows lengthened as the sun set over the Judaean hills behind us. I said goodbye to the busy little town of Es-salt, rising in rude and rugged tiers on the mountain side, where Dr Bird and his charming wife at the CMS Hospital had nursed me and David back to health. As we reached the plateau before Amman, suspended in the sky like a ripe peach, hung an enormous blood-red moon, trailing wild clouds and larger than any setting sun I had ever seen (but for the fact that we were travelling east I would have taken it to be 'the greater luminary'). Fat and monstrous, dominating the twilight, it sat as though ready to burst in a thousand violent fragments on Amman. The barren hills cowered under its menacing light. Was it an omen? The journey to Beirut on the following day was not trouble-free; we broke down short of Damascus and had to stay the night there. Would the moon cast a shadow over the entire journey? Embarkation at Beirut, although a complex job requiring tips and patronage by the Embassy, was accomplished without incident, the car was dumped aft as planned and a hatch booked. Our fame spread, for by the evening we had received visitors, the most welcome being the Chef from the First Class Kitchen, bearing a fruit flan.

After a windy night on the deep, the morning saw us in Port Said, surrounded by Arabs in bum-boats shouting their wares. Then came Alexandria and the start of our land trek of 3,500 miles.

No need to detain you in the Customs shed. Even bouncing along the ancient tramlines of Alexandria was preferable to the prolonged business of total unloading, inside and out, and convincing Egyptian officials that we were not mad, only British. We paused to lunch under the shade of a few eucalyptus trees and drew into the side – on to an unfriendly nail. Puncture Number One. I saw a long line of desert punctures stretching away into the future.

The road now ran endlessly between the desert and sea: neglected tarmac with enormous uneven potholes gaping all over the surface at irregular intervals is far worse than dust and stone roads. Shortly after El Alamein the car was so shaken that the rack not only deposited its contents on the bonnet but parted company altogether with the roof. In Mersah Matruh the punctured tyre was quite briskly repaired but at the Sollum border the Customs Officer had retired to bed for at least two hours. He lived at the other end of the bay, but I am afraid, not deterred, we roused him from slumber waving an Egyptian £1 note rather conspicuously. Fortunately not even Denis completely understood his Arabic: it was better to be leaving the country rather than seeking admission. At length we were climbing Hell Fire Pass with its superb view of the arcing bay, a dazzling golden blue in the overhead sun.

We needed to do at least 200 miles a day, according to the schedule, consequently at the pace required by these roads more motoring time was needed. (We were not to know the cost of forcing the pace but a light sea breeze did make midday travel not too uncomfortable: at the peak hours of heat it was actually cooler to move than to stay still, however shaded the environment.)

The Italians had quite a feel for beauty in their Libyan buildings, notably Derna and Bardia, with their arcades and oleanders; but our next objective was the Roman city of Cyrene. Charming though the riviera peninsular at Derna was, it was even more delightful to pass through the lovely wooded hills of Cyrenaica. Shortly before the city, Denis detected the site of a Roman conduit which we explored, very much impressed by its size and vast arched roofing of stone.

The dreaming remains of Cyrene stand on the edge of the plateau where a little stream bubbles out of the hillside and carves a course through the limestone to the edge. The little fountains with their delicate spouts and troughs breathe the atmosphere of naiads and the worship of water sprites. The plateau falls steeply to the coastal plain which glistened in the afternoon heat haze. Some of the villas whose mosaic floors we admired must have enjoyed idyllic views of the sea. The remains of temples were impressive and in particular the magnificent and largely intact Forum in the upper part of the city, but it is the Paterian quality of idyll which makes this city so much more alive than Pompeii for instance; ancient worship seemed quite vividly congruous in Cyrene. However, Christian worship had been neglected by us, so entering Benghazi on a Saturday evening we sought and found an English church for the morrow. Army HQs also permitted the use of the officers' beach for camping that night.

After a freshening bathe and settling down, a rowdy group of officers turned up, obviously the tail-end of a party in need of a douche, flashed their head lamps on us and made disparaging remarks about 'wogs' who had the cheek to bed down on their beach: but they were too happy to investigate further, and none of us was disposed to effect an introduction.

Roman cities really set their mark on this part of the journey. These gracious ruins laid out with a sense of their living quality in carefully planned gardens, are perhaps the best memorial of Italian occupation. At Leptis Magna, the city of Septimius Severus, statues and frescoes were mostly preserved *in situ* or within the living context of some ruined house, bath or other public building. The streets with their arches and colonnades had a nonchalant charm, especially in the glowing sun of an early evening. At Sabratha, beyond Tripoli, some mosaic floors are open to the sky, one actually bordering the sea which conjured up an exquisite picture of the house, raising the walls and decorated frescoes spontaneously in one's mind, the streets seeming to echo with the patter of donkeys' feet and the cries of vendors; the eye even imagined stately Roman matrons and the dignified movement of white togas passing by.

The port of Leptis where we camped provided good bathing near the former harbour; the sea was phosphorescent: I had never before enjoyed flicking little drops of blue luminous water through the air, my body glowing in the dark. We ate silently in the night, stilled by the sleeping majesty of the ruined city.

The day before we entered Tunisia four Europeans had been shot in their car, so to our disgust the police refused to allow camping and we were advised to find a hotel. It had been a bad day. The pleasant off-sea breeze had changed to a desert wind which is hardly a wind in the usual sense, just a steady imperceptible and relentless flow of hot air, drying up the atmosphere, scorching your face and body and inducing a sense of suffocation. One's temper deteriorates and it brings on a headache: with the movement of the car, it seems to roar past and its rough caress is so disagreeable that you soon shut all the windows: this increases the impression of slow asphyxiation. If you get out, it blows sand all over you and into your food and drink.

We were heading for the magic city of Kairouan, only recently opened for the general public to gaze upon its sanctity: but not for us. The fan-belt broke and the belt included in the spare-parts kit proved to be designed for a lorry. A charming Arab truck driver towed us quite some distance to the nearest garage. There was no likelihood of reaching Kairouan, so the Roman amphitheatre at El Djem had to take its place; a very fine and better preserved version of the Coliseum with beautiful graceful arcades. I inspected the lion pit and reflected on what I would do with the Hillman agents who had supplied the spare-parts.

Teddy seemed to be very happy and was as competent as ever in the kitchen. The strain of sharing life with three articulate and self-willed males was not telling on her unduly and the discomforts and improvisations of our desert journey never once affected her temper. She enjoyed the bathing and was no mean swimmer. There were times when I wondered if I had accepted the situation too easily, had been a craven lover; but then to have accepted it at all was perhaps an indication of emotional reality. Indefinable threads of feeling still linked me with her and sometimes I wished they were stronger. At the same time I sensed that the next step had to be faced alone.

Carthage proved a disappointment the following morning. It was heavy and lifeless compared with the Libyan ruins; but a boy showed me a charming little clay oil lamp, engraved with what resembled a dog curled up asleep. Perhaps the kind used by the Virgins (wise and otherwise) of the parable. He wanted very little for it.

We were now thinking of making an extra detour into the desert beyond the Atlas. Everyone wanted to see the real Sahara and to visit an oasis. I had a special desire for Biskra where my father had spent several months in 1939. An early start the following morning brought us to the lovely mountain country round the frontier at Ain Draham and soon down to the coast studded with little riviera ports, harbours nestling under the steep side of rocky promontories. Taking the corniche road through the precipitous wooded cliffs to Bone we were again blessed with an off-sea breeze and the bright mornings were deliciously fresh. Algeria is green and pleasant, strikingly colourful after the arid and unvaried contrasts of the desert: after the riviera scenery came rolling hills, grassy and wooded, with little stone villages reminiscent of the Yorkshire dales. This 'Tell' country at 3,000ft has much the same climate as England, but soon snow-capped mountain peaks and rocky serrated ranges with knife edges appeared on the horizon.

The road wound up and over the mountains, through the Alcantara gorge and on to the broad, reddish terrain of the desert, weaving over and back across a little railway; the level crossings here were far from level. At one of these, with a loud crack, the front of the car took a sideways plunge, and scraped along the road on the offside wing. We came to a halt just below the little house of a crossing keeper. It was blisteringly hot. One of the wheels was flat on the road; the front suspension had gone. We were stranded about 30 miles from Biskra. The time was about 11.30 a.m. At about 3.00 p.m. Denis and I got a lift from the first lorry to pass. Its cabin was hotter than the desert. The crossing keeper had generously allowed us to shelter, providing water and other necessities, so David and Teddy could be left with him while they looked after the car. In Biskra the sun boiled the streets and little white houses shimmered like molten metal. It was siesta time: the few passers-by stared at us curiously. Our lorry driver had obliged us by finding out where the manager of a reputable French garage lived; we waited diplomatically so as to avoid waking him, and stood ourselves and the driver food and an iced beer – ambrosia and nectar for mouths as rough as old rags. Parting with the usual cheerful exchanges of an Arab encounter, we set off hopefully to the house of the garage manager. It was difficult to get an answer and when it came, of no use whatever. The man clearly did not want to be bothered, and ended up by suggesting that the car might be put on to a train. He did not say how that engineering feat could be achieved without a crane. The door was firmly shut.

Denis, using his Arabic to good effect, now discovered there was a little Arab garage in a back-street. There we learnt that only 'le petit' could help us; but 'le petit' was out on a job. We must wait... Since clearly we were stuck for a while, rooms in a hotel would be required. Returning to the garage an hour later . . . no 'petit', but a lot of friendly badinage; perhaps he was just a myth? Still, we were now committed to this strand of hope. Our real worry was how Teddy and David were managing. Perhaps they had abandoned hope?

Had been carried off by the Bedouin? Would the crossing keeper shelter them for the night? How could Denis and I get back to them?

Towards dusk, a dark, tousle-haired lad of about seventeen dashed wildly into the little garage; cries of welcome went up on all sides. He had a companion about his own age. Here was 'le petit'. Denis explained our predicament: 'le petit' would come at once. He threw some tools into the boot of an old car. We all piled in on top of one another, and the car went – like a bomb. It was a terrifying drive, but it was still dusk when we arrived. Teddy and David were safe.

At once 'le petit' was under the car, prodding, examining, lifting . . . he was a little genius. With some unskilled help from us in lifting the front and holding it, he and his companion got the wheel under the car and temporarily attached again so that it ran freely. Darkness was almost upon us when I climbed gingerly into the driving seat and very gently let the clutch in. We moved – and I followed him slowly into Biskra.

After a late breakfast at a cheerful pavement café, feeling our lives were in the hands of 'le petit', David and Denis went and looked at the old oasis while Teddy and I dropped in on the garage to see how things were going. How many days would it take? Oh, le petit would have it ready by the afternoon. This was incredible; but on our return at 3.00 p.m. the smiling lad invited us to get into the car; and drove it furiously out into the town regardless of traffic. How had he done it? A few nuts and bolts, he explained. I was none the wiser: but began to express our gratitude. 'First,' he exclaimed, 'We must go to the Garden of Allah and pledge friendship for all time.' Though a little anxious to get away we felt this superb gesture must be accepted, and soon he had whisked us to an attractive oriental garden at the end of the town to eat icecreams together while David took photographs. Names and addresses were exchanged – he was Halimi Raschid.

Our parting was touching, for somehow Halimi managed to convey the impression that we had done him as much of a favour by needing him as he had by responding to our need. He had done such a good job that when we reached the Hillman Agents in Algiers some 300 miles later they could not improve upon his 'nuts and bolts': they lasted another year before finally giving up – 5,000 miles on! The Christmas after we got home, a small crate of dates arrived at Liverpool for David – with affectionate greetings from Halimi Raschid.

We were now well behind schedule so had a continual sense of racing against time in order to make sure of our passage at Ceuta. Fez was to have been a long day of browsing but instead became an afternoon and evening complicated by an interminable visit to the Spanish Consul for our Moroccan visas.

Nonetheless Fez left an indelible impression of veiled beauty and the fascination of an unsolved maze. Would that we might have remained longer in the dim warm light of bright painted tiles on the walls and floors of tiny mosques, but with a sense of urgency we pressed on, spending a few moments on the wind-swept shore of Larache facing the Atlantic breakers, before we turned inland through the greeny-mauve peaks of the Rif and the last primitive simplicity and squalor of such market places as Tizi-Oosu. Late that evening a sudden hunch impelled us to inquire about the time, since our ferry boat left Ceuta the following morning: Spanish Morocco was an hour in advance of French Morocco! With no place to camp along the steep sides of the road we at last turned off straight into an Arab village. Not daunted by the dusty laden car and four grimy Europeans, the whole village turned out to welcome us. Men helped with the beds, women provided grapes and soon we had settled down for our last night in Africa, decorating the small square with the litter of our equipment, secure in the warm embrace of night and the friendship of a score of strangers.

The Rock of Gibraltar arose out of the sea like a goddess veiled in the silver mists of early morning. There might have been no crossing for the AA had forgotten to make our booking, but the ferry company had been obliging and soon we docked in Algeciras. Setting foot in Europe brought decision uncomfortably near. The demands of the journey had mostly thrust doubt and fears into the background, but there were times when I had felt overwhelmed by the sensations of panic or a feeling of unreality about my impending ordination. Sometimes I became irritable, and we couldn't agree where to pitch camp. A kinder providence would intervene to settle us in some wood or field, beneath the ruins of a castle or beside some soothing river. It was vain to seek the help of man in a matter between myself and God.

For one holy moment the tension eased at the top of Gibraltar. Away to the south the powerful African shore raised its granite head and was answered by the sturdy affirmation of the Rock. Passing between the Pillars of Hercules, the rough waters of the Atlantic are tamed and transmuted into the delicate blue sheen of the Mediterranean. Though some of the harsh infertility of

Africa stretches into Spain, there is a softening of line. Rough Moroccan terraces and sprawling unkempt Arab bazaars give way to orderly little farms, whose terraces climb tidily up the hillsides, and neat little villages huddle around bright, painted Romanesque churches. Granada is the gem. There, under glittering porticoes of many-faceted archways, through cool tiled and vaulted saloons and sun-drenched loggias, by graceful fountains, gardens and still pools, the Moorish and the Latin meet in creative profusion. You may say, 'There is nothing classical about the Alhambra', yet I sensed a spirit of classical coherence. A pity that the Moorish style is supplanted by the depressing monotony of such buildings as the Escorial.

A morning with El Greco at Toledo and an afternoon at the Prado produced an aesthetic surfeit, so the next day I was seeking the prayers of St Teresa at her walled and castellated town of Avila. Of all women saints I admired her the most, so imaginative yet so sensible, so determined and so humble, and one who had suffered from incompetent advice.

After Vittoria the weather broke and we entered a green and verdant Basque country, rain dripping from every tree and swirling down in foaming torrents from the hills. It accorded well with a mood of melancholy and apprehension, but ordinary people were warm-hearted: at Bayonne a farmer allowed us to use an empty cottage. We had been soaked at the narrow frontier bridge and bedding was still wet from the previous night, but the house was dry and our peasant neighbours helpful.

At Lourdes the atmosphere was strangely heavy and unedifying. The shops were garish with the knick-knacks of Romanism. I bought a fairly tasteful glass figure of Our Lady. The route from the town climbed out past 'The Immaculate Conception Garage' (!) on to the wide vistas of the Massif Centrale.

Driving on to the sterner air of Albi we admired its austere but noble Cathedral fortified by Puritans against Catholic Crusaders. For me Le Puy's sedate Romanesque grandeur and the soaring aisles of Bourges represented the best in mediaeval religion.

A swim in the Loire, while camping in woods by the river's edge, ended a day of basking in the secular sunshine of the chateaux at Chenonceaux and Amboise; and our tour of castles ended in the Lionheart's fortress, Chateau Gaillard. Heavy iron clouds hung over the Seine, recalling Ludlow or some misty English keep, but the final lap was enlightened by the brilliant flourish of luxuriant rose windows at Amiens Cathedral.

The rain poured down mercilessly as we settled for the night in a Dutch barn! Hay bales offered the only protection. Why had I left Jerusalem? The others were not too despondent. Teddy was looking forward to marriage; Denis to his new life in the States. Even David was no longer a companion in doubt for he had decided to be ordained in Liverpool and to serve in the parish of his second home, the Shrewsbury Boys' Club; a dog-collar with a difference. Was I committing the folly of abandoning a limited but real good for an unknown perhaps forbidden fancy? Would it be another false start? On the Gibraltar crossing we had seen the Rock rise like some Venus from the blue waves. In the approach to Dover I came up from below decks as though from a tomb to see the white cliffs emerge a muddy grey in the downpour. Dover castle was concealed in the mist. While wrestling with the baggage, disembarking, saying farewell and setting foot in England again, one thing became unexcitingly clear: I would return to College and be ordained.

Looking back I asked, what was gained from Jerusalem and the journey? Something about faith that Jacob must wrestle with the Angel to secure a blessing: that to believe could never be to know, and that acceptance of uncertainty and surrender to the unknown were as much a part of vocation as decisions. Christ had come alive for me in his own land, renewed my affections through Teddy and my desire to love God, and to communicate that love and knowledge if I could. Also I had found that I could teach at the Secondary level though not so that I accepted Denis' view that I should make teaching my career. In general, I had greater confidence both in myself and in other people. Things I had lost or forgotten through ill-health had been recovered, and truths learnt 'in purgatory' as it were, since the 'angelic experience', were now grappled more closely to my soul. Would inward peace come when the straits of ordination had been passed? Perhaps not even then: but that risk had to be taken.

The author (aged nine) and sister Pat with the author's father

St George's, Jerusalem 1953, with the O Level class

The author aged about sixteen or seventeen

The author's mother in 1939

Interior of All Saints Belhus Park (1956-62)

Some of the boys and parents at Miserden Camp 1959 (author at the back)

The author's first wedding, to Gill, in 1961

Hatfield Heath Vicarage (1962-76)

*(on the left, Bess, the author's housekeeper,
centre is Clara Coleman, PCC Secretary for fifty years)*

The author's second wedding, to Wynn, in 1977
(Penny, Alex and Timothy visible behind)

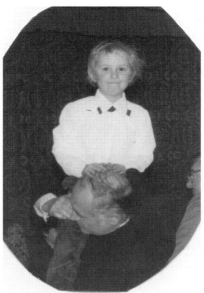

'I solemnly ordain you my Dad'
Timothy and the author at the wedding reception

The author and his wife in 1993

Peter Shepherd and Katie Taylor, two of the author's grandchildren

PART II

To burn fiercely for an immense beauty is not always a harsh and deadly fault, if it so softens the heart that a divine arrow may then easily pierce it.

Michaelangelo Sonnet 260
(The Poems. Ed. Chris Ryan pub. J.M. Dent)

CHAPTER IX

WANSTEAD

In a forest of hands my priesthood was born. To change the metaphor it felt as though I were back in the womb, for there were so many hands that my head was pressed down into a cavernous darkness and the words of the Bishop came from a great distance:

> Receive the Holy Ghost for the office and work of a Priest in the Church of God . . . Whosesoever sins thou dost forgive they are forgiven . . . and be thou a faithful dispenser of the word of God and of his Holy Sacraments.

Altogether a happier occasion than twelve months previously when I had been made a deacon, for I was far more certain that I had done the right thing. At the deaconing I think it was chiefly my pride – the feeling that I could not go back now – which had kept me steady in the Ordination Retreat; together perhaps with my being chosen to read the Gospel at the Ordination Service which I took as a sort of encouragement. Nonetheless I was still uncertain about what I was doing and couldn't deny a certain amused relief that the correct answer to the Bishop's question: 'Do you think that you are truly called . . . to the ministry of the Church?' was the almost noncommital: 'I think so.' (The inflection of voice is not prescribed.)

A year as a deacon had made all the difference. Immediately after ordination the dark past melted away and the first days in Wanstead, NE London, were bright with the sense of a new beginning. Two definite gifts were given me in ordination: the Devonport promise of increased confidence was confirmed – I knew more or less what to say and to do in situations as they arose (with bewildering novelty, unexpected frequency and often total lack of warning); I was amazed to find that I was saying or doing something

117

appropriate. Then, secondly but no less valuable, I began to care for people, quite warmly and spontaneously, a kind useful gift, becoming a glutton for new contacts. (Also I ceased to want to smoke!) I visited systematically down the streets of my area in our parish of 20,000 people, finding an almost intoxicating satisfaction in the immense variety of acquaintance and friendship available to a parson. Far from being a barrier, I found my dog-collar opened doors and encouraged confidences. All this activity may have been an aspect of the psychology of doubt and I was being impelled to go and prove myself– but it all felt a lot simpler and pleasanter, arising from choice rather than compulsion. Teddy came to see me before her wedding: a kind gesture and I could not bring myself to feel reproachful for she said: 'You are so marvellously happy! I am glad,' and I could not deny it. She was quite radiant, too.

I was very lucky in having an experienced vicar[21], who rode us (eventually three curates in all) on a light rein and not only gave us responsibility but listened to our suggestions. Of course I was often over-zealous and presumptuous, but he was tolerant. Wanstead was a mixed parish, mainly fairly well-to-do people but a substantial minority of artisans moving in from East London and a small group of old retainer families surviving from the days when they looked after the wealthy who had now moved out. It was a valuable cross-section and one could not get into a fixed manner of approach to people with such varied backgrounds: I found I liked the younger artisan families, who had moved out of the East End, but they did not always feel settled in the slightly rarified atmosphere of this suburb.

There were two churches with differing traditions of churchmanship, which I also liked. One had a somewhat 'High' congregation, with a Sung Eucharist, the other – a fine Georgian church with majestic portico – was essentially eighteenth century and carried a safe Matins congregation. It is difficult to say which I enjoyed serving the most. At least it saved me from becoming narrowly partisan, as there were zealous protagonists of both wings and it became only too evident how easily Christian charity could be dissolved in the party spirit. A Church School, aided not controlled, and therefore open to Church teaching, gave a fine opportunity and the pleasant experience of working with a happy and intelligent Christian staff who were keeping up a

---

[21] The Revd Canon Alan Gates, later Rector of Blakeney, Norfolk.

good academic standard. I could not help being immensely and at times overwhelmingly grateful to God, who had given back more than double for all the trouble.

The only cloud during this happy period was the feeling that perhaps I might be meant to remain a deacon: that maybe the priesthood was not a prize for me to grasp. I had met a perpetual deacon at St Mary's Portsea and he seemed very happy. It is commonly supposed that deacons are rather frustrated creatures – eagles with clipped wings – but I must confess that I loved being just a deacon and had no great desire to be ordained a priest. There was so much in the children's work, the visiting, teaching and preaching, that there seemed no necessary gap to be filled by taking on priestly duties and I feared rather than desired the celebration of Holy Communion. However, I more or less accepted that it was probably best to follow the normal practice and go ahead in a year's time. A month or so beforehand I began to look forward to it.

I wanted to celebrate, not at Michaelmas as was first suggested, but on an ordinary weekday in case I went wrong. Far from being a terrifying ordeal, however, the first celebration of Holy Communion was a most wonderful experience – quite unsensational, no highlights (those were more evident in the first Sung Eucharist) but immensely and deeply satisfying and full of meaning. I was grateful to be a priest. The more I was involved in this angelic mystery the more profoundly thankful I became. Soon came the rather touching experience of conducting a marriage and then I was allowed to prepare adults, most of whom I had found in the course of visiting, for Confirmation and First Communion. This was also deeply interesting, especially as I felt and observed the growth of spiritual fellowship, an authentic 'being knit-together in the Spirit', in the Confirmation groups as well as the 'aha' situations when people excitedly saw a spiritual truth for the first time. This encouraged my belief that small groups thinking and praying together might achieve more than mass movements: it was after all the apostolic method and I found that many other priests were experimenting with similar ideas through the Cell Movement and SCK (Servants of Christ the King). Attending a Billy Graham rally I was not impressed, but we carefully followed up the neophytes referred to us by the Crusade.

We formed four 'cells' during the next year, partly to deepen the understanding and faith of those already practising the Way and partly to help the newly-confirmed and those on the fringes who needed not so much to be preached at as to experience the meaning of the Church in genuine fellowship. These groups continued to meet for some years – and for all I know may have their successors now.

After eighteen months in this parish I was approached by the Principal of a Theological College with a view to joining his staff, but was most unwilling to return to the limited field of mainly academic work. I resisted the invitation until good manners and my former College Principal indicated that at least I should go and visit the place. Then I was glad to find that in the meantime an old friend had recently entered the lists. He was far better suited to the work and with relief I returned to the parish; but the episode had thoroughly unsettled me and I began (quite literally) to dream of new housing estates! I had already sought the Bishop's advice on the college post; both he and my vicar suggested that I was better suited to parochial work; and what more fascinating than a new housing area? A month later the Bishop asked me to look at one in South Essex – All Saints Belhus Park.

Mile upon mile of entirely new building gives a most astonishing and exhilarating impression of virgin ground and new life, accentuated by the sight of hordes of young children. Here was a courageous piece of new settlement by the LCC with open prospects in all senses. This new town was surrounded by fields and woods, the air was fresh and comparatively clean, and there were about 23,000 people, predominantly young married couples, making a new start. I saw David, the Priest-in-Charge and learnt about many of the problems, one of which was that I had to live in a council house. I can't say I was appalled by this: it seemed quite a good idea that a priest should live in the same conditions as his people, though I could understand the difficulties David and his wife with two small children would have. Every time a caller came to see him there was only the kitchen for his wife and children. Once again, I was not sorry to be a bachelor.

The most unexpected experience was my first view of the church, a dual-purpose sanctuary cum hall, as I had been warned. I had expected the worst: I found a gem. The sanctuary was broad and spacious, forming a bright chapel to seat at least thirty in the week, the hall was finely proportioned, parquet-floored with a large stage at the west end. But most striking of all was the effect when the floor to ceiling doors (no flimsy curtaining or partitioning) rolled back to disclose a harmony of hall and sanctuary, focusing on a superb Rood Cross hanging over an austere free-standing altar inscribed with the Chi Rho. Where had I seen it before? Perhaps I was deceived by the distant memory – was it the altar of my epic poem where the Knight had 'blended his yearning essence with the flame', as I had written so long ago at Oxford? Fifteen years' pilgrimage had found its destination: I had no doubts this time.

CHAPTER X

BELHUS

From my pocket-handkerchief sized council house garden I could see about forty other similar-sized gardens and a large school playing field, yet a great sense of space prevailed. A Cockney boy coming to visit commented: 'What bags o' sky you 'ave 'ere!' My parsonage house was a typical '50s council house, three up and two down, at the end of a terrace. There was a 'front room' large enough to take my baby grand, Aunt Nell's little sofa and an easy chair or two: a rather bigger kitchen-dining room at the back; upstairs one large and two smaller bedrooms, one of which, overlooking the playing field could be made into a study. At thirty-one I had my first house and I loved it. The Cub Mistress came in to clean and occasionally cook: she thoughtfully found me a kitten, black with a clerical collar, who on seeing me, scrambled up and nipped my ear – so was christened Nipper – an engaging little companion.

My immediate neighbours were an Irish couple with six children – the LCC had exported the largest families to this estate – their dad usually had one over the eight on a Saturday night so a pre-Sunday vigil on my side of the wall was almost inevitable. I enjoyed a gap between the north wall and my other neighbours – a family with five children. Both families were somewhat 'disturbed' and in time shared their troubles: the Irishman's wife was later confirmed – as were the quieter couple who moved in when she left. Probably more than 2,000 children lived in the vicinity of our street, Foyle Drive, and that was about a quarter of the total – some 9,000 children were funnelled daily into eighteen schools, four being secondary moderns (a few went to grammar schools in Grays Thurrock and Hornchurch). The males mostly worked in Fords at Dagenham and had to walk a mile or so to the nearest bus stop unless they had cars. The women also had some distance to go to the shopping centre or one of the three shopping parades. For them it was not at all like home – neat box-like terrace houses, spaced along straight concrete roads in the silent countryside, far from the noise and vitality of the East End and connected with cultural and social roots by little more than a telephone and a half-hourly Green Line bus. Few pubs assuaged the isolation, and inadequate street-lighting failed to make the nights companionable. Fresh air, new houses and magnificent schools did not wholly compensate for the absence of 'Nan' (head of many an East London clan) and the rest of the family. All the same, a minority of new householders lovingly developed gardens and redecorated their homes with appreciative care.

The vicarage side of Belhus was surrounded by woodland which was accessible and fields which were not: children who had played in the London streets before coming down still had to play in the streets outside their homes, though they were safer where houses were arranged round a T-shaped dead end, called a banjo. It took time and pressure to get enough purpose-built play space within the estate, and I had to promote an agitation for the central coppice to be thinned out and converted. Soon we had set up clubs and a football team and two or three hundred youngsters were involved in uniformed or non-uniformed organizations. A Youth Club for the estate's teenagers was run by a church member at the largest secondary school.

I have already mentioned the good impression made by the Anglican church building, a warm autumnal shade brick, standing on the other side of Foyle Drive not far from my home. Built in 1953, its main hall was about 50' x 30', entered by doors at the front side and the back where there were toilets and a kitchen. The west end had a sizeable stage and the east had a sanctuary about 30' x 25' with the fine free-standing altar already described. When the doors between sanctuary and hall were folded back, because ambos on either side were stationed in the hall, it felt as though the hall was taken up into the sanctuary rather than a holy area tacked on to the hall. People who came to weekday events in the hall found it relatively easy to come through the same unassuming doors to try out a service.

The 5,000 houses and flats of Belhus had been built on the parkland of a fine Elizabethan mansion, Belhus Park, between South Ockenden and Aveley, two large villages with ancient parish churches. The pastoral responsibility for the new estate was given to St Michael's Aveley and the vicar there had conscientiously visited as the houses went up. Father Ovenden, a compassionate high churchman of the sort East Enders were accustomed to, set up house meetings and established contacts that helped people to sense a local church presence. He found a remarkable elderly Plymouth Brother, Harry Lobley, an Essex countryman, to lead a Sunday School; Harry's warmth and love for children, and his simple and manifest sincerity won a steady following. Fr. Ovenden's curate, David Wainwright, discovered two other valuable allies, the Headmaster of a Primary School, Jim Ellis, who was a Reader and ready to preach and assist, and a very competent pianist around whom he could build the music of a sung Parish Communion. Marjorie Jose, although an honest agnostic and unbaptized, responded sensitively to the liturgy, and her children came along with her. Tony, an eleven year old, had unusual musical gifts himself and the other three good singing voices. Jim Ellis was very soon playing a major part in the liturgy and also on the Church Council.

Another woman, Judith, had experienced an unusual conversion just before I came. Her father had been a minister in the German government who fell foul of the Nazis. He had been arrested, and in some way I could never understand, Judith had to stand surety for him when he was released on bail. However he decided to escape, imperilling Judith's own life, so she courageously made her way to Switzerland in considerable discomfort and danger. Reaching England after the war she married an intelligent young Canadian by whom she had a daughter, and came to Belhus: but she had not been able to forgive her father for his treachery. One night she lay awake pondering how she might forgive him when she saw clearly in front of her a great gaping wound and she heard a voice saying, 'Put your hand in the wound and be not faithless but believe.' She found herself rather bizarrely thinking 'Oh, that's St Thomas, where surgeons put their hands in wounds' and then came to herself feeling that she could at last forgive her father.

After her baptism and confirmation she became a vivid spark of light in the church. I was quite fascinated by her, but in several ways she reminded me of Peter Brook and some wariness arose to interfere with my desire to trust her wholeheartedly. We exchanged ideas and hopes for the church quite ardently and I tried to interest her husband in what we were doing, but Judith's absorption in her new faith made the church his rival, and anyway he was more interested in Labour politics, an interest we had in common. Judith gave herself generously to people in need and strongly backed any plans to deepen our spirituality through Retreats and Quiet Days (held at the peaceful church of North Ockenden). She helped with a class of older girls, though they found her wavelength a little hard to attain. I admired and even envied her devotion but also failed often to understand her, although her charisma undoubtedly blessed us all. After a while her marriage began to founder and she left the estate to live first in Harlow as a licensed church worker and then in London, where she ministered to the homeless and drug addicts around the Soho region. There I visited her, and was impressed by the sacrificial character of her life; she had learnt the guitar to help in her ministry to teenagers. Her daughter stayed with us briefly in a later parish, when the family broke up and now I have lost both memories and contact. I used to fear that she might draw me into something very demanding, and in my heart there may have been a spiritual jealousy of her selfless dedication to Christ in serving 'rejects' and the poor – to the point of risking her own safety and security. I have a persistent sense of having failed to obey Christ's teaching on 'becoming poor'.

Licensing me as Priest-in-Charge on St Luke's Day, 18 October 1956, the Bishop preached on the text 'We are fellow-workers with God' (I Cor.3:9). The next morning I had a visitor – Tony's brother – thirteen year old Michael Jose. I invited him in and at once he stated his business. 'I want to be a fellow-worker with God,' he said simply. 'Can you suggest how I go about it?' Feeling slightly winded, I asked him if he had been confirmed and in that way committed himself to Christ? He hadn't but he thought it would be a good start. Michael was the first fruits of a harvest that exceeded our wildest expectations. Like many other lads that followed his example, and also brought their friends, he became a server, finding his place in Christ's Liturgy, and helped us set up an open organization for youngsters, the Friday Club. Tony, his younger brother, became joint-pianist (later organist when the Lord Lieutenant, Sir John Ruggles-Brise, gave us the mellow-toned mid-Victorian Bevington from his home, Spains Hall); with Marjorie he played for our first venture into opera, Britten's *Let's Make An Opera*. Her husband, Jack, a gentle and thoughtful member of a printing works and a keen trade unionist, gradually joined in and was eventually confirmed with Marjorie. As with many of the families the children took the lead but when the parents decided to commit themselves they too were steady and generous with their time and energies.

In 1956 there were about thirty coming on and off to church or receiving ministry in their homes or on week days in the house churches. By 1959 it was about ninety. A year or two later over a hundred would regularly squash in to the little church and one year I was astonished that nearly as many communicants turned out on Low Sunday as on Easter Day. Casting around for help I happily landed a Church Army Sister for whom the diocese was to pay and the LCC agreed to provide a flat. Now living in retirement, Winifred Bowmaker, at ninety, is still a strong-minded and compassionate Geordie. She was experienced in several areas of church work, specially valuable for the care of women and girls. Her approach was not confrontational. 'I notice you stayed at the side of the hall during last night's social,' I commented. 'Yes,' she replied, 'they come and talk to me there.' They did indeed, especially the teenage girls, and they were not alarmed by a basically downright and fairly rugged character who said what she thought, but usually with a pinch of humour. All this stood her in good stead when enduring the vicissitudes of life on a council estate – and also a vicar who at times knew rather too definitely what he wanted!

A year later the Bishop asked us to train a young deacon, who was interested in coming because he was fond of the daughter of one of our parishioners. He was a conscientious learner, but having an evangelical background felt out of sympathy with our sacramental tradition. Sadly the relationship with the girl did not flourish, so one thing and another led him to decide to move when he was priested. I felt somewhat bereft – but meantime a fine elderly priest working nearby but due for retirement, asked to come and help. Etienne Watts had been a distinguished figure in Christian Socialism in Lancashire and had helped in the 1930s hunger marches. He suffered from Parkinson's disease, but he and his wife were game for a lively parochial setting. The LCC generously provided a flat for them too. Etienne helped with a House Communion nearby and was pastorally available on the opposite side of the estate from the church. His dry humour and integrity were attractive to our Londoners.

Pastoral needs were immense, chiefly because people were cut off from their roots in London. They had relied on the extended family; marriages were under strain from the long hours of shift work and the large number of children, six siblings being not unusual, all having to be despatched to school each morning and shepherded to some degree in the afternoon and evening. With no friendly corner shop, mothers had to walk some distance, pushing a pram, to the nearest shopping parade, and social life was minimal, except with new neighbours, who were not always congenial. At one time more were returning to London than were coming out – it was too expensive to return to the East End each weekend!

Parents with large young families, however willing, cannot take a lead in a new community. Father is tired by his travelling, mother by coping with the children and shopping. If the children are old enough she may take part-time work, and that will help meet the expense of furnishing and maintaining the new house or running a car that is not a luxury in view of poor local communications. But anyone showing public spirit is inclined to be put upon, and finding they have agreed to do too much, react by withdrawing altogether. Moreover, leaders tend to come from the families most likely to move through change of employment. Better jobs often mean a new locality.

One street had some thirty larger houses, suitable for professionals and middle-management; Jim, the headmaster living in one, two or three GPs in others (all but one moved out) and six of the houses were LCC Children's Homes each housing 6-8 youngsters and a house parent. Several of the other householders, like Ken and Mary Banyard, with seven children, were incredibly willing to help with uniformed and other organizations, but the brunt of leadership responsibility fell on the East Enders.

Political leadership was provided by several hard-working councillors, especially Jack Evans[22] (on Thurrock Council). His son John joined us, ran our bookstall and later married Barbara, one of the choir. Hugh Delargy, our MP, was genuinely concerned for the estate; but a major endemic weakness was the LCC's refusal to accommodate the new generation in Belhus – all housing was to be reserved for London overspill. So John and Barbara had to begin married life miles away in Ilford, losing their friends, family support and church as they set up home in foreign territory. When so many older people were still longing for London, the younger generation who grew up in Belhus and were fond of it, had to move out. They would have happily settled to provide a firm core of Belhusians.

Family and marital upheaval was frequent and in the absence of supportive relatives, the church was quite often a first resource. We found ourselves caring for young orphans of the storm sometimes actually having them to stay, and each week some hours were devoted to divided families. I shall not easily forget being telephoned about 10.30 p.m. on a Sunday evening. A woman asked me to come quickly. She had her neighbours from three doors away in her front room and her husband had announced his intention of leaving that night with the neighbour's wife. I found them as she had reported, and succeeded in delaying their departure for some time. They seemed, however,

---

[22] Jack, though not a Christian was heard to say, 'On this estate the only real community is the Church.'

impervious to argument, like possessed beings. It mattered little to either that they were leaving two small children apiece, and one child was ill. I prayed inwardly for help, and about 1.15 a.m. the man collected his car and prepared to go. I said to the woman, 'I expect Ann (the sick child) was crying today.' 'Yes,' she said, unmoved. 'You won't easily forget her tears' I retorted. She shrugged her shoulders. A minute or two later there came a piercing shriek. It was the voice of her child, and it had penetrated to our room from three houses away. She recognized it, blanched, and ran for the door. I said to the man, 'If you've any guts, you will let her sort this out. Why not go and spend the night with your people in London?' He half assented, and went out, but I knew where he was going. He went to the woman with the child. I waited, and then stood in the door to see him return. He came back slowly and said, 'Alright, Vicar, you win'. I watched him pile a suitcase into the car and drive off alone. After some weeks of sorting out, both families went on living in the same houses, more or less at peace. Later I dined with each of them. One family started to come to church, irregularly; the other rejoined the Methodists.

Such episodes immensely increased my own faith and undergirded the work, but the calls were frequent and I felt untrained and inexperienced for marital counselling. Yet there were remarkable compensations. Just as these couples were enabled through the church to find the way out of a crisis, so others discovered faith and a genuine community of mutual compassion at All Saints. Men responded through practical concerns. Bill Thomas, a docker, happened to see me taking some coal to an OAP. '*We* should be doing that sort of thing, Vicar', he said, and promptly enlisted four or five others who named themselves The Good Samaritans. They built up a regular clientele, monitored their activities in a weekly meeting, and although none had much to do with the church at the start, every one of them was confirmed during the next few years; their wives too, helped with Sunday School (Bill's Eileen became the church Sacristan) or joined women's charity or leisure groups.

The same happened over running an annual church Holiday Camp. An original team of six couples, who came to help with sixty boys at Miserden, all eventually became communicants and ascribed the beginning of faith to our daily evening prayers in the beautiful little church at Miserden. Thanks to Pat and her good neighbours, the Rector and a farmer, Martin Partridge, together with the Miserden Park staff, I had negotiated a twelve days' sojourn in the meadow below Miserden church, the estate providing vans to take the boys on various expeditions during the day. Bill, having cooked for the Eighth Army during the War, volunteered to be chef, and with a small team fed us each day in the old school house at the centre of the village. Miserden House provided washing facilities under the tolerant eyes of my sister's staff. No rain fell on us and there were few troubles, so when in 1960 Martin Partridge offered a more suitable field at Birdlip and a large marquee, we prepared for an even larger contingent and wider explorations. However, having settled a camp of about ninety, this time the weather was more typically West Country and just when we had opened up the marquee for airing, a sudden torrential downpour flooded everything. The Birdlip villagers responded magnificently by opening their houses to take the boys and dry out their damp bedding and clothes.

The experience decided us to transfer the camp to Church Army huts at Seasalter on the Kent coast near Herne Bay, where girls could also have their own quarters and families be accommodated in caravans. I think our largest camp was about 120. Visits to Canterbury Cathedral were combined with other excursions, but the beach provided the chief diversion: the only crisis I recall was the temporary loss of one boy and his later retrieval from the police. All in all, the planning, running and enjoyment of these holidays, brought church people closer in friendship (though the opposite could occasionally threaten). It introduced non-Christians, or those initially 'not interested' to the Christian community, and refreshed those who were 'over-worked and under-paid'. One coloured lady from the East End had had a rough time, but after bringing her two boys and a girl, felt a different person: later the children came for holidays at my next parish.

The operas brought in people with fewer 'outdoor' interests. It was perhaps over-ambitious to attempt Britten's *Let's Make an Opera (The Little Sweep)*; but we had such a remarkable reservoir of youngsters and some genuine musical talent that it was worth tackling. Benjamin Britten himself wrote a letter of encouragement, the text of which is as follows:

THE RED HOUSE, ALDEBURGH, SUFFOLK

15 June, 1960.

My dear Mr Smythe,

Please forgive the delay in answering your interesting letter, but the preparation of the Festival here has taken all my time.

I was very impressed by what your sister Pat told me of your work, and more impressed still to read the moving account of it that you enclosed. I am delighted that *Let's Make an Opera!* went so well and gave the children so much pleasure. Perhaps one day *Noye's Fludde* would fit into your plans, which is in a way more fun for a greater number of children.

Some day I hope it may be possible for Peter Pears and myself to pay you a visit and see something of what you are doing, but life is incredibly complicated and this may not be for a little time. In the meantime if there is any way in which you think I can help your work, please let me know.

With best wishes,
    Yours sincerely,
        Benjamin Britten

We gave three performances of *Let's Make an Opera* to raise funds for World Refugee Year, my godson, Nigel Banyard, playing Sam the sweep boy, (a 'refugee') and his mother, Mary, Miss Baggott. Young Tony Jose and his mother were probably right to settle mainly for Gilbert and Sullivan in subsequent years and to consolidate an outstandingly loyal and hard-working group. In 1990 I attended a party celebrating the performance of thirty different operas since the *Little Sweep* in 1959.

Lest it be thought that the church grew solely on a diet of light-hearted activity, I should mention the Franciscan Mission we mounted the same year. The Society's Father Guardian, Oswald, brought a strong team to stay with us for a fortnight. As in the Plymouth Mission, which had meant so much to me while at college, each morning a briefing session prepared the team for the day's visiting: children's meetings were set up for the afternoon, and the main service took place in the evening – on the whole well attended. Oswald deliberately eschewed a rhetorical style, concentrating on basic teaching. It gave us all a 'shot in the arm' and drew a number of serious enquirers who were later confirmed. To help us look after the influx, the following year a new staff member, Peter Mason, came from Mirfield, as a result of my going on retreat in 1959 and seeing Fr. Hugh Bishop. Peter settled happily into the flat vacated by the first curate, and rapidly with the congregation, who took to him at once. He responded imaginatively and warmly to the pastoral opportunities and by the time he was priested in 1961 had become a much-valued colleague. He also took over my morning at one of the secondary modern schools. Belhus had eighteen schools, four of which were secondary: I was soon invited to be a governor of three of them. The fourth even more valuably engaged me to teach, which gave direct contact with staff and youngsters. One master became a server and a good friend. I remember another male teacher who had come to discuss something at the Vicarage, meeting one of my churchwardens who was large, muscular, full of cockney vitality, and drove the largest Esso tanker I'd ever seen. The teacher was fascinated by him and commented afterwards, 'Your church has real people in it.'

1959 was a remarkable year, and concluded with my moving into a vicarage. As the dual purpose church had been so satisfactory I asked its architect to design a simple parsonage house to be built in two stages, partly for financial reasons. Rather unusually the diocese agreed and in four months, benefiting (like the camp) from the fine summer, a vicarage went up with hardly a drop of rain on it, and at the cost of £3,500; later completed with another bedroom and study for my successor and his family. Its hallway facing east had a two-storey length window by which the house was flooded with light. The sizeable sitting room with 'picture windows' on the south side and the kitchen-dining room on the north-west were handsome rooms, one with a Yorkshire stone fireplace, the other with a boiler-stove. In between on the west was quite a large room for my study, destined to be the future dining room – and used as such for parties. One large and two smaller bedrooms with a bathroom and WC were supplemented by another loo downstairs and a useful utility area by the backdoor.

The council house had begun to feel rather inadequate for the volume of visitors that now circulated through it, and of course now I had room for a housekeeper. Nonetheless I felt something valuable was being lost by moving out of the council terrace. A 'vicarage' spoke of status and professional distance between 'them and me', that I was part of an officer class no longer living with the people as a working man; I was to live in a privileged way, and like other professionals was 'detached' and would probably move on. However, I liked the quietness of the modest home next to the church building and got a farmer to plough up the land around so a garden could be begun – not as vast as the average rectory garden.[23] With a larger domain to care for, I looked for a housekeeper and found a unique treasure. The Banyards previously mentioned, who helped with uniformed organizations and did so

---

[23] The local magnate Sir Francis Whitmore presented some trees and kindly presided over a planting ceremony on a wet November morning.

much for the opera, had a granny living in Liverpool. I had met Bess two years earlier when she visited them shortly after her husband's death. She came again this year and she decided bravely to be my housekeeper. Settling into the new vicarage with Bess in charge completed the *annus mirabilis* 1959, exactly 200 years after the original *annus mirabilis*!

Strange how gifts are poured on us in phases of good fortune! In the summer of 1960 an Ely College friend, Victor de Waal, having tested his vocation as a monk and returned to the world as Precentor of Kings College Cambridge, decided to get married to a history don, Esther Moir. They married in her home county, Hereford, and held a reception in London. There I met Gillian Deby, a speech therapist and a friend of Esther's who was completing a degree in theology at Kings, London. I was immediately charmed. After the party I obtained her address from Esther and with trepidation telephoned from the Thompsons' in Wimbledon, where I was staying the night. Yes, she'd be delighted to meet for lunch the next day. She was all I'd hoped for; and she even agreed to motor back to Belhus with me and see the parish. I think Gill recognized at once that she would have something of a rival in the church; but we faced that – gradually – and the next few months provided gracious opportunities for meeting. It was high time to enjoy some personal life and here was someone who could understand and accept me, and whom I found altogether attractive, amusing, thoughtful, sincere and genuine, warm-hearted with people and totally loveable. Sadly she had been born with a defect in one leg, which involved regular treatment, but that seemed a minor problem. In all other respects, at thirty Gill was fit and vigorous. I was but thirty-five and Belhus had done my own health no harm at all, apart from some chronic tiredness. A year under Bessie's care had been recuperative. I checked out my mental health with a visit to Dr Desmond Pond: he was positive!

In November 1960 I proposed to Gill and was accepted: she came to Belhus to celebrate but that night I had a most frightening dream. I was fighting to get to Gill through a wall: after great efforts I burst into the room and found her dead with an equally dead embryo. This so shattered me that I shared the dream, and my terrified self, with Gill in the early morning. After some hours we agreed to postpone the engagement – I feared that my chronic doubt and anxiety would return. Shortly afterwards I went on retreat with the Franciscans at Hillfield, Dorset, and the experience was helpful. On my return Gill remained as loving and supportive as ever. Christmas was more cheerful than I'd expected, and a fortnight or so later we met for lunch at a pleasant pub near Epping Forest. There I renewed my proposal and Gill responded, 'I feel much happier about you now'. We planned our wedding for May 1961.

Gill was a worshipper at the Grosvenor Chapel, not far from her London home, so we had decided to hold it there. Her vicar agreed to share the service with Canon Sidney Evans, Gill's spiritual adviser and Dean of King's College, London: Gill's mother Renie began preparations for a wedding breakfast at a club near the chapel; I had already met her and her barrister son, John. Gill's father had died a few years earlier, and Renie had not fully recovered from her bereavement. The parish rolled on relentlessly through Lent, Holy Week and Easter, with delightful interludes but before Pentecost fell upon us I heard that Gill had to go into hospital again for the removal of another fibroma from her leg. Every one assured us that she would be fine for the wedding. The operation took place in her home town, Sheffield, under a surgeon she knew well. I travelled up to see her, and was met on Sheffield station by an extremely agitated Renie. She tried valiantly to prepare me for the bad news, but not surprisingly broke down to say that the growth had for the first time proved malignant. Though I recalled the nightmare, my predominant feeling was of refusal to be discouraged. It had come about that Gill had read her hospital notes when they had been given her to take to another department. Though the family was very distressed about her knowing, I was glad that there was no pretence between us. We had barely a month before the ceremony, but Renie and I enjoyed the final touches. Friends of my sister, who owned Heligan House, near Mevagissey, lent us a flat there for our honeymoon, surrounded by vast and glorious rhododendrons. The Grosvenor Chapel choir was able to come up with the music I wanted for our Nuptial Eucharist, part of Howells' Mass and John Ireland's 'Greater love . . .' May 24th dawned in brilliant sun: the day was a halcyon blue throughout.

Gill's operation had taken its toll and walking was troublesome: but no one guessed it from her enchanting smile and game manner. John Deby gave her away: I was groomed by Alan Thompson, who made a witty speech and, after a final clear-up at her flat, Gill and I were off to our first night stop at Virginia Water *en route* for Mevagissey. In Cornwall, Heligan and the coast were superb: it was hot enough for a swim, though I got a slight chill which gave excuse for an extra day in the warmth: that meant a long journey on a holiday Saturday with the deadline of a parish welcome, but we made it through West Country 'back doubles' to reach the party in time. I apologized for our rather battered condition after the trip, to which Gill interjected, 'Speak for yourself', which immediately endeared her to my Cockneys.

The following five months are hard to write about. It was going to be difficult to say goodbye to Bess, but Gill invited her to stay with us as long as she wished while planning her next step. Ironically this was a blessing because within the month Gill began to feel very ill. Our GP, David Pedersen (who had for a time lived near me on the Belhus estate) arranged for an investigation at Barts Hospital. It was feared that the malignancy might have spread, and a later visit there established the presence of lung cancer. Unfortunately Renie and John were determined that Gill should not be told, and I rather weakly went along with it; I defended the decision when challenged by Sister Bowmaker, but I now think she was right. It was probably through determination to make our remaining time as carefree as possible that I resolved not to share the implications; and indeed we had lovely days together, one of the best being an expedition from Barts to Wimbledon Common in the sunshine. It brought together present joy with memories of childhood happiness.

Gill had now to stay in Barts – 'Bring her champagne: it helps', said the ward sister, so I visited most days and life in her pleasant single room became a continual wedding toast. I asked Canon Evans to come to anoint Gill, and together with Renie we received Communion. I was thankful for the sense of spiritual warmth, and also that the illness was not causing any physical wasting. Gill had a gloriously robust presence, fine dark hair, a Gainsborough-like profile and eighteenth century natural elegance, but her breathing was now being affected. For short periods she returned home, where I was trying to keep up with parish work, and now recall with shame the nights I heard her groan and simply went off to sleep again through sheer tiredness. I felt the inadequacy of my love. We had a happy visit to friends in Surrey, where she felt relaxed and hopeful: but by early October there seemed no hope of taking the autumn holiday we had planned. One night after visiting Barts I felt I must stay: the ward sister offered a bed after I had seen Gill fall into a peaceful sleep. Early in the morning sister woke me and said I should come. Gill was very quietly leaving us. I kissed her forehead and held her hand: she sighed gently and died. Sister thoughtfully left and I could kneel by Gill and weep: I hadn't known that you could feel as though your heart was actually breaking.

It was St Luke's Day and I learnt that the chaplain was saying an early Eucharist. Thank God for that. I hoped the same sense of oneness we'd known at the communion when mother died, might come to assure me of her peaceful and true presence with me in Christ. It came only partially – the world was too fractured and awry. I went off to tell Renie and John: what a painful early meeting! The rest of that week remains in darkness, except for the funeral service taken by Sidney Evans in the Chapel of King's College, London.

Mercifully the de Waals took me to their home in Cambridge for a few days, where I had the company also of their first baby, John, godson-to-be. Later Renie and John Deby came to stay at Belhus, but it was a very sorrowful time. I remember some relief through playing my recording of Delius' 'Sea Drift': the poignant bereavement of Whitman's seabird was almost a solace in mutual loss. Renie took long years to recover, the turning point being when she came with me on a pilgrimage to the Holy Land in 1967. John was deeply bereft too, but graciously handled probate and much other business: it was good to have Gill's family to remind me of her. Pat, though supportive throughout, had to be abroad on show jumping events and wrote sympathetically from Japan.

I was very thankful to be living with men and women with whom I had shared closely the last five years. It is always hard to know how to respond to another's loss: their warm but unintrusive concern reinforced Bessie's profound comfort given also at a silent depth more companionable than words. Returning to the humdrum jobs shared with understanding colleagues is more healing than the condolence of official and church bodies, though I was grateful for it – contrasting with the local press, who blazoned across a front page VICAR'S DOUBLE FIFTH: Gill had died on October 18th, the date on which I had become vicar five years before: we had been married for five months.

A year or so before, I had protested at one of the editor's reporters badgering a local woman when the news came through that her husband in Kenya had taken his life. She had declined to be interviewed, so the man went to find out more about them from their neighbours. Consequently the woman's children first heard of their father's death somewhat crudely from the neighbour's children. I asked the editor to soft pedal the reporting to spare the widow. He said he would, but instead put it on the front page. Sensation took priority over compassion: I dare say he had resented my intervention. I now had some fellow feeling with that widow in the way the press handled our grief; she had had worse treatment than I.

I found comfort in writing music for the psalms: so many express with penetrating power our deepest feelings of joy, sorrow, protest, anger and despair. I borrowed a method initiated by Pere Gelineau in taking one verse as an antiphon, a sort of chorus repeated after a few verses, and providing a chant to go with it. The evensong congregations sung them with feeling giving the psalms a new resonance. Several other priests, notably Peter Graham and Douglas Bean (Ely colleagues) used them in their eucharists and Alan Wicks, Canterbury choir master, tried a few at choir festivals. I discovered last year that one large and lively parish church continues to use them.

Several projects helped to divert attention from the sense of bereavement. We had decided to build a church hall to complete the church campus. Another large batch of confirmation candidates brought the total over five years to over 400, half of whom were adults. Our interest in the church overseas increased with several fresh contacts and visitors. A notably effective speaker was John Bodger, Secretary of the New Guinea Mission who for the next ten years stimulated interest by his vivid accounts of the work in Papua. However I was greatly in need of support in our own mission field and was relieved when Sidney Evans suggested that one of his theological students, David Gamble, should come to us after ordination. This coincided with my recognizing that once again I was doing too much: in my 1962 diary the first half year is full of lists! I realised this was a way of escaping from bereavement so resolved again to consult Dr Pond who put me in touch with Fred Roberts, a priest psychotherapist in our diocese.

Fred was Vicar of Hatfield Heath near Bishops Stortford. He was working to qualify as a psychotherapist, and looking after a village of some 2,000 parishioners. I saw him before Christmas 1961 and then fairly regularly through the first half of 1962; even today I am not sure how much he enabled me to work through Gill's death. I found a few sessions with Dr Frank Lake of Clinical Theology probably more effective: but Fred did convince me that I needed a change. In fact he sold me his parish.

Half way through our sessions he decided to take an opportunity to qualify at Boston University. Would I care to consider coming to Hatfield Heath? The idea was startling especially when David was due to arrive shortly. On the other hand, it was exactly the sort of charge I would like – limited numbers, social and economic variety, one school, an attractive church requiring little maintenance, liturgically what I was used to and rural without being the back of beyond: the vitality of Harlow New Town nearby, lying between Stortford and Chelmsford. The decision was very hard: finally Fred accepted the Boston offer and declared he was leaving in June. The Wardens and PCC had to know my decision or the diocese would step in to make the appointment. I consulted the diocese who were not pleased to hear about this private disposal of a benefice, but after trying to persuade me to take a larger parish near Maldon, the bishops had to admit I needed a change and there wasn't anything else quite so suitable.

I agreed to be considered for Hatfield Heath provided I could postpone my arrival until a reasonable time had elapsed for receiving and training David Gamble. Unfortunately I could not get a postponement later than November, and of course had to share this with David: he might prefer not to come. However, he had got to know both Peter and Winifred in his visits to Belhus and felt they would carry on effectively any training I began. I am still uncertain that I made a right and just decision; eventually I had to face the sorrow and anger of my Belhus people, and the indignation of the Hatfield Heath PCC for what in those days was considered a big gap for them to manage alone; but today an inward angst and doubt arises from the question: was I not meant to remain much longer as priest and pastor of that wonderful company of loveable Cockneys? When I went there the wife of Aveley's Vicar had commented 'What those people need is someone to love them'. Why was I deserting those I loved, just when I'd lost a wife? The truth was: I was exhausted and felt empty.

Going through the painful disengagement from Belhus I tried to assess what the six years with them had meant, and this I will summarize:

At Wanstead I found the parish ministry absorbing and manageable: at Belhus it had become fascinating, compelling, galvanizing my over-intellectual heart, emotionally stretching – stretching and challenging to my intellect too in order to encompass the way such people thought – with Marjorie Jose one evening I felt my mind going ever deeper into her mind, responding ever more sensitively to her words and, relying on something beyond reactive thought, I knew directly what she was searching for and how to reply. I came to trust insights and awareness that I hadn't before. In the exchange with Marjorie, and beyond it, she found her way, as several others too, into a unique and personally authentic faith.

At Wanstead I had, with the senior curate, practised the traditional healing ministry through the laying-on of hands and anointing after preparation. At Belhus this dimension of the work came to occupy a more central place: taking communion to sick parishioners had brought physical and mental improvement in health and often a return or beginning to personal prayer and church attendance. Laying on hands before a major operation became a regular event at the Family Communion – when one man, a bus driver with apparently chronic and life-threatening kidney deterioration was anointed and then went to be operated on, the surgeon found that the condition had vanished. He had appeared yellow and emaciated at our service and a few weeks later he turned up looking a cheerful colour, a picture of health. He was so grateful that he volunteered for Sunday School teaching and later became our treasurer. He lived for another thirty-five years and his widow is now church warden.

On another occasion my GP, no great believer, asked me to go to a dying woman. She had had one leg amputated and the other was gangrenous. He thought a clergyman might be a comfort to the family. When I arrived, she was unconscious, her pulse had virtually ceased and her face was 'falling in', as it were. The family agreed to anointing, and when I returned with the oil the signs of death were unmistakable. They appreciated the service and joined in the prayers: I invited them to call me in the night if they wished; but no call came and when I visited the next morning Daisy was sitting up. She smiled and as I approached, whispered 'I feel wonderful'. Privately warning the family that this might only be a temporary remission, I was surprised on my next visit to find her knitting, and soon she was up and about. Some months later she was confirmed and became a communicant. My GP commented, 'Medically speaking, Daisy should not be alive.'

These events, and others not dissimilar, enormously enlarged my faith and my confidence in the ministry. I believed that Christ's Spirit would continue to show me what I was there for, however easily I might get distracted, confused and exhausted. I came more to believe that the Holy Spirit worked as much through the ordinary functions of the church as through certain gifted individuals. Having been brought up with some suspicion of 'priestcraft', and as a historian aware of the weaknesses and crimes of the institutional church; knowing too the self-concern, rigidity and blindness to human needs of some churches, it came as a surprise that healing power and a genuine community could arise from our frail efforts, and I was astonished for instance, that our Ford workers would join public processions of witness to challenge often scornful anti-church attitudes of their work mates. Here were ordinary people often in demanding and creasing conditions finding time and energy for Christian faith and togetherness; coming to classes, attending house communions etc. giving and receiving mutual affection and support, and moving out into their communal lives to share their love and their belief.

For myself all the learning had been immensely enriching, and at times painful. Weaknesses of character had been pointed up, and only partly addressed; a dream at the time had me administering the Holy Communion not with bread but with drawing pins. I had to acknowledge over-directiveness, and the occasionally ruthless autocracy and self-glorification of my leadership style. Incompetence too, had been shown up in individual care and counselling: I had not acquired adequate listening skills and was far too ready to provide quick answers in place of empathy. I lacked sensitivity in handling groups, small or large, and would easily become defensive: inadequate self-awareness led me into emotional errors and disasters in relationships.

Yet viewing the Belhus experience as a whole (while reversing into the new prospects) I saw that some of the talents with which I had been fairly lightly endowed (the adolescent dilettante-ism) could usefully contribute to a parish ministry. Music, drama, teaching skills, oratory and rhetoric, meditative reflection, even a taste, perhaps a gift, for friendship, and a loving concern for the well-being of youngsters, not to mention an interest in orderly administration, all had a place, provided one or two of these did not become dominant at the expense of the others.

Above all, I had experienced authentic affection, loyalty and love, tolerant acceptance of my strengths and weaknesses, and having endured my own excruciating loss, had become more available to fellow sufferers. Mysteriously, people were able to pick up and use constructively their feeling that I knew something about what they were going through – and could share their pain. But I was aware of having neglected the capacity for sustained thought and hoped that Hatfield Heath would give time and opportunity to recover this. Spiritually, it was hard to say what progress I had made: I tended to leave such judgement to the spiritual guides that had felicitously come my way; Fr. Oswald SF, Norman Goodacre, Peter Morris (later of Pleshey), Fr. Christopher Bryant, SSJE amongst others. Making a retreat with the Cowley Fathers before starting at Hatfield Heath I was conscious chiefly of darkness – it was a typically gloomy November in a gloomy building: darkness and not knowing.

CHAPTER XI

HATFIELD HEATH

Six intersecting roads made a star-shaped village round some twenty acres of grassy heath land. This was Hatfield Heath. The roads ran between Sawbridgeworth and Chelmsford, Harlow and Gt. Dunmow, Bishop's Stortford and Ongar: at times a busy junction. A line of shops stood along the north side, a bakery, general stores and post office, a builder's yard, a butcher, a restaurant and the vicarage: another butcher and a garage stood on the Heath's west side, and several quite substantial Georgian-style homes on the east with a fine timbered house or two accompanying the very large United Reformed Church. In the centre of the Heath stood a modest and quite tasteful mid-Victorian Anglican church. Most people lived on the six roads fanning out from the centre, in houses of every age, shape and size; Lea Hall, a mainly Elizabethan mansion and two late medieval timbered buildings on the Dunmow Road being the oldest. To the north stood the fine old farmhouse of Corringales at one end, and the Ryes Hall at the other. Beyond ranged the bosky acres of Hatfield Forest. Three other impressive farmhouses with farm cottages, indicated the working presence of agriculture. 1930s and 1950s council estates stood at either end of the village: several 1930s bungalows witnessed to the presence of the retired, mainly in the Chelmsford Road, and substantial executive houses betokened managerial and business people along the Stortford and Sawbridgeworth roads. Shortly after I arrived, new private estates for 'first time buyers' were going up to attract young newcomers. All this made for a community as varied as Belhus had been monochrome – and with one tenth the population.

In the vast Victorian vicarage with four reception rooms and nine bedrooms, Bess and I were not alone. Before we left Belhus, a young widow who had lost her husband in a road accident came to help Bess in the house. When Eileen heard of the proposed move she accepted our invitation to take some rooms in the new vicarage with her two boys aged five and two. She would be nearer her elderly mother. Fred had questioned whether this arrangement was entirely fair to Eileen, like myself newly widowed, and on reflection I am not sure that it was. However, after three years she found a house of her own in a neighbouring village and soon afterwards remarried, another widower, with three children. Meantime she, Robert and Stevie happily enlivened our lives.

Bess, in her quiet way, soon became part of the village scene, and learnt to paint in oils, later exhibiting in the WI Essex Exhibition. During the next six years she made the Vicarage a secure haven from which parish, personal and diocesan enterprises could be undertaken, providing hospitality for business meetings, occasional gentlemen of the road, family gatherings and godchildren, backing up the work of visiting local invalids and hospitals, and handling callers with tact and kindliness as pastoral demands steadily increased.

It was not a feudal village: the Elizabethan Hall was occupied by the owner of Kraft Cheese, the social mix being paralleled in the church membership: one churchwarden worked at the bakery, the other was the proprietor of a large Stortford garage; both resourceful, loyal and effective colleagues. The Church Council was drawn from all strata and included a youngster or two, all being ready to take some part in the 'management', so that in time specific responsibilities could be devolved on to four separate working groups. These dealt with Worship (higher profile with 1960s experiments), Finance Planning, Mission (local and overseas) and Social Affairs (crucial for relations with village organizations). Each group handled both self-generated and referred business, keeping the Council informed. This set me free to visit fairly widely, to promote Children's and Young People's activities, as yet limited, and to improve inter-church relations. I also vaguely toyed with the idea of developing the Vicarage and its grounds as a Christian community.

Shortly after arriving at the Heath my desire for stimulus to study was answered by an invitation from the Vice-Chancellor of Oxford University to preach a University Sermon. This honour had probably come through friendship with my old tutor, Tom Parker. As it would take place early November I resolved to relate my words to the doctrine of the Communion of Saints and to a theology of Christian community. I settled to fairly wide reading, the Fathers, the Schoolmen and more recently, Bonhoeffer, Thornton, Merton and Teilhard de Chardin, taking as my text a phrase of de Chardin's, *'The consummation of the world is a communion of persons.'* Dining with the Vice-Chancellor the evening before was almost as formidable as delivering the sermon in the University church, but he was very gracious; as likewise was an interesting fellow-guest, a scientist researching DNA. The sermon was published in the Church Quarterly Review (Oct.–Dec. 1964).

Inter-church relations were, however, a priority issue. The Free Church had arrived in the village long before the Anglican. In 1662 a dissenting[24] Vicar of Hatfield Broad Oak brought his congregation to the Heath, where they built a modest tabernacle. Although C of E Christians lived in the neighbourhood, the hamlet was predominantly Congregational. The church was built in 1859 to the dismay of many local people and thereafter the two religious groups were barely on speaking terms. People I met could recall members of the two denominations crossing the road to avoid speaking to one another. Providentially a new URC minister, the Revd Sidney Wheale, about my own age, had been appointed the year I arrived, and his views were unusually ecumenical. Slowly we brought the two congregations together, first by ourselves meeting regularly for prayer and discussion, and then by instituting joint worship, and joint action in the care of the sick and the housebound. In time visiting newcomers was undertaken by laity from either church on behalf of both.

The Roman Catholics were served from Dunmow by a lively young priest. The Heath had a few mixed marriages so that a degree of mutual exchange took place and I got to know Fr. Jack Harden through playing tennis with him at the home of a Roman-Anglican couple. Jack and I went on a Scottish holiday together later on: we only fell out briefly on Loch Tay, I think, on the subject of the Immaculate Conception! Sadly he was moved to London the following year.

Tension of a secular character also existed between the village and the church, because the latter was considered to have hijacked the village hall – a timber and corrugated iron structure that had many years earlier been donated to the village, but, because its maintenance had fallen largely upon church people, appeared to be managed by the church. Controversy also surrounded the ownership and use of the Institute, originally the earliest church school building, but with the construction of an Aided School it had been let to a

---

[24] A number of C/E priests refused to accept the church settlement and revised prayer book when Charles II returned and were evicted from their livings, becoming the original nonconformists or dissenters.

village Men's Club for billiards and social evenings. The members were naturally suspicious when we wanted to use it for the new Sunday School, to run alongside the Family Communion, and a Youth Club on some evenings. However, a workable compromise was negotiated over a year or two, and legally safeguarded, and the help of several newcomers to the village enabled both Children's Church and the Youth Club to get off the ground. Robin Parkinson was an exceptional pioneer in the children's work, later joined by Alice Hackett; and their husbands, Commander Parkinson and Cyril Hackett pioneered the Village Hall.

When the church recognized officially that the old hall belonged to the village as a whole, a new era of co-operation could begin with the joint planning of a modern village hall. An impressive programme of fundraising was launched, culminating in an Annual Village Festival, begun in 1969 and still running. The Hall Committee has looked after the management of the building so well that it is now worth over £50,000. Later in the '70s, as part of the broadening of interests and responsibilities, the old Church magazine was turned into a village publication, edited also by an enthusiastic newcomer, John Paine.

Meantime beyond the parish our new bishop, John Tiarks, wrote to his parish priests 'the church, a traditionally inflexible institution, fashioned for stable times, has now to adapt itself to a socially fluid society', and summoned his clergy to a conference at Clacton in Butlin's Holiday Camp. This was partly to make recommendations on how the diocese should celebrate its impending Golden Jubilee, but in general to look at the functioning of the church in Essex, and, in particular, to move towards a policy over infant baptism, in answer to general dissatisfaction with both indiscriminate 'christening' and rigoristic refusal to baptize any but the children of regular churchgoers. At Clacton each morning we four hundred clergy were roused in traditional Butlin's style, and through the day divided between small group and plenary meetings. Only a ripple of support arose when I pointed out that Jubilee in the biblical sense had to do with 'release from obligation'; could we perhaps celebrate by reducing the number of committees and easing the weight of institutional 'busy-ness'? but the bishop's useful proposal of a Diocesan Self-Appraisal to begin in the parishes was accepted by a large majority.

Shortly afterwards John Tiarks appointed me editor of a diocesan publication called *The Essex Churchman*. With the help of a thoughtful cross-party team (Peter Elers and John Gunstone on the 'catholic' side, Paul Berg and Richard Bewes on the 'evangelical'), and advised by Michael De-la-Noy, a new *Essex Churchman* was brought to birth with photos, reviews, controversial articles (rather on 'New Christian' lines), achieving a circulation of 112,000. We attempted to monitor the appraisal process and to promote greater lay participation and frank comment on diocesan affairs – not always tactfully. When my editorial expressed some indignation that a maverick Archdeacon had been using his visitations to sow doubt about the Anglican-Methodist Reunion proposals, the *Daily Telegraph's* Peterborough picked this up in his gossip column under the heading 'Dog Eats Dog'. It had never occurred to me that my comments might be construed as the Bishop attacking one of his staff! I 'gat me to my Lord [Bishop] right humbly' and apologized, to be greeted by rich laughter and the remark that everyone had been highly amused at Diocesan House. It was slightly alarming that the Archdeacon himself died shortly afterwards.

In 1964 Inter-church Travel invited me to lead a group on their prestigious Voyage of a Lifetime for some 250 'pilgrims' chiefly by boat; not only the Holy Land, but Rome, Greece and Syria were to be visited[25]. Quite a few people from the Bishop's Stortford area joined my party and it became an opportunity for genuine pilgrimage. I enjoyed sharing my feeling for the holy places, but Good Friday and Easter in Jerusalem became additionally poignant when an elderly pilgrim fell from her donkey while riding into Petra and died on Maundy Thursday. Mervyn made a dramatic and quite moving occasion of this in the Church of All Nations that evening. (I found him rather remote as a person, and in my mind distinguished on this journey chiefly by the episcopal purple trunks he wore whenever he bathed). Bonuses on the journey included an interview with Pope Paul VI, a visit to Sparta and to Baalbek on the way out, and following the usual tour of Galilee, a Grecian round via Salonika, the Meteora Monasteries, Athens and Corinth. After such a classical feast what could be more apt than to sail up the Aegean and into the lagoons of Venice. The leaders were all exhausted so ICT generously bundled us into comfortable sleepers and we awoke for the channel crossing. The parishioners mostly found their faith strengthened by the experience and it was a climax in the life of Clara, our PCC Secretary of nearly fifty years in the job. Two years later I led a much shorter pilgrimage for a small group which Renie decided to join. Wonderfully, all her bitterness about

---

[25] led overall by Mervyn Stockwood, Bishop of Southwark.

Gill's death was taken away and she became a much happier person in the remaining ten years of her life.

In 1966, one of Renie's friends, a well-known eye surgeon in Sheffield reduced the 30 dioptres optical divergence in my vision to 3 dioptres, enormously easing the strain and making it possible to correct the remainder by reasonably light prisms.

Nevertheless, I was aware in myself of some tension manifested chiefly through weaknesses such as forthright or tactless intervention, impatience, insensitivity in relation to women and a predilection for escaping into the company of children. To gain better self-understanding I had joined one of the Clinical Theology Groups begun by Dr Frank Lake and found it challenging, fascinating and on the whole edifying. A surprising by-product was to discover salvation doctrine in terms of psychodynamic theory and experience: for instance, the concepts of justification by works and by faith acquired fresh significance through studying the origins of chronic anxiety and depression, which arise from inadequate or perfectionist parenting, and consequent compulsion to achieve and to vindicate oneself. Finding personal peace in Christ acquired fresh meaning as I worked through my own dynamics, began to let the compulsions go and accepted more thoroughly Christ's free justification, gaining release from years of trying to fulfil all the expectations of others and of myself. I became more available to other people as they were in themselves, and not as objects of obsessive 'do-gooding'. The Clinical Theology training helped me to begin to listen more deeply and more thoroughly, and to enable parishioners to discover and use their own insights and resources. To my surprise people also came from outside the parish and, without my desiring or seeking it, a counselling ministry began to develop. I also discovered some skill in teaching pastoral care, and was used by Dr Lake to conduct courses in Essex and later in Kent and Sussex. Both these developments were signs for the future.

Our healing ministry flourished, supported by a prayer group who also visited the sick. A dramatic moment took place one Whitsunday when our doughty Reader (and former headmaster) Ralph Dix had a stroke during the service. He was standing for the Sanctus, but valiant sidesmen caught him and conveyed him safely to the vestry. I continued the service, asking all to pray for Ralph and before the communion laid hands upon him. When the GP arrived he was pessimistic and arranged hospital admission. However, that afternoon Ralph woke up, commented favourably upon the nurses around him, and returned home a few days later, to continue his life as a great raconteur for at least another fifteen years.

In 1965, John Tiarks summoned the clergy to a second Butlin's Conference, devoted wholly to the formulation of a baptism policy. By now we had been goaded into action by the rigorists who were promoting an initial replacement of baptism on demand by a non-sacramental service of thanksgiving and blessing. The bishop was determined that decisions should be made as much by the laity as the clergy and to that end set up a painstaking process of consultation. I had to speak at several meetings culminating in three Synods of laity and clergy gathering in Archdeaconries. Over 1,000 actually attended these, (576 laity and 477 clergy) and overwhelmingly agreed that Holy Baptism was rightly given to children, but should not be administered without careful preparation; also that it should normally take place in a public service of regular worshippers. An optional service of Blessing should be officially provided but not be required use by those who accepted preparation for baptism. Guidance on what the preparation should undertake and require was provided by the committee of which I was a member; and the Bishop wrote a Pastoral Letter to all parishes asking for loyal acceptance of the policy. In practice, 'conservatives' and 'radicals' continued to wrangle, to the detriment of the average parishioner, but having insisted on baptism preparation at Belhus and been rewarded by a sizeable number of parents seeking confirmation and improving their church involvement after it, I felt that a moderate policy on these lines would eventually win the day. John Tiarks found that it took all his energies to keep laity and clergy working together, and pointed up the anglican need to find a mature lay-clergy partnership.

Difficulties in such partnership were also reflected in the parish as the C of E moved into the reform and updating of its worship. From 1966 onwards the Alternative Services and a new lectionary were authorized. With us, a BCP Sung Family Communion at 10.00 a.m. had become the norm for most Sundays, but this had left those used to worshipping at Matins feeling deprived. Some of them transferred to the regular Evensong and others preferred to receive communion at 8.00 a.m. but there was a movement for a monthly Matins. House groups were set up to study the new services and to my surprise were generally in favour of trying the first of the new Communion services, Series Two, at 10.00 a.m. The new lectionary, later modified and made part of the ASB, (Alternative Service Book authorized for 1980-2000) was introduced in 1967 and I enjoyed preaching on the subject matter provided as the distinct theme for each Sunday. Here was a chance to engage in progressive and sequential teaching at the best attended service, and we were probably amongst the first to reproduce copies of the readings for people to follow and take away. Newcomers liked the new service, quite a number were prepared for confirmation, joined the team of those who read lessons or served, and swelled the numbers so that I was grateful to have the school headmaster Don Foster to assist at the communion.

Luckily I did not lack opportunity teaching the young. At Hatfield Heath, unlike Belhus, I had to be chaplain to a large 'top-drawer' school for girls who were quite unresponsive to teach, though later their confirmands were more interesting. Don Foster, who was also church council Lay Chairman, an invaluable support who didn't mind saying just what he thought, allowed me to teach juniors RI, junior science and history. This put me in touch with village families in a fresh way. One day a mischievous imp of about eleven redeemed a gruelling history lesson by coming up to say, 'Thank you for teaching us, Vicar'. She was no creep, so I cherished the feather in my cap.

Each summer a Children's Church Week helped to vary the long holiday for some 30-40 children with activities and outings every day; usually crowned by a Pageant. In effect this took the place of the Belhus Camps (village families did not need country holidays) and every year drew in children and new families for the start of church activities in the autumn. As a number of my godchildren and Belhus Homes children came to stay during most of the holidays, particularly in the summer, they got to know Heath friends, especially during the Church Week, and developed their own interests in the village.

Three of these lads gave me a diary when they came for a half term break in 1965. I had never before 'written up' each day and it didn't last very long then. My diaries have simply recorded appointments and information; but for a while I noted main activities and made a few comments. Selective quotations over a month may perhaps help to give a sense of the personal and parochial mosaic at the time.

Feb. 21-26.   Impressed by band at Beat Service, especially drummer.
              First visit to Lionel, POW victim of Japs, pre-war extreme
              poverty – v. humbling.

Hospital visits incl. Roger[26], planned a holiday to cheer him.

New youth group, thoughtful exchange on prayer.

Printer, Stubbs came to instruct me over *Essex Churchman* layout & paste-up.

Yet another cremation, hatefully synthetic feel at crem.

School[27] confirmation interviews refreshingly open now.

War on Want fundraising – raised some interest visiting the pubs – terrified at first.

March 2-4.   House communion on new estate. Had a sense of entering calmer waters.

Inner message, 'Do not be strange with yourself'. What does it mean? Less compulsive visiting etc?

Little Miss H dying: lay on hands. Schizophrenic lad on the brink again: see family.

Gs took me to *Romanoff and Juliet*, Harlow Playhouse, a good lark. Met cricket club to plan Open Air Service.

March 5-15.   Miss H remarkably better: can't last. Felt wretched after row with parents of non-attending choir girls.

Spring has burst through, warm and balmy, but Bess ill: lots of sick visits.

Began Pilgrims' Progress lent course with children. Sixteen Downham girls made confession before Confirmation.

Lionel got more Jap horrors off his chest: plucky chap.

Miss D. calls to confess to 'church phobia'; needing to talk.

Introduced Gelineau music, mixed reception: second beat service OK but drummer got lost *en route*.

March 16-21.   V.g. doctor-clergy group, four GPs hope to plan course. Am feeling rather limp.

Chapter [deanery clergy meeting] tackled Chris Wansey re infant baptism – smooth but intransigent.

---

[26] Roger's brother had been killed while motor-biking along the Heath. Roger had suffered multiple fractures and was in hospital for nearly a year.

[27] The private girls' school, Downham.

Discovered no banns called in other parish for next day's wedding: groom dashed madly to London Registrar. Nearly fainted in pledging troth to very large and much older bride.

Newcomer Cyril Hackett offers help with Youth Club, very pleasant: reminds me of Belhus men.

Visited Belhus orphaned boy and girl now in Brentwood home. Clocks forward, lost the hour and half the congregation.

Rather before these events I visited the Community of the Ascension to see whether I might have a vocation to their order with its particular focus on work with youngsters. However the Bishop thought I should be concerned with other people's vocations and put me on a Committee for fostering them. I found myself involved in a large conference at Selwyn College, Cambridge, entirely for Sixth Formers. Essex Schools had responded well, the exchanges with such bright youngsters were crisp and testing, and a follow-up workshop was held at Hatfield Heath, several village families housing the students, and the Vicarage providing seminars and meals. The young men and women used the opportunity to help clarify their personal aims and afterward a few continued to write. My colleague Jean from the diocesan education department commented, 'You really came alive, and so did they, when you were in exchange with them. Are you sure you shouldn't be teaching?'

About the same time a London surgeon who lived locally and came regularly to our early communion became friendly and urged me seriously to consider swapping my clerical horse for a medical charger. 'You should go to Harlow Tech. and get yourself qualified in physics etc. I will help you to become a GP.' So, while being required to help Sixth Formers to assess their possible spiritual vocations, the old demons of doubt about my own vocation were rearing their heads. In fact, I was beginning to feel frustrated, though not discontented with the parochial ministry. I had reached an impasse with the Church Council over the next step in parochial growth and development. In my view our need as a church was to embark upon a deepening of our commitment and spirituality. I suggested we engaged in either a parish mission or stewardship training. The Council reluctantly allowed representatives from these projects to address them, but were not convinced. Later they agreed to engage in a Parish Life Conference but I do not recall the outcome.

A fresh dimension to pastoral work emerged when the local GPs accepted invitations to a regular meeting with trained parish visitors and myself. One GP, Angela, began to attend my Clinical Theology sessions; the others provided pastoral support for villagers. Angela later became a personal friend and joined us on holiday, opting eventually for a career as a psychiatric psychotherapist. We enjoyed the companionship and intellectual exchange but as Angela said, two relatively lonely people have to be wary about the degree of committed relationship they enter into: she remained a good friend until her early death some fifteen years later. So in effect my personal life had reached a degree of stagnation, although I remained very content with, and greatly appreciated, Bess's unfailing loving kindness and support. We had others to live in and help run the house and garden, chiefly young couples who couldn't find housing. One baby was born in the Vicarage, and for some months we reached a maximum of seven adults and seven children actually resident. Personally I had been attracted to one young parishioner, a leading member of the United Reformed Church, who had acted extremely well in a village play I produced. Later she married a young farmer. A liaison had also grown between myself and one of the 1964 Holy Land pilgrims. Working for a well-known publisher she had given stalwart help with *The Essex Churchman*, but it was too soon after Gill's death and this was very difficult to explain.

In my mid-forties with no clear way forward and a feeling that soon I would need to move on, I began to explore the possibility that I was meant to lead a celibate life either in a religious order or in service with an overseas church. I have already mentioned a visit to the Community of the Ascension in Birmingham; I liked Michael and Peter Ball, its founders; but sensed no clear direction. It was impressive that the missionary societies were throwing off their old 'colonial' style of white autocracy and replacing it by the encouragement of co-operative autonomy. The Papua and New Guinea Partnership particularly attracted me, interest nourished by their Secretary, John Bodger, but my heart was moved by the reports of South Africans suffering under apartheid and I felt that there our Church was effectively fighting injustice. Could I help them? (There was also a family link in South Africa, my favourite uncle, Nicco.)

My own seventh or jubilee year in Hatfield Heath would arrive in 1969 so why not anticipate by a few months and take a sabbatical? How could it be managed? As though in response to my restlessness, our most recent Belhus curate David Gamble let me know that he was unhappy in his second curacy and would like somewhere to mark time: taking care of Hatfield Heath appealed to him, if the Bishop would agree. But, having disposed of my immediate responsibilities and income, was there a Bishop in South Africa who would have me? And would Bess remain to look after David until I returned? John Tiarks graciously accepted the idea, although I was handing back to him a number of jobs: he even made a personal donation towards my expenses. A letter to the Archbishop of Capetown, Robert Selby, could now start the ball rolling towards the Southern hemisphere.

The ball did not roll freely. At first I received a welcoming acceptance: the incumbent of a predominantly coloured parish was planning to leave for a sabbatical in England about the time I wished to come. This prospect sounded ideal and plans were laid for David's caretaking and for travel by air (for one moment as I paid the price of the ticket it occurred to me that I was mad: luckily I had combined the visit to the London travel agents with a musical trip for a small group of parish youngsters: I could not flinch in their presence!) Then, a few days later the Archbishop wrote saying that the Capetown clergyman had changed his mind: would I go wherever I might be needed within his jurisdiction? The open-endedness was daunting but I agreed, hoping that a similar parish would be found. It was not: the Bishop of Bloemfontein had asked for me to back up a young curate, Donald Lowe, whose vicar had moved on, leaving him alone with a large parish. My heart sank, I was to go to an all-white congregation in the homeland of apartheid, the Orange Free State. Yes, it was where Nicco had farmed: but he was no longer there. However I felt I should regard this direction as the divine will. The impressive certificate of permission to absent myself from the Church of England arrived from the Archbishop of Canterbury (not to exceed nine months) and Bess decided on her own sabbatical with her daughter in the Lake District while I was away.

The parish was inclined to believe that I would not return, or only in order to settle abroad. I had no such expectation, though equally no idea what might transpire. I did, however, feel immensely grateful for what Hatfield Heath had provided and that the parish might yet be a launching pad for the next stage. The future was open, and I could bring to any new work fresh experience of how to run a parish, new concepts of effective pastoral care, greater self-awareness, albeit with a sense that spiritually I had grown a little stale. I wanted time to clarify the jumble of new theological ideas I had recently acquired (John Robinson *et al*) and stimulus to re-invigorate the practice of prayer and meditation. I also felt the need of external challenge from the real world, having for six years settled into rather a cosy rural ministry. Carrying far too many books with other baggage when my dear friend Cyril Hackett dropped me at Heathrow, I had to unpack and jettison a small load for him to take back. I embarked somewhat dazed, and a few hours later watched a brilliant and tempestuous dawn break through Mediterranean skies.

CHAPTER XII

SOUTH AFRICA – AND BEYOND

Becoming airborne over a mosaic of bonfires and fireworks, I took off from Heathrow on Guy Fawkes night 1968, landed in Johannesburg (96°F in the shade) and was greeted by Michael,[28] a local priest who had generously offered to meet, entertain and despatch me to Bloemfontein. There I would assist the overworked parish priest Donald and his wife, Mary, living in the white town and caring for St Margaret's church. The parish was linked with a Bantu township nearby where Kelham Fathers ministered. In place of the coloured community in Capetown I had originally hoped to work with, I was given Anglican Afrikaners and small association with a black congregation in the Bantu township. This latter also contained a school for Bantu children at Phahameng which Chelmsford diocese supported. Donald travelled to several outlying Bantu communities involving trips of over 100 miles; he also had diocesan duties. Residing at first with the jovial Bishop, Freddy, and his kindly wife, I later transferred to St Margaret's Rectory, where the parish had ensconced a charming couple, Saxon and Briony, he being an organ builder whose business took him all over the Republic. The Bloemfontein culture shock, symbolized by park seats and bank entrances that warned black people not to use them, was gently offset by the courtesy of these new friends, and the warmth of Donald's family life. Sitting in the rectory garden with a book in the cool of the evening, while plucking fresh apricots from leafy foliage nearby, made up for the fierce heat of the day and the distress of seemingly insoluble pastoral situations.

I was soon involved in work which brought association with illness and death, and human closeness in distress; also in house meetings which opened up mutual friendship (one family lent me a car). It helped me towards understanding this tense and complex society, where some of the most gentle

---

[28] later Michael took me to the Drakensbergs for a two-day trek, mainly round Cathedral Peak.

and charming people I'd ever met appeared to acquiesce in blatant racialism and injustice. In practice, (I discovered) a lot engaged in works of charity to mitigate individual hardship; but nothing could blot out the meagre accommodation for lesser breeds at the foot of many an opulent garden. Everywhere a barely acknowledged fear lurked and not many were prepared to name it; though amongst those who identified and fought for just causes, the Anglican Church appeared to have an honourable part.

The white church had an interesting range of membership and was quite active. Of about 250 members a third were professional, managerial or self-employed; a fifth, clerks, salesmen, reps; and nearly a fifth artisans, skilled mechanics etc: six farmers and retired people made up the remainder. The Eucharist was well attended and an atmosphere of genuine devotion and friendliness prevailed: the introduction of a new Family Communion attracted nearly 200. I formed a small choir to contribute towards it. At Evensong, also popular, the men outnumbered the women.

Bloemfontein sprawls beside a massive flat-topped mountain over which animal and floral wild-life flourishes; the town is full of colour, exotic gardens, subtropical trees and shrubs, but the brilliance struck me as brittle; though the little street of old Afrikaner houses where Saxon and Briony later moved, with great generosity taking me too, had charm and character.

On one visit to the Bantu township I became aware how I had myself become infected by the fear. Driving through the shanty houses of corrugated metal, rough timber, jerry-cans and other unlikely materials ingeniously pressed into construction, I lost my way; the awareness that I did not know this particular meeting place of several baked-mud roads struck me as catastrophic. All the tracks were humming with lively black Africans and for a moment I became convinced of their hostility: it seemed only right to expect it. Mercifully the need to get somewhere overcame the emotion; I got out shakily and spoke to the nearest and very large male; with ease and courtesy he told me the way. I felt humbled and ashamed at my fear.

Unexpectedly, people from both parish and SSM community asked for fairly prolonged counselling care. In retrospect this was a pointer to the future. Even more so was the outcome of a visit to Robert Selby, Archbishop of Capetown, when he offered me a job: to become pastoral carer in the archdiocese for all coloured clergy and their families. I was staggered that he should think me suitable and qualified for this immense task, and also doubtful of the wisdom of entrusting it to an expatriate. It was a curious message to send the coloured clergy that none of their white colleagues would undertake such a task; and looking ahead at the need to set up long-term care, and knowing that the Afrikaner government would not hesitate to send me home if I offended, I wondered how secure such work would be. I consulted Tom Winter, a former fellow student, Capetown vicar and brother of Bishop Colin Winter who had been expelled by the government: he urged me not to accept, agreeing my reservations and knowing my ignorance of the republic. In spite of the Clinical Theology training I felt unready for intensive pastoral counselling, but when Robert Selby took me to visit a coloured clergyman and his family I was very aware of their isolation and unhappiness. It felt dreadful to reject them and yet I knew it was not for me. The Archbishop wrote renewing the offer when I was back in England and addressed the letter to '*Canon* R. Smythe' (a carrot I wondered?).

The Capetown visit had been an after-Christmas break, primarily to enjoy the company of Nicco my favourite uncle, who had farmed in the Orange Free State for some forty years and retired with his wife to a pleasant Capetown flat overlooking the sea. The drop in temperature was an immense relief and the Cape was a lot moister than Bloemfontein. They took me round the whole Cape area from the heights of Table Mountain to the intimate little ports like Hout Bay, and from there I spent a few days with another uncle and aunt at Somerset West. They lent me a car in which to visit a large coloured township at Paarl where another Chelmsford priest was wrestling with the appalling poverty and deprivation of his parishioners.

Chelmsford diocese also supported a coloured township near Port Elizabeth (Gelvandale) so I routed myself there on the way back to Bloemfontein staying with a delightful Hatfield Heath family with two girls and a boy of whom I was specially fond. Gelvandale's lively parish and intelligent young parish priest were impressive: but I was told many tales of oppressive police tactics and the discontent and frustration of local priests.

A month or so later, Nicco and Mary came to Bloemfontein, arriving for a Sunday when I was preaching at the Bantu township church. A vast basilica taking several hundreds, it was lit by windows made from the ends of beer bottles, effecting an agreeable, gentle light and aptly redeeming the cause of much Bantu violence and misery – the beer bottle. Nicco was visibly moved by the fervour of the music and singing, saying that in all his years as a farmer with Bantu workers he had never felt closer to black people. My time with them was beginning to run out and I was feeling almost exhausted by the continuing heat. Mercifully the rain came, after about four months' drought, and I stood in the rectory garden simply soaking it up.

A really delightful young girl, a Sunday School teacher at St Margaret's was killed in a road accident. It was the worst of several bereavements and I became very close to her parents as they grieved and slowly adjusted to the acute pain. The church mourned with them; many had loved Grace. The funeral took place on my mother's birthday and brought a deepening of my own grieving for both mother and Gill. It seemed that this sabbatical had to do with healing the losses of past years.

On return from Port Elizabeth I began to hatch a plan to go home after Easter 'the long way', that is, to circle the world, via family in Bulawayo, Salisbury (now Harare), and Nairobi, friends in Ceylon, New Guinea, Australia, New Zealand, the USA, and contacts which might make stepping stones between. Thanks to all these good people there gradually emerged a possible route (through East Africa to Delhi and Sri Lanka; Bangkok, Papua, the antipodes, a Pacific island or two, the USA and home) to be accomplished in three months if I were not to exceed the archiepiscopal permit. The absorbing practicalities of journey-planning helped to assuage the sadness of goodbyes, the congregation sending me off on Easter Tuesday 1969. Adults and children who had become affectionate friends joined in a heartfelt farewell and gave me an inscribed fountain pen.

This time I stayed in Johannesburg with the sister of a Hatfield Heath parishioner, whose very lovable family took me to the Voortrekker Monument at Pretoria the next day. It was a profound reminder of what I was leaving. Twenty-four hours later I landed on the green and lush plateau of Bulawayo in Ian Smith territory, where Tim Gibbs, son of Humphrey Gibbs the Governor of Rhodesia, was waiting to drive me to his farm. His Manager was Gavin McColm, my South African aunt's brother. He had found me a comfortable rondavel for a few days. An expedition to the Matopos Hills, monumental puddingstone rocks, bare and bald plateau scraped out by glaciers, gave time for learning.

'Little yellow-skinned bushmen developed a remarkable civilization here beginning in the fourth or fifth millennium BC until the Bantu arrived in the ninth Century AD.' said Gavin. 'By the start of our millennium they had

158

perfected painting on cave walls so liquid that brush strokes are still visible, but the paint never ran nor has it cracked like oil paintings.' I thought the paintings both naturalistic and impressionistic with a fine sense of movement. 'They mastered perspective and foreshortening before Mantegna's breakthrough in Padua,' continued Gavin, 'and it can probably be said that their work is the purest expression of original art in Africa.'

I learnt also about Matope who founded the Monomatopa empire in the fifteenth century. Its wealth was based on some 600 goldmines exploited with the help of Arab traders and Indian mining engineers. All this was achieved without the invention of the wheel or writing. I also learnt something about Rhodes, when we visited his grave up in the hills. It confirmed my dismay at what he aimed for and how he went about it. He had sown the wind and Southern Africa was reaping the whirlwind.

On a visit to the St James' Mission at Nyamandhlevu I met Fr. Boatwright and heard of his work amongst non-Christians in the native reserve helping them to farm what used to be barren scrubland. His schools educated the children for a better start than most had elsewhere. A day or two later I could also fit in 24 hour visits to the Victoria Falls and the Kariba Dam: at the Falls you are welcomed by a rainbow corona; then staggered by immense silver white sheets of roaring foam and peer into giddy depths from precipitous heights. You end up in a small park with a witch doctor, an enormous black cauldron containing a seething mass of simmering mealies and a large notice which says 'Customers Park at their own Risk.' Kariba was a mighty engineering feat: set in little Mediterranean hills, bathed in a ripe plum sunset the evening I arrived; the shores of the lake yielded their best treasures next morning in the form of enormous stately elephants. In the town was a little church built entirely by the workers on the dam in their leisure time.

Nicco's daughter Suzanne and her husband lived in Salisbury and I had not seen her since she was undergoing secondary education in England. Though happy to meet up, they were unhappy in Rhodesia: and not long afterwards emigrated to the USA, where it was far from easy to resettle. Humphrey Gibbs and his wife had kindly invited me to lunch at Government House, opportunity for an interesting exchange, but I was struck by their sadness and depression: the country and people they loved were being done out of their heritage and they were powerless to help. I left the town feeling a sense of cul-de-sac: later on it amazed me that such a state of affairs could last another ten years.

A flight over the sandy red Limpopo snaking through dark green and buff-coloured scrub, brought me to the bright flamboyants and poinsettias of Blantyre in Malawi to meet an English team working amongst impoverished and malnourished families in the nearby highlands. All too soon I had to embark on the next leg, to an old friend, Paul Hardy, Chaplain to the University at Dar-es-Salaam. He lived in a pleasant bungalow surrounded by palm groves near Oyster Bay, the most impressive of his colleagues being Bishop John Sekumo. After watching Bishop John preside like a stately eagle over his diocesan synod I was not surprised later to hear he had been appointed Archbishop of Central Africa. Paul took me into the high land behind Dar-es-Salaam to see the University, which dominated the hills under an enormous stone canopy of immense presence with an exquisite view of the ocean. Tanzania struck me as a country which might succeed in modelling a new style of African government, though Europeans tended to see no further than the 'scandal' of Nyerere's use of China to build his trunk rail line.

Kenya was modelling a more Western style of representative government under Kenyatta's benevolent autocracy. My cousin Ken Stovold, Archdeacon of Nairobi, had hopeful words about the country's future in spite of the chronic threat of tribalism . . . I felt his optimism confirmed by several days in the Mount Kenya (Kirinyaga) diocese with its Bishop Obadiah Kariuki, to whom I brought the greetings of my own bishop. Chelmsford diocese had helped to fund some ventures and to train their youth officer, Eshban Githinji, who took me off to remote towns and villages to meet youngsters and to give talks on church history. The number of young people aged 14 – 25 who had recently joined the church was impressive and so was their thirst for knowledge. In one village they had brought a very English bed for me to sleep on in a thatched rondavel; but so enthusiastic were the questions following a lecture that I did not get the benefit of much slumber. Both the Anglo-Catholic Tanzanians and the young Evangelicals of Mount Kenya struck me as holding keys for the future in Africa: but I needed far more time to reach an informed judgement of this.

Ken Stovold and his doughty CMS missionary wife, Hilda, drove me through the dramatic Rift Valley (not unlike the one I had known in Jordan) near the three mile crater of Mount Longonot and the several million flamingos that turn Lake Nkuru a brilliant pink. We passed acres of fine tea plantations to their bungalow at Kisumu by Lake Victoria. During the brief stay I explored the lakeside and bestrode the equator nearby; I also preached at the Sunday evening service on 'the lakeside commissioning' of the apostles in John 21: all through this leg of the journey I was reading Marsh's fine commentary on John's gospel. Back in Nairobi a visit to the remarkable Starehe School showed what Kenyans and Europeans could do for disadvantaged youngsters, and a trip to the local safari park where we encountered a large pride of lions and herds of beautiful giraffes, led up to the flight to India via Addis Ababa and Karachi.

On arrival in Delhi I was arrested and detained. The quarantine authorities discovered the vaccination reference in my yellow fever card was defective. (My arrival coincided with Indian outrage at the UK government's handling of the Ugandan Asians issue.) I was bundled off to the isolation hospital, where I was allowed to telephone the British Consul for advice and help. He promised to get in touch with the London Fever Hospital: I had no idea how long this would take. After an uncomfortable night I waited hopefully, chatting with fellow patients and somewhat consoled by the premature breaking of monsoon rains – no sightseeing would have been possible that day. About 4.00 p.m. the Consul arrived with the vaccination batch number and I have his typed statement that he witnessed my payment of 25 rupees for overnight accommodation – an addition of injury to insult! I booked in at a comfortable hotel and arranged a car trip to Agra.

Next morning dawned in clear blue skies, and a pleasant Indian driver arrived punctually to take me through rather barren villages with muddy ponds and water buffaloes to the Taj Mahal, immaculate and with few other visitors around. In the stillness and bright morning light, pointing up every coloured stone, the serenity and beauty were palpable. My driver found me an outdoor restaurant for a late lunch and, after another tour dropped me off at the Delhi Red Fort for an absorbing *Son et Lumiere*. This brief taste of India left the elusive flavour of a breath-taking immensity, contrasting extremes, affable talkative people, and the sublime meditative purity and grandeur of Jehan's tomb, whose carnelian, jade, lapus lazuli and other mosaic wreaths continued to dazzle my inner eyes.

Then, taking wing to Colombo into the warm embrace of Lakshman Wickremesinghe, former fellow student at Ely and now Bishop of Kurunagala, witty, profoundly genuine, compassionate, and energetic in a laid back way, I found an ideal companion for touring Sri Lanka. Hoping to repay his hospitality by a few preachments, I got my leg pulled for trying some Singhalese words: we laughed at the faded glory of the Queen's Hotel in Kandy (like taking tea at the Grosvenor Hotel in London), respectfully admired the Temple of the Tooth, especially the superb teak pillars, the Audience Hall paintings and its almost gothic gargoyles and the university buildings at Peradenya. I relished in particular the magnificent botanical gardens with their plethora of orchids and avenues of tall trees.

We drove through lush paddy fields via fine local temples, intriguingly shy villages hiding within groves of tall palm trees, and handsome villagers (not at all shy) and came to the massive statements of Buddhism at Pollinaruara and Anaradhapura.

Galvihara's three vast Buddhas (standing, sitting and lying down), the Samarthic figure which expresses great compassion, and a Buddha presenting a flat hand towards us to imply the message Fear Not – all these spoke of an impressive and attractively powerful spiritual presence which became embodied and personal when Lakshman introduced me to the Custodian of the Chief Temple, Sri-Sumama-Revata-Kayakathero, a man of evident spiritual force and character. I was almost too awed by his presence to take part in their conversation.

After visiting one enormous dagoba and its superb carvings, Rubens-like temple statuettes with plump bellies and dancing feet cavorted all over my imagination for some days, subdued a little by the evening sunset at the lake and Rest House near a mighty rock-hewn statue of King Prakzama the Great, glowing in the sun's declining rays. Most of what I'd seen related to the period 400 BC – AD 600, after which came a Christian presence, beautifully represented by a museum Nestorian cross, a copy of which Lakshman had had woven into his vestments. An orphanage at Talava was a more modern Christian presence and the children sang very sweetly to us. My interest was captured by a visit to the ashram set up by a young Sinhalese priest, Yohan Devananda; early the next morning we took part in an alfresco Anglican eucharist there, attended by local Buddhist monks. Equally contemporary, but secular, was my farewell to Sri Lanka; paying respects to the Bandaraike monument and lunching with the Speaker of Colombo's Parliament.

Few lands had been so pleasurable to visit. To my great sorrow Lakshman died a few years later. While there at the time I suspect I picked up an infection, because my brief call at Bangkok included a day in bed – when solicitous

Thai attendants kept coming to ask me if I required a masseuse! Luckily I surfaced in time for the mandatory trip through the canals to the Floating Market, delighted by the vigorous and colourful family life going on in the waterside homes as we passed by; and to see the brilliant green, blue and red mosaic stones and fearsome animal statues of the great temples.

On Ascension Day (in spite of the airline losing my booking from Manila and allocating a rough place in the fuselage!) I landed in Papua New Guinea at Port Moresby to be greeted by Archbishop David Hand, whom I'd last seen in 1939 at an Old Boys' event at Greshams. His cheerful, corpulent figure did not quite match my idealized memory (enhanced by the reputation that had been wafted to the UK). David was all courteous welcome and, after giving me a little time to recover from the journey, invited me to celebrate the festival eucharist at the altar in his chapel nearby.

Papua in 1969 was on the verge of self-government under Australian oversight. This had been achieved in barely eight years and it appeared that its rapid maturation had owed much to the Christian Church. PNG had also consistently sought multiracial equality in everything; government, transport, public eating and assembling, minority racism being dealt with firmly. Equally remarkable was the degree of ecumenical tolerance and co-operation. The RC Archbishop did not permit his priests to poach on Anglican areas and the French monastic orders tended to regard Anglicans as the Church of the country. As in East Africa the churches appeared to enjoy the support of many young people.

Papua consists of a series of high mountain ranges and thick bush, so that it was normal, and often only possible to travel from A to B by plane or boat. Soon I was transferred to Dogura, the spiritual centre of the diocese and the site of an impressive cathedral. Approaching the massive wall of mountains east of Port Moresby, I wondered how our little Cessna could possibly get above it; but seeking out a narrow cleft at some five thousand feet we broke through into a series of high contour valleys with precipitous walls rising on both sides. Soon the Cathedral appeared below, standing on a plateau surrounded by thick forest: we bumped down on some rough pasture, took a jeep up on to the plateau and were surrounded by a cheerful and unusually varied crowd of staff, students and other visitors including an old friend, John Bodger. He introduced me to my bedroom, furnished simply by a bed of interwoven branches surrounded by wooden uprights, open to the rest of the ménage. There was hardly room for my case, but that night I slept well and woke to a twittering chorus of banana birds. John and I walked to the beach where the first missionaries, Albert Maclaren and Copland King had landed in August 1891 and explored the little villages where John had been the missionary priest. I was impressed by the fine physique of the Papuans. During three weeks in Papua New Guinea I gave a hand where I could. The school at Dogura had 450 lads and 250 lasses; I preached on Whit Sunday at the Cathedral, and taught briefly at the Martyrs' School, under the shadow of Mount Lamington whose eruption in 1951 killed between three and four thousand people including all but one of the church's ordinands. The survivor was George Ambo, first Papuan bishop and then Archbishop, whom I was to meet later. The headmaster Ronald Morris (still active today) was particularly pleasant and interesting: so also was Fr. Eric Cassidy, the Principal of the Theological College, who later invited me to consider joining him as Vice-Principal. Bishop David talked of combining this with the job of Sub-Dean at the Cathedral – but vocational issues did not clarify until later in this tour. Nevertheless New Guinea, the other side of the world from home, did become the locus of decision.

At 4.00 a.m. one morning we set off for the mission motor launch, *The Maclaren King* skippered by a Cretan, Harold Parasco, and standing by at a rocky inlet. (Today his son is the skipper.) A sturdy swell on the Pacific accompanied a watery sunrise and in the mist Mount Goodenough, a 9000ft volcanic monster, reared directly out of the sea. Flying fish and porpoises entertained us and coral 'mushrooms' protruded around the island of Ipoteto. For twelve hours we hugged the coast until reaching a fjord where *The Maclaren King* could harbour. Papuan lads appeared to carry John ashore and we climbed steeply up to the mission station of Sefoa. The priest John Read, and his wife Sheila, had not expected this visitation, but greeted us kindly and escorted us to a neat village and their beautiful children, Alban and Crispin, bright vivacious little blondes. An early rise for communion in magical shimmering light began a day of lively discussion about local conditions and prospects, in a languid atmosphere. Re-embarkation followed for Wanigela further up the coast, a Melanesian pictorial cameo of palms, white sands and massive koleas of brilliant red and yellow, sporting butterflies in exotic colours almost the size of blue tits. There, housed in a capacious little bungalow of sago sheets, we looked out over the village and its playing field, later wandering through the surrounding scrub to the sounds of cockatoos knocking out their messages on the trees and the warbling notes of the leatherhead. Using the earth loo under a spreading palm I met a spider of formidable size. At night the flying foxes flapped around the trees, and thunder rolled about the mountains.

A new church was to be consecrated at Kokoda, famous as the place where the Australians stopped the Japanese and frustrated their planned invasion of Australia. Japs had already swallowed up Malaysia, Indonesia and the Philippines and so unprepared were defences that they seemed unstoppable. Failure in New Guinea could have spelt the end of free Australia. It was one of the decisive battles of the war, though barely appreciated in the West. The New Guinea Mission lost a number of priests and staff in the invasion and their memory was to be enshrined in the new church. Now, many of the current personnel were summoned to the new church. We were expecting to be collected from Wanigela by the Bishop's aeroplane, but a radio message alerted us to the grounding of this plane through engine trouble and the apparent cancellation of our trip. However, the following morning a low flying aircraft intruded upon breakfast and landed noisily on the playing field carrying the District Commissioner on the first leg of his return to Australia. He had picked up the Bishop's message and diverted the plane to collect us for Kokoda – such was the local camaraderie. Thrusting a roughly made sandwich into my pocket and leaping to our quarters for my case, I managed to scramble aboard the little bi-plane before the pilot's patience expired. Soon climbing over Mount Lamington, we peered into its smoking mouth, and, crossing the impenetrable dense forest (I wondered what a forced landing would be like), arrived at Kokoda in time for the ceremony.

The consecration of the church was a prolonged and colourful affair with processions and fervent singing all presided over by Bishop David and Bishop George Ambo. An alfresco feast followed and an hour or more of dramatic and energetic dancing by fully armed warriors, in their war-paint and traditional dress: altogether a powerful gathering of about five hundred people. My attention was specially caught by the beauty of the reredos (local art, I think) and the great frame, about ten or twelve foot high on which the congregation had hung their offerings – fruit, vegetable, flesh and fowl for the main part.

Shortly afterwards an expedition took place to a remote village, whose priest, I believe, was in need of help. My memory is chiefly of wading through a river in flood up to my chest for about fifty feet – and emerging festooned with leeches, to be removed smartly. Later we came to Popondetta to stay with the Archdeacon, John Sharpe and his wife Jean, who entertained us generously and gave a run down on the northern area, including a courageous new initiative in the furthest mountains where pockets of cannibalism were still rife. John Sharpe, however, revealed that he was not advancing on that front, but intended to return to England and undertake a course of training to improve his pastoral skills. He had several prospectuses and waved one at me about the Richmond Fellowship. I had told him about my own uncertainty over the next step, but was surprised when he said quite firmly to me, 'I think this is the sort of thing you should consider'.

The Richmond Fellowship was the child of a pioneer nurse Elly Jensen, who had felt scandalized by the failure of local authorities to set up the half-way hostels for discharged mental health patients that Parliament, recognizing the urgent need, had encouraged them to provide through a recent Act. So she opened her own home in Richmond, under licence, and began to take such patients. Helpers eventually joined her and after much pain and harsh learning experiences, other houses were set up and rehabilitation methods developed. Recently they started a training college in Addison Road, Kensington, to run a Human Relations Course designed to provide basic training in the care of disturbed people and to access the fruits of their experience more widely, especially to workers with voluntary services, such as the churches. As I read about this course the idea that John could be right formed in my mind; could this be a pointer to the next stage? I took the prospectus, mulled it over and resolved to investigate on my return to England. Suddenly I had the shape of a purpose for the future; but I said little about it. Crossing the Owen Stanley range back to departure from Port Moresby I felt quietly thankful and hoped I might survive to see it through.

Papua New Guinea was hard to leave but I had an Australian date with another Ely man, Robert Waddington[29], so arrived at Cairns in Queensland to be met and whisked up to St Barnabas Ravenshoe, a Bush Brotherhood school where Robert was Headmaster. He was proud of his speedy coupé, almost too rapid for my stomach on the 270 hairpin bends to the 3,000 ft plateau. The school was a campus of large and small huts surrounded by fine rolling hills brightly heather-clad. The boys (10-18) came from all over Australia, their families, white and coloured, glad of the quality education. At Ely I had written Robert a song to words by Paul Dehn called 'In the Spring'. I was pleased he wanted to correct his transcription and to sing it

---

[29] later Dean of Manchester Cathedral.

again. He also asked me to take a class of intelligent if slightly cynical Six-Formers, eighteen year olds whose focus was already on future jobs rather than academe.

The next leg took in Sidney where kind friends opened my eyes to the harbour's grandeur, and saw me off to stay with a farmer in Taihape, New Zealand's North Island. The Duncans had stayed with us at Miserden and after taking a bus from Auckland past the great white smoking volcano, Ruapehu, I enjoyed seeing them again, although slightly dismayed to find that my notoriety had preceded me. I was reported in the local press to be preaching at the parish church a day or two later.

My reward was an expedition into the North West mountains to see the glow worms in the Waitomo caves. A warden showed me a female glow worm, like a small dragon fly with long legs, and explained how she 'lights up' to attract the male – producing a beautiful glow from the ignition of her waste matter; this also attracts edible insects to commit suicide on her long acidic threads. A resourceful lady putting to good use her humblest bodily products.

For the final days I will use a letter I wrote at the time for the Hatfield Heath parish magazine:

The last instalment of my journey home from Africa left you in the glow worm caves at Waitomo. The next day I returned to Auckland for the night flight to Fiji. My object was to stay at the Theological College at Suva and to see something of the Polynesian Church. However, I had reckoned without New Zealand Airways. The Comet on which we were to have flown, had been replaced by an ancient Electra, which developed engine trouble half an hour out of Auckland. We had to turn back, jettisoning trails of flaming fuel on the night air. At the Airport we waited around for two hours, somewhat chagrined by having just missed our dinner on the plane, until we were taken off to a hotel, resuming the flight at the crack of dawn.

'It is an ill wind . . .', because I found by arriving in the morning at Fiji I connected with a little local plane which got me to Archdeacon Jeff Sexton at Suva in time for an interesting visit to a number of churches and colleges. I won't bore you with details, but I can say I was most impressed at the moment of efficient church work being done by both Fijians and Indians (who are nearly 50 per cent of the population in

Fiji). I took messages from New Guinea to students studying at the main college.

I was now on the direct line home passing through Honolulu, San Francisco, and New York. Although I was to take services and preach several times, this last fortnight had more of the character of a holiday. It started well with the traditional greeting at Honolulu Airport and a circlet of frangipani. I stayed at the Diocesan Centre and took a service for a Japanese Priest, whose family was extremely charming and interesting. A Japanese businessman took me out to a traditional Japanese meal, another family took me to swim on the famous Waikiki Beach (I envied the superb surfing) and I spent the evening in a club for ex-drug addicts, run by one of the Churches. A walk with Judy in the hills overlooking Pearl Harbour brought home to me a bit of war history[30].

San Francisco is magnificent. The two bridges, the Golden Gate and the eight mile long bridge across the bay, are amongst the most impressive constructions I have ever seen. The city is built on fairly steep hills running down to the sea, and little trams charge up and down ferociously. It has fine buildings, but I was staying at the YMCA in a rather rough area, and as I left the taxi driver said 'every day you stay there you are pushing your luck', and went on to describe the nightly murders!

The next stop was Denver in the shadow of the Rocky Mountains, where I was staying with an administrator at the University of Boulder. I visited the University and its Chaplaincy, but perhaps the most memorable episode was a day tour chauffeured by her father, a ninety-two year old ex-lawyer. We did at least a hundred miles of mountainous roads, first to his log cabin and then over precipitous heights to over ten thousand feet. The views were magnificent, especially of the snow-capped mountains, but there were times when I kept one eye on the brake! I took two services and preached to a large congregation at one of the suburban churches. The Vicar got me involved in a heated argument about South Africa, having invited me to talk to his confirmands.

New York I dreaded somewhat, and arranged for only a short stay with friends who live on the edge of Harlem. But it was far less terrifying

---

[30] Judy Austin YWCA Executive Director at the University of Hawaii.

than I expected, and visits to the United Nations and to the Empire State Building were nearly as worthwhile as the superb boat trip round Manhattan. The skyscrapers, lightly touched by mist in a shimmering blue sky, stood like the giant ramparts of a modern Babylon.

I am astonished to find that my diary does not actually record the day on which I landed at Heathrow: it was in the first week of July – and I remember clearly that I went straight to the Richmond Fellowship to enquire about the Human Relations Diploma Course, before reaching a warm and happy reunion at Hatfield Heath with Bess and David. Within a month Bess had mounted parties to resume contact with parishioners and friends who could hardly believe I had returned. We were in the middle of Children's Summer Church, and soon after I travelled to Sheffield to help with an ACCM Selection Conference and to see Gill's mother. I was back in the saddle: but what new horse was waiting to be mounted?

CHAPTER XIII

RICHMOND FELLOWSHIP AND WPF

Desire to enter a new world could hardly be more colourfully fulfilled than by walking up the stately, yet half-secret incline of the approach to No. 8 Addison Road, Kensington. One's vision has already been arrested by the sheer size of the white and dark-green marble building rising up by the pavement. The horizontal green lines almost evoke the cathedral at Siena – would have exactly if they had been darker. The entrance is distinguished: tall black panelled doors, with marble pillars in a solid and sophisticated porchway – and behold! as they open, a phenomenal hall. You wonder if you have been transported to Ravenna. The proportions and domed ceilings are vaster and on the shining mosaic walls are figures, not Theodora and Justinian, but larger than the rulers of Byzantium; not symbols of a Christian Empire but pagan Greek characters of the Argonauts. The theme is none other than Jason and the Golden Fleece, with Jason and his crew sporting, not the lineaments of Aegean heroes, but the faces of Mr Debenham (for whom the house was built) and his many children. What more apt a symbol of the spirit of Edwardian entrepreneurism than the Golden Fleece!

Steps lead from an elaborately panelled hall to elegant rooms, including a lounge adorned beautifully by a walnut dresser and light panelling of exquisite texture. Uniquely delicate almost Arabic tiles decorate the lower walls everywhere, in dark greens and blues. Stately stairways lead to fine bedrooms lit by large windows of leaded lights and covered in silky wallpaper. The bathrooms, oh joy! have vast bulbous baths, ornate china basins, enormous polished brass fittings, and stately polished-wood lavatories. The original parquet floored and large, low-windowed dining hall makes a magnificent lecture room, current residents taking their meals in the vast servants' quarters below, approached by narrow and rather precipitous stairs off the great hall; for below all this majesty lurks a penumbral world of kitchens, long, illuminated and carpeted corridors leading to offices, counselling rooms, training quarters, all reigned over by the elegant aristocratic yet kindly Russian 'princess', Thuria, like a Queen of the Night.

Such was the background of the Human Relations Diploma Course where we lived two days and nights each week, under the tutelage of Bob Bocock, lecturer in Sociology at Uxbridge University, Dan Miller (American) lecturer in psychology and John Wickens, our course tutor, an agreeable young Anglican priest, trainer and lecturer in pastoral skills and counselling. The small rooms off the subterranean corridors acted as a sort of catacomb for mysterious group rites, debriefing of role plays, presentations of one-to-one exchanges in the Houses and casework supervision, not to mention personal therapy.

For another two days we dispersed to our placements in the Halfway Houses. These had originated with the Anglo-Dutch nurse, Elly Jansen, when in 1959 she courageously opened her home in Richmond to patients discharged from mental hospitals. She did so because everywhere local authorities were tardy in responding to the recent Mental Health Act's provision for community care, which included setting up half-way houses. A new awareness had grown that many patients were obliged to spend fruitless periods in hospital when the acute stage of their illness was past and they needed a gradual but down-to-earth chance for re-entry into community and working life. Elly Jansen's plan relied on the provision that discharged patients could be subsidized by their Local Authorities and preventative care could be offered to avert a return to hospital.

It was a plucky and humane vision, but for some years beset by enormous personal strain, including the anxiety of neighbours to these houses, and considerable financial stress. Nonetheless in the ten years before I became a 'Richmond fellow', eight homes in the Home Counties together with others in Chester, Southampton and Oxford had become established, four were becoming viable during the previous year, including one in Manchester, and several were under negotiation mostly with guaranteed finance. In 1965 about 140 people had been accommodated: by 1969 the number had exceeded 300 – mostly aged between 20 and 40, including adolescents, ex-alcoholics, mothers with young children and those diagnosed psychotic (2/5 of total). Over 100 had found full or part-time work while residing. It was a remarkable achievement, crowned by the acquisition of 8 Addison Road as administrative headquarters, an in-service training centre for the staff (both central and in the Houses) and – enlightened inspiration – a college where an accredited training could be offered to those working in caring professions who wanted to improve their pastoral skills, and to learn from face-to-face experience with suffering people.

Elly herself lived at No. 8 with her husband, George, housed in a remarkable if slightly bizarre structure called The Pavilion, jutting out into the garden and evoking mildly oriental associations. On the rare occasions when we saw Elly, though small in stature she radiated an aura of authority, almost 'tyranny' from which I developed a sort of Turandot fantasy. In this she was, I think, a projection of what the Diploma Course inevitably did to us, namely to present a bewildering range of theoretical and experiential questions which could seem unanswerable, and yet our very survival depended on risking a response.

In the London Houses we slept, ate our meals, met with the staff and took our leisure with the residents. It was a challenging experience and you never knew what Pandora's Box might open up before you. House meetings were held regularly where language and silence became powerful vehicles of corporate and inter-personal life. Raw emotion, often more negative than positive, poured out for mutual ingestion and digestion, revealing springs of motivation and roots of personal disturbance and unhappiness in relationship. It was my first experience of large group therapy. In the college group-work theory was propounded and experienced in a small group with Dr Robert Andry and also in occasional large group exercises.

The one-to-one exchanges which inevitable arose in the Houses were powerful learning occasions and could be recorded verbatim for study in John Wickens' pastoral training group. I have a record of almost the earliest confrontation in my first House – one resident is complaining about his treatment when another, a woman, recovering from a breakdown and rather volatile, suddenly shouts at me, 'You are not very holy,' and when I react defensively, 'you are not a priest either or a man,' and she refuses to attend the House meeting if I am there. We are eventually reconciled and her guns are turned on a fellow resident. It usefully pointed up direct teaching about aggression and paranoia, giving it a three-dimensional, flesh and blood feel, with time for reflection on my own reactions and response. Residents, like many disturbed people, had a keen instinct for one's weak points, as the attack on my sense of vocation illustrates.

At No. 8 I shared a bedroom with John Fielding, a gentle Midlands minister,

I warmed to Dick Cory, a Marist Father from Dublin and John Gildea, another Irish Religious. I found John Hackett, an Anglican priest in Surrey, interesting and thoughtful, Jim Little from the USA, lively and amusing, John Foskett, later Chaplain to the Maudsley, impressive on all counts and Jim Reid, a Free Church 'Bishop' from Australia, a likeable man of integrity. He discovered Bill Kyle and went to help at a new counselling venture in Westminster Central Hall: through him I eventually found it myself, but that's a later story. I remember Jim Reid chiefly for a ribald error. 'Down under', what we in GB call sellotape they know as Durex. Jim innocently asked for Durex in a Kensington shop just before the festive season. 'Oh, we don't stock that sort of thing; you need a chemist,' replied a rather shocked assistant. 'But surely you have that sticky stuff; I want the sort with Happy Christmas printed on it.' He told the story against himself with a straight face. The nun, whom we called Sister, was very alert and never allowed us males to get away with our chauvinism. One fellow student, Graham, was a consummate musician and played the piano beautifully. In all, it was a widely talented and varied group, though somewhat too male. One day Hoult Taylor, music master at Greshams, came to goggle at No. 8 and to eat with me in Kensington. He had hardly changed over the years, as warm and perceptive as ever. 'This new work of yours is right for you,' he pronounced. I was glad.

Back at the works, Bess had returned to the Vicarage. David and I shared the liturgy and the pastoral work: we mounted a link with an East London parish, St Cedds Canning Town, joining them for their Eucharist and vice versa: their people came and holidayed with our 'Hatfield Heathens'; the parish began to understand better what East London life was like. Meantime, more newcomers arrived with fresh building in the village and from these new adult confirmands, including some youngsters, came forward. Amongst them was a young haemophilic lad. His mother decided to join an enquirers' home group and, much to her surprise, to share with them some of the excruciating stress of caring for a haemophilic child (and in her case earlier a brother too). She came into counselling to work through the surfacing pain, and I began to learn more thoroughly how to respond to such trauma and to enable healing to take place.

It was valuable to understand a bit of what caring for children with congenital illness e.g. cystic fibrosis, was like. In general, parish visiting became less a matter of 'tea and sympathy'; better orientated to the real needs of the parishioner, with more appropriate response on my part.

During the first term of the training, David had provided invaluable backup, but shortly before Christmas he was offered his own parish in Chelmsford, and, of course, had to say goodbye to us. The farewell took place on the last Sunday of the year and I had to face 1971 as a solo vicar. Mercifully some temporary help arrived – Donald Lowe, just returned from Bloemfontein gave me a week, and in the summer the Bishop sent us briefly a young curate, another David, who had found his training parish unsatisfactory. From June to early October he lived with us at the Vicarage, undertaking a lot of parish work, excelling in dramatic presentations with the youngsters, and finally moved to a second curacy in Canterbury diocese. But with no help in the first six months of the year life was excessively demanding and somewhat uncomfortable, as my hips were deteriorating through osteo-arthritis. A group session at the RF had forced me to recognize that I seemed to be going the same way as my father – an unwelcome perception and hard to accept.

By extraordinary and malign coincidence my father-in-God, John Tiarks, was falling a victim to Parkinson's. Accompanying him to meetings I had observed his limp and felt apprehensive about his gaunt and hollow-eyed look[31]. Was I about to lose him? With noble courage he continued in office for four years until retiring in 1971.

During the second term, in addition to the 'housework' I spent most of one day a week at Claybury Hospital and there saw Dr Dennis Martin's concept of a therapeutic community in action. I attended one very able psychiatrist-therapist, Dr Pippard's small group, watching his delicate handling of paranoid patients. It threw astonishing light on the behaviour of several parishioners! My own therapy was increasing self-awareness and self-monitoring – several parishioners helped by commenting, with gentle approval, on my handling of pastoral situations and less pressurising style of work. At Claybury I met young medics training to be GPs. They were impressed that the Church was encouraging its men to improve their pastoral skills and lamented that I was getting a whole term at Claybury whereas they were only allowed a day or two in a few weeks. Later I gave a lift (*en route* from visiting my bereft mother-in-law in Sheffield) to three young doctors. They told me about their very pressurised lives, and I confessed that the idea of training for medicine had always been an attraction: counselling was to me just a second best. 'Oh, don't you get misled by that idea,' said one of them. 'What you are doing for

---

[31] Gordon Hewitt *History of the Diocese of Chelmsford* p 190

people's minds is a lot more important, so press on with that!'

The Richmond Fellowship was setting a high standard of professional competence and integrity: I was grateful for, but rather daunted by it, and concerned whether the free and easy openness of much parish pastoral care would be lost in stricter observance of appropriate distance, recognition of boundaries and awareness of underlying dynamics. However, Clinical Theology had taught much about handling transference and the inevitable half-acknowledged projections upon the person: now it was chiefly a matter of developing more sensitive awareness and use of professional supervision.

About this time I delightfully acquired a new godson aged seven whose family lived in the village, and our mutual exchange in preparation for baptism was unusually refreshing. Matthew was baptized at a memorable Easter Midnight service, later joined the choir and assisted in the church for some years before going to Agricultural College. His family allowed him to visit the Vicarage, Bess became very fond of him, and he even came on holiday. It was a charming relationship for me, though not so ideal for him as he had to endure being teased at the village school as 'Vicar's pet'. However he refused to be discouraged; and became a unique example of loyalty in a child, as well as very good company.

I was particularly glad of this, only occasional though it was, because Bess had decided it was time for her to retire. She was now eighty and had given me more than ten years of service and companionship. Her Lakeland daughter and son-in-law had prepared a pleasant pad for her at their Ullswater home, and I hoped to visit them regularly. Many villagers came to say goodbye on August 9ᵗʰ 1970, and it felt as though an era was ending. I missed her no end. Her successor Mrs Zuniga brought with her a little daughter, Francesca, so the tradition of vicarage children continued, and in addition the second floor was occupied by a pleasant young couple with a baby. Mrs Zuniga was an ardent charismatic and 'danced in the Spirit'; in general she found our church to her liking, but she did not approve of the ancient lead plumbing in the Vicarage, so the signal for her rising each morning was a mighty cascade of 'water in the water pipes' (Psalm 42). All taps were discharging the baleful accumulation of the night.

Shortly after the end of the RF course, in September 1970, the curate of Writtle, a large active parish near Chelmsford, invited me to train a pastoral visiting and counselling group, and in the autumn the first term of a six-month course began. This was to become a significant strand in the pattern of my future life. At the same time another strand materialized as a slender thread in the form of a letter from Bill Kyle, the Methodist Minister friend of Jim Reid, engaged in setting up what came to be the Westminster Pastoral Foundation.

Bill Kyle was a remarkable man. The son of an electrician in the Plymouth dockyards who had emigrated to the USA in search of work, he never lost his affection for Alabama where he was born in 1925, the year of my own birth. He had been notably influenced by the outgoing warmth of Southern Evangelicals, and later returned to the USA to complete his training as a counsellor and obtain a doctorate. He and his family had come back to England before the war, during which Bill worked as a marine engineer. At its end he 'candidated' to be a Methodist Minister and while training met an outstandingly gifted woman, Benita, who became one of those greatly valued early Medical Social Workers. As his wife, Bennie's faith and warmth strongly backed up his work and enriched his personal development. David Black, in his story of the WPF, entitled *A Place for Exploration* published in 1991, describes Bill in these words, 'An apparent conventionality and actual great personal force stood Bill in good stead in dealing with a wide range of people from clients and trainees to church leaders, businessmen and parliamentarians . . . He was enormously kind and, in a man well endowed with earthly appetites, it was moving and impressive to see the continual and very real (not obsessional) dialogue he maintained between his energetic responses and his deep Christian conviction . . . He could be manipulative and seductive . . . His playful teasing could become irritating. A man so politically skilful, however kind, also could not but find himself giving priority to choices that put him in touch with the bearers of wealth and power; but . . . I have never known a man who so genuinely put himself at the disposal of those who needed him. Almost without exception those who knew him use some word like "pioneer" or "entrepreneur" to describe him. He had the gift of initiative, of involving people in his projects so that they became not just interested but active [and] in some way promoted the work he was engaged in.' [32] That is precisely what Bill did for me, quite painlessly assuming that I could do what he coolly expected of me, whether it was going into counselling at the deep end, leading a seminar, promoting the WPF to a prestigious outside body, lecturing at short notice, joining a committee, though I did draw the

---

[32] David Black *A Place for Exploration* (Westminster Pastoral Foundation, 1991) pp 7-8

line at his describing me as a 'psychotherapist'.

At first I came to Westminster one day a week and saw two or three clients, a number which increased to six by the end of the year. I was staggered by the variety of traumas, and the degree of disturbance meant that nearly all required over forty or fifty sessions. Bill found me a Supervisor, David Holt (who had trained with the Jungians at Zurich) and contributed towards the cost of weekly therapy. I saw my first client in December 1970. She had undergone nearly twenty years of psychiatry and had recently overdosed again. She also inflicted physical damage on herself. Interestingly her GP had always wanted her to go into psychotherapy but her consultants had insisted on heavy medication, ECT and narcosis. Now her minister had consulted Benita Kyle, who saw her for assessment and passed her report to me. I was not too hopeful: however, we got along better than expected and an interesting four months ensued during which most of the symptoms disappeared; and she achieved greater independence from continually warring parents. Counselling ended at Easter, and a review session in August seemed to confirm the improvement.

Meantime the first long-term work had begun at Hatfield Heath in February 1971 with a homosexual man who wished to change his life style, and this lasted until 1973 with gradual resolution of mountainous problems. With four other WPF clients who received counselling, two improved and two did not. My first couples also were counselled, over about six months, and several suffering from depression and panic attacks. Bill later gave me rather daunting work with an MP (he had been a Cabinet Minister) and his wife, and another fairly high-powered government figure. The wife of the latter presented me with a fine collection of prayers and spiritual writing she had herself collected, which I continue to treasure: equally treasured are the few relationships that blossomed into friendship after the therapy had been completed. I became particularly intrigued by the way that, without any conscious evangelizing on my part, several clients found a religious component in the ultimate resolution of their problems.

Neighbouring priests and GPs also began to refer people to me at Hatfield Heath, though I had to be careful that this did not spread into parochial prime time; and the Warden of Lee Abbey asked me to come at regular intervals to be available for members of the Community. These visits to Devon continued, eventually leading to an offer of the position of Chaplain, which I regretfully declined. Lee Abbey is an impressive experiment in Christian life together, and several friendships arose from the contact.

One day I had a call from the Jordanian Embassy. Would I go to see an Arab doctor at Risley Detention Centre. He had asked for me after his arrest for an apparently motiveless attack on babies in a Blackpool Hospital. Ahmed was one of my former Jerusalem students, now a fully qualified eye surgeon who had suffered a paranoid schizoid episode some years earlier, had recovered and come to practise in England. He had warned his hospital that he was fearing a recurrence of the episode, but was refused sick leave. When arrested he was conducting a delicate operation and was quite unaware of having gone into the children's ward the night before and committed the crime. I saw him at Risley and came away feeling that our Health Service could have looked after him better and so prevented this tragedy. My view was publicly confirmed in a television documentary by Ludovic Kennedy. I suspected that his illness partly stemmed from his people's sufferings in the Arab-Israeli conflict. He was sent to Broadmoor where I visited him several times. There he took a course in printing and when fit again was eventually repatriated to Jordan.

At home a few self-referrals showed me how counselling could be combined with the priest's healing ministry especially when a block on forgiveness was a component. One woman with a handicapped child was unable to forgive either herself for what she felt was her responsibility for the child's condition or her own mother for contributing to it. Slowly, very complex feelings around this were allowed to surface, prayer began to help in the process of inner acceptance and finally she decided to be confirmed. The sacraments of confession and communion became a lively reminder and renewal of her sense of having been forgiven and a strengthening resource for her own forgiveness of others. A married man came because he wanted to prepare himself for an operation which might prove fatal or at least damage his brain. We discovered that inability to forgive his father was a great block to his faith. Counselling sessions brought the origins of hatred to light; it was acknowledged and absolved in sacramental confession and the evening before the operation he received the laying on of hands and anointing. His reconciled father was present. The surgeons were entirely successful and a year or so later the man was confirmed – though unfortunately he couldn't get on with the vicar in his nearby village (transferred father trouble?).

I visited my own 'second father' John Tiarks and his plucky, vivacious wife Gwyneth in their retirement, and in January 1974 he died – Gwyneth too after only a few months. They were inseparable. Their stalwart and restrainedly affectionate friendship had been like manna in wilderness times. Meanwhile from the last year or more I had been obliged to take services seated, so a more sedentary ministry had become generally inevitable through osteo-arthritis, preaching from a three-pronged 'shooting stick'. The choir paid unwonted attention in the hope that I would fall off – their expectation was rewarded, once! Our new bishop, John Trillo, had kindly permitted a priest, who had no living of his own, to help regularly with services; during 1974 he began also to undertake parochial work – and the diocese and I together produced a stipend for him.

Came the 74/75 winter and Bess decided to move south from the harsher clime of Ullswater. She visited the Banyards and stayed more comfortably than at the Vicarage with friends at Hatfield Heath. Her heart had been giving her trouble and quite suddenly she died. That morning I felt I must look in before leaving for the WPF. I don't know why, but without thinking I gave her a blessing and a warm farewell. An hour or so later she told a mutual friend how much this had meant to her: and that afternoon she quietly left us. Few people had ever given me so much loyal, loving and gentle care.

The arthritis was rapidly decreasing my mobility. A national health surgeon at the Herts and Essex, Bishop Stortford, was monitoring the condition quarterly. Sleep became rather disturbed though an electric overblanket helped, and accompanied me on residential forays; a Lincoln Conference for Clergy, the Eastbourne CT 3rd year, Salisbury and Lichfield Training weekends, and other overnight invitations to speak or train, a suitable power point being a condition of acceptance. Relief was in sight when the surgeon John Read proposed to operate on one hip (nearly collapsed) on June 27th, my fiftieth birthday. Friend Peter Morris anointed me in Sawbridgeworth Parish Church on the 24th. The evening before the operation John visited me in the ward and announced – a threat or a promise? – 'If you behave yourself I might do the other hip as well.' When I woke up he had; I was without an undercarriage and shouting some unclerical language about the discomfort.

'Simultaneous bilateral' hip replacement has many advantages over the two stage procedure, and in this case was amply justified when I could walk on crutches a week later and on sticks from July 14th. At the end of the month I drove myself down to Pat's for a week's break and was joined by Matthew, good company as ever. I took another break there early in December and recalled an intention to write a poem. Some of it had emerged a few years earlier, but the operation had in effect pulled together a number of ideas and focused the feeling of multiple bereavement – the loss of important parts of the body is usually an occasion for some grief, though in this case it was a loss that also brought new hope. The poem brings together the deaths of brother, father, mother and wife in the context of a walk with Esther de Waal the previous autumn, across the fields to Bardney Abbey, a ruin near Lincoln[32]. Esther had herself suggested writing about feelings I had shared with them; the sight of a monastic millstone and the crumbling pillars of Bardney, scattered around like bits of bone, triggered off the flow of words.

BARDNEY ABBEY
(written for Esther after an operation)

The damson dappled sky of December's evening
Congeals and lingers – defies approaching night.
In the brown eloquent Cotswold mud with lengthened stride
I trudge firmly (two neatly fashioned joints
No longer strangers to their bone are
Anchored by plastic, steel and tenuous gut)
Body moving in painless equilibrium –
Though mind and feelings jostle rudderless
Like thick purple clouds on the sluggish wind.

Two months before, the rich October foliage
Beech rust, flame red ash and yellow brown sycamore,
Had uttered a promise of harvest gold: evoking
The question, what should this body be doing?
Hope, daring, dread and a quickening spark
As we trudged (I a little less firmly then)
In the dusty chaff and dark earth of Lincolnshire stubble
Looking for Bardney Abbey.

My usual sense of direction brought us to earth mounds
(Ironic to find my way calmly on contours

---

[32] Esther's husband Victor was Chancellor of Lincoln Cathedral.

But get so clumsily lost on the spiritual journey).
A broken thicketed field strewn with remnants of
Mediaeval rubble suggested little to build on,
Except for some regular, parallel molehills covering
Fragments of buried pillars: gaunt masonry
Footing the framework of a dead monk's cell . . .
This was not the topography I sought:
Sole crumbling pediment and derelict millstone
Spoke of failure, death – something broken and buried.

That building's collapse echoed an agony of birth:
Mother's bewildered cry, a dying brother.
'He's dead, but the baby can't feel it' they said
Turning to hug their sorrow. I was left in the howling
Grief tunnel, man's or God's mercy past belief.
The death my doing? O Cain! Killers deserve no breath;
Riven by guilt, must ever take what's given.
'Must take'? mistake? Most stuck in rumination . . .
        The wind has risen on the brow
        I trudge the ridges' turned up plough
        Scudding clouds in keening rune
        Opal-white, thin menacing moon;
        Trees' torn hands in wind-lashed sky
        Rip my breast in dirge's cry . . .

God! Do I have to take what you give?
When now to live
Is sullen anger, fury half-crushed,
(Bones lie scattered before the pit)
For she my life is dead.

Do I accept that you have taken
The rib and broken
Bone from my own side? Left me free
Among the dead: not free to die,
Though she my life is dead.

Can I be reconciled to death
Of brother, half-breath,
Fragile bone? Father's crumpled frame;
Limbs twisted, fixed by pain,
Which gave me life . . .

What of that crime, her violent end
Who bore me?
Loved me (loved too much).
Fair golden head, crushed by the roadside
Dead, dead.

Dissolve, you bones of mine, calcified loss!
Lie in the dust, like stone crumbling on ground,
(Love grinding upon millstone cross)
Urns of cremated ash in holy mound.

Can new pillars rise
Built of new stuff, a sacrifice
Of flesh and blood – in surgeon's newfangled guise?

       Darkness as I trudge alone .
       Bardney stubble, Gloster stone,
       Both the same when nothing's known
       Of love's rebirth or rising sun.

So I'll take my metal thighs
Built upon the death of bone;
Work with them till the warm globe's rise
And beget a son – my own.

Quite an angry bit of verse which also opened up a degree of desolation and the inner solitude of my life. I still longed for a family and was more in need of mature companionship than I cared to acknowledge. Would 1976 bring an answer or would I have to continue to trudge alone?

CHAPTER XIV

ENDS AND BEGINNINGS

In September '74 I had been blessed with a new housekeeper, Nancy Edwards, who saw me through the months of extreme discomfort before the operation and was an invaluable support during convalescence. Her patience and reliability were exceptional, and I have known few more considerate and tactful helpers.

With Bill and Benita Kyle, and the WPF, came a whole sheaf of new friends. Chris Fenton, the other Anglican priest in the outfit and a qualified analyst had begun counselling in January 1970 and was soon running the group therapy section. Chris shortly gave up parish work to focus on a private practice which included WPF. He was joined by an RC priest and group psychotherapist Gregory van der Kleij, now Prior of the Community at Turvey, and later the group department was taken over by Tom Hamrogue (regular fellow diner on the nights I had to stay in London) a whimsical Irish wit and excellent company. Another Anglican priest, Peter Liddell, having trained in New York joined as a tutor in 1976. David Black, now an experienced psychoanalyst, came as one of our earliest students, soon to exhibit exceptional gifts. Like another of our therapists, Mary Pett, he had spent a year or two at the Findhorn Community, famous for converting part of the Moray Firth near Forres into a sub-tropical paradise. Our Consultant Psychiatrist, Sasha Duddington, varied the religious orientation by being an Eastern Orthodox Christian, and provided steady professional earthing until his death thirty years later.

Two distinctive characters from the analytical world, David Holt and Wendy Robinson, both keen to point up the ontological or spiritual component in our work, added piquancy to the climate; and able women like Moira Duckworth, Una Farrer and Ruth Archer balanced an initially over-male WPF cast. Our guru was Martin Israel, who gave meditation groups and spiritual consultation. Through Bill's contacts with the USA, impressive men like John Maes and Edward Thornton visited us to lecture. A frequent visitor who became a colleague was the Canadian John Millar. He assisted chiefly in group work and also lectured and took an interest in the affiliates. John actually travelled to Bishops Stortford to see me in hospital and with his wife Robin came to stay with us. During the surgery a sense of support from both Foundation and Parish was palpable. (One parochial client was so 'supportive' that she managed to get herself admitted to the same hospital and had to be discouraged from bedside visits.)

One of the therapists, Helen, an Australian, was particularly good company and visited Hatfield Heath: she later married a well-known child psychologist. Meantime David Black became a source of stimulating companionship and comforted me by saying that W B Yeats remained a bachelor until aged 51. It was prophetic; for shortly after going on holiday with Gregory in the autumn of 1976 I became aware of a blossoming relationship nearer home.

Ten years earlier the Taylor family had taken a pleasant Georgian-style house on the other side of the Heath from the Vicarage; Dick Taylor was with United Glass in Harlow, having left Rickmansworth where he'd been working with Whitefriars. He attended church and soon became a sidesman, and his son, Alex, volunteered as a crossbearer: his daughter, Penny, later joined the choir and they were both prepared for confirmation. Wynn, their mother, was more interested in young people's activities, offering her services transporting young church members for their Saturday Swimming Club at Harlow Baths. She also took elderly ladies to a Day Centre. During my sabbatical in South Africa the family helped with the Village Festival's inauguration, and soon after my return Wynn was elected to the Church Council. In 1971 Alex became a boarder at Bedford School, and the next year a hoped-for almost despaired of, third child arrived. Timothy was christened that summer, fifteen and twelve years younger than his brother and sister.

Dick's health had given him little trouble but on June 27th 1973 (my birthday) he suffered a massive coronary thrombosis and died. On the 28th I drove to Bedford to collect Alex as Wynn had more than enough arranging a funeral and looking after a 13 month old baby. During the following months many parishioners attempted to support a very shattered but plucky forty year old widow, and naturally I was amongst them. I got to know some of her family, and took mother and child down to see Dick's crippled mother in Bournemouth. Nonetheless the relationship with Wynn was no different from that with other bereaved adults. Sadly, a year after Dick's death, Wynn's father died (and Timothy lost another very significant male) depriving her of valuable advice and support. Curiously before he died he had said to Wynn's mother, 'She'll marry that vicar before she's much older.' Neither she nor 'that vicar' had any such expectation, but Wynn did begin to come, with Timothy in pram, to a weekday communion: she also took over organizing the magazine distribution and then became the PCC Secretary. Being rather dyslexic she had fairly frequent recourse to the vicar for 'minute checking' and other parish matters, and joined the Pastoral Care Group for some training in parish visiting. Our paths crossed quite often, and by mid 1976 it was not unusual for us to discuss such things while walking her dog in Hatfield Forest. Occasionally after Evensong I was invited to share an avocado or a boiled egg. Our friendship grew as gently and inevitably as the turning of the spheres.

I have a happy memory of taking her and the lad after Christmas, to her mother Joan who lived in Hathersage – my first view of that gem set in the craggy wooded heights and precipitous edges of the Peak District. The visit was partly to see my ailing mother-in-law in Sheffield: Renie had contracted cancer the previous year and was now almost bedridden. Together we received communion in her home and found a sense of peace and affection between us. It was a goodbye rounding off our years of shared sorrow and recovery: she entered a local hospice in Jan '77.

The crucial diary entry is 'Jan. 11 supper at Wynns', for I know that it was then I made explicit what was virtually known between us already – and even to Timothy, for he decided to get out of bed to join the party and sit on my knee. From then on he referred to 'our wedding' – it was apparently as much his; and we asked ourselves: Why wait more than the time needed to read the banns? So the date was set for Friday, February 11th. Incredibly not a soul had guessed what was going on – except perhaps Nancy, though she never let on. Even the most perceptive of village gossips, present at the Sunday Eucharist when I read our banns, was amongst those contributing to the audible gasp. It certainly helped to boost the congregation on the following Sundays.

The diary entry for February 11th is actually 'to Whatcombe for five days'. So uncertain about the future had I been during the previous autumn that I had accepted an invitation from Reg East, the pioneer and Warden of Whatcombe House, a charismatic community in Dorset, to spend a few days with them with a view to membership of the Community and possible chaplaincy. In 1976 it had looked like a good solution for the lone priest. A particularly close friend, John Gunstone, had been a founder member and at Whatcombe had met a late-in the-day wife. (He and Margaret couldn't come to our wedding because they were expecting a baby). Now in January I had to say to Whatcombe, 'I am marrying a wife and cannot come,' but forgot to alter the diary entry to 'Wedding Day'.

Although the diary is choc-a-bloc with visits and meetings during the month between engagement and marriage, and on Jan 25th Renie died so that I was travelling again to Sheffield, somehow we managed to arrange the Nuptial Eucharist and a party in the Village Hall not only for our 100 guests but also to include any of the village who cared to come. My sister Pat's children, Monica and Lucy, were considered too busy at school to be Wynn's bridesmaids, but she and her Swiss husband came, having arranged to meet 'at the first pub in the village'. Unfortunately Pat approached from the west and Sam from the east so they spent a frustrating half hour at the hostelries at either end, at least consoled by refreshment, eventually meeting in church just before the service. Penny and my goddaughter Kate Pederson made elegant bridesmaids in strikingly original dresses preceded by Timothy as handsome pageboy accompanying his four year old cousin Arabella (one of the dozen or more nephews and nieces I had acquired): but the sartorial prize went to Wynn in full length, long sleeved, gathered, sandy-gold dress adorned with Aunt Dorothy's amethyst pendant, brooch and bracelets. The diocesan bishop, John Trillo married us, the suffragan bishop Jimmy Adams delightfully offered himself to preach – well, as ever – Victor de Waal, (then Dean of Canterbury) was my best man, and Wynn's brother Jonathan gave her away.

Who can do justice to the memory of his wedding? Certainly not I; but in retrospect after twenty-five years it remains fresh, bright and serendipitous, as though chanced upon by happy accident. Almost the best memory is the sheer delight when Wynn and I walked from the church to the new Village Hall. The school lunch break had just begun and as the children spilled out of the classrooms they surged towards the railings cheering and waving – we felt like royalty. Villagers had clubbed together and bought us a dish-washer – what good sense! As it was presented our local builder announced, 'I shall install your new machine at your convenience' – cheers all round. Afterwards young Timothy toured the assembly of guests sitting on my shoulders with his hands placed upon my head as though in blessing, or perhaps ordaining me as his adoptive parent. With his permission the process of actual legal adoption was undertaken in front of a friendly magistrate some months later. However, the crowning of this event came one afternoon when he was about six. We were walking together to the Post Office. 'Dad, you know you adopted me that time we went to the man?' 'Yes indeed,' I said. 'Well,' said Timothy, 'I think I will definitely adopt you.' Slightly winded I replied, 'That's really good, I'm glad.' It was especially graceful because he did have problems about my not being his 'real father', which we had to talk over. My difficulty, I explained, was that if I wasn't a real father then perhaps he wasn't my real son. One day I rather clumsily invited him to consider the possible advantage in some circumstances of having two fathers (we retained his two Christian names and added his natural father's surname so, like me but more felicitously, he bore three initials) but not long after he found his own solution. 'My first father can be called "father" and you are my Dad.'

Alexander was quite sure he had no need of any more fathers, but was relieved to feel a lot less responsible for his mother. He and I both worked on the business of becoming friends, mercifully achieved mainly through his forbearance and steady good will. My step-daughter had far greater difficulty in accepting emotionally her mother's remarriage. Her father had been the most important person in her young life and losing him at the age of twelve had deeply scarred her. Though she generously said she was 'over the moon' because of the marriage, at heart she couldn't help feeling I was an interloper who had supplanted Richard. Who can cavil at the profound loyalty and devotion of a daughter? At no time did she withdraw her love and her helpful cheerfulness.

A few months after our marriage Penny was offered by her school, through an American Minister, the chance to continue her education for a year in the United States. She accepted the opportunity eagerly and the challenges she had to face through this bold step helped to mature a courageous sixteen year old and perhaps heal some of the trauma. When Wynn travelled to Harrisburg for her graduation in 1978 she found a confident young adult who had weathered storms that might have thrown a much older girl.

For our honeymoon I had suggested Bath, my early love, and found that Wynn took to its charm immediately. The weather was crisp and bright; the Cotswolds green and fresh, and the hotel near the Royal Crescent (that immaculate terrace overlooking the city) exceptionally comfortable: but the holiday was brief because, months beforehand, I had been booked in to lead a pilgrimage after Easter. This became Honeymoon Part II – and I don't know which was more demanding; for Wynn suddenly to assume the role of Vicar's wife, or to travel in strange parts as a tour leader's spouse, expected to 'know all about it'. Her problems of adaptation and diplomacy were outstanding and she was a lot more patient than I with tetchy and often pressurising pilgrims. Returning to the Holy Places was not an entirely happy experience for me; everywhere especially at street corners young Israelis stood alert with machine guns: but a number of former St George's students sought me out and arranged a lunch party, with regrets that Arab custom forbade them to invite a lone spouse; so Wynn received in lieu a lavish and colourful box of sweetmeats.

Wynn found the alleyways and the people of the Old City as fascinating as I used to, and enjoyed Arab food, our hotel meals being rather dull and Western. Her brother, Jonathan, turned up on a business visit for his Sheffield firm and took us on a separate visit to Bethlehem without our pilgrims. The untrammelled quietness of the church of the Nativity was deeply moving, and the three of us were profoundly refreshed by a long silent stillness in St. Jerome's cave next to the stable chapel. Later Jon and Wynn climbed some way up the Mount of Temptation with its dramatic views of Jericho and the Dead Sea, but most unforgettably moving and impressive was the visit to the last ditch fortress mound of Masada.

Hebron, with the tomb of Abraham and the patriarchs had a genuine Old Testament flavour and was marked by a young Arab selling me a black Russian-type fur hat of camel skin, which is still in regular winter use.

Passing through Nablus *en route* to Galilee, disaffected Arabs put a brick through a window of our coach, a sharp reminder of the Holy Land reality, not so different from the tensions at the time of Christ. A high point for us, in more ways than one, was our arrival at a hotel near Safed at 5000 ft with a remarkable bird's-eye view of all Galilee – lake and mountains: snow capped Mount Hermon shone majestically to the east seeming (although 9000 ft) to be little higher than ourselves. A brief note awaited us in the hotel, 'Little brother is watching you' – Jon had been there on a business meeting. Renewing my love of Capernaum and its environs I was glad that Wynn was as affected by the lake's beauty as I; and she too felt the celebration of an open air eucharist by the lake's lapping waters near the Loaves and Fishes church a fitting conclusion of the tour.

Timothy had manfully put up with our ten-day absence, having also had to endure the five days in February, and now had to enter hospital for the removal of his tonsils. St Luke's allowed Wynn to be with him and I got to London once to see them. In the autumn he'd begin at the village primary school. The pace of work was increasing even beyond the earlier months of the year; in fact between the wedding and mid-July I undertook over 400 hours of counselling. Now we learnt that our invaluable assistant priest was to be appointed a vicar elsewhere and I must manage alone.

I have mentioned the training courses at Writtle promoted by the curate, Bill Cummings. Now an energetic and enterprising new vicar had been appointed to Writtle and he planned to set up a local Pastoral Foundation on WPF lines to serve the Chelmsford area and beyond. The men and women I had trained could be used more systematically: a local GP and a church family had both offered useful premises for counselling. The training could be expanded on WPF lines and accommodated in a local hall. The vicar, John Potter, enlisted my support and urged us to consider moving to Writtle to counsel and teach. At the same time expansion was being planned by Bill Kyle; the Central Hall rooms were too cramped for development and the Hall authorities were being strangely hostile. Bill learnt that the Roman Catholic Sisters of the Assumption, Kensington Square, were looking for new occupants of their very fine teacher-training college. The Sisters had become enthusiastic supporters of WPF and did all they could to encourage the agreement of the lease: but it took a year to complete.

Meantime Bill was appointing new staff and in the autumn offered me a post as supervisor: this involved regular meetings with counsellors to monitor their work, and could be combined with the weekly sessions with clients. By now I was seeing over ten a week in London and four or five locally. Together with teaching, counselling and supervision of counsellors at Writtle, a viable full-time job was emerging. Undergirding this would be specific involvement with All Saints Church at Writtle, so that I would remain a 'practising priest' in the local liturgy, in preaching, teaching and sharing pastoral care. Testing out the idea with our bishop I was pleasantly surprised to find that it made sense to him; at least half of my work would be in the diocese and I could be available to him if required. Others in the diocese were not as positive, I think partly because the Writtle Pastoral Foundation could appear to be a rival of the Chelmsford Cathedral Centre set up by Canon Dick Herrick (for whom I had lectured in the early 1970s) though there was pastoral need enough for both of us and more: but the Centre guru was Dr Pierre Turquet of the

Tavistock Clinic, and he had unfortunately taken against the WPF. I was only just becoming aware of the wheels-within-wheels in the psychotherapeutic world. In the diocese itself some disapproved of psychodynamic counselling, feeling that it might 'supplant' Christian faith.

Though far from unhappy at Hatfield Heath, we were aware that our new family life was to some extent being eaten away by the responsibility for two thousand parishioners, once again my sole charge and I rather older and without help. It might be said that they were my proper concern and both Writtle and WPF should now be dropped: but I had in fact come to question whether sixteen years in the same parish should be extended. Moreover, in my view marriage is as much a Christian vocation as the priesthood (both sealed by a solemn sacrament) and that my family should be considered as equally a commitment given by God. Even without the day in London there still seemed too little time for the family, especially to be with Timothy. He was beginning to find the village primary school, notably his unwanted celebrity as the vicar's son, both difficult to understand and at times uncomfortable. Not for another two years were we to become aware of the root problem, namely severe dyslexia, which aroused anxiety in the school situation and could sour his relations with teachers. All these considerations suggested that a change was due, and the possible combination of so many of our prime interests and needs pointed to the Writtle-Kensington option: but could we find a home? The search fell largely upon Wynn, but was not prolonged, for our plans were, it seemed, confirmed by a remarkably suitable one going up for sale on Writtle Green itself.

The Green is triangular, sloping towards an attractive pond at the eastern apex. At the top south western corner, at the end of the fourteenth century there had stood a pub, The Black Swan, now converted into two private houses, both handsomely timbered and 'Essex tiled' with exposed beams, seventeenth century sash windows and Georgian doors. No. 27 was on the market at a remarkably attractive price to get a quick sale. Entering it, you found a large oak panelled hall with Jacobean fireplace and chimneybreast (with Wynn's refectory table and leather chairs a dignified scenario for formal dinners), and to the left of the front door a charming study with Georgian alcoves and a casement door into the garden – chiefly lawn and shrubs of a manageable size and condition. Further up off the hall came the sitting room with exposed brick inglenook fireplace (later Roman bricks from the first Chelmsford were discovered in the chimney, so skilfully designed that any log fire could be kindled from ashes!) Family life could be nourished by such a room, which also had a garden exit, and family appetites by the adjacent breakfast room, divided from a spacious kitchen by timber uprights salvaged from ancient boats and forming a partial screen to the kitchen. This had a fixed wooden dresser and other accoutrements including iron hooks of venerable age from which pans (or hams) could be suspended. The utility room was unceilinged and open to the tiles. Viewing these, simply laid upon the roof beams with nothing to secure them, we wondered what happened in bad weather. The answer came soon. The snow filtered in to lightly carpet the freezer, floors and walls, which were of wattle and daub, but the tiles stayed firm. And what about the little black bodies scattered along the walls, death watch beetle? Yes, but apparently they had been around for centuries.

Upstairs, more joy with capacious main bedroom and equally large guest room over the front: then two delightful sunny rooms for Tim and for Penny when she returned from the States, and on the second floor an intriguing den approached by its own secret (because only a rough door like a cupboard's indicated the way up) stairway, just large enough to provide a home base for 6' 4" Alexander (and later bequeathed to Tim). The garden even allowed room for a double garage. What man could be more excited about the prospect of owning such a house? All my earlier accommodation had been rented or tied to the job. In my 53rd year, thanks in part to the sale of Wynn's Hatfield Heath home, I joined the property-owning middle classes beloved of Mrs Thatcher.

Our move took place in deep snow and upon icy roads. Timothy and I had to go the long way round by Ongar, bearing two reluctant cats. Wynn and I had both been given male kittens a year before marrying, a tabby and a white half-Siamese; but neither favoured a merger and they barely tolerated one another. 'Tiger' at Writtle adopted the family next door (they allowed him to sleep in their airing cupboard) 'Ponto' pranced everywhere energetically and later adopted the dog when she arrived the next year. In spite of the weather, and helped by a log fire in the inglenook, the house felt homely from the start; but the term began almost immediately with instant preparation for delivering the initial lectures – in a cold church hall. Wynn had a major task with endless unpacking and sorting out, and Tim tried out his new school with some apprehension.

Hatfield Heath and I found it hard to separate: almost as we were moving a young former parishioner who used to live at the Vicarage and had moved away overdosed and her mother and I had a sad vigil at Kings College Hospital in Denmark Hill (opposite the hostel where I began in London). Through clergy shortage I had to return quite often to take services during the interregnum until after Easter, when the new incumbent arrived: but by Holy Week I was also involved in preaching and celebrating at Writtle. Soon this became the norm and I felt established in the church there as well as in the 'village'. In June Wynn travelled to the States for Penny's graduation, and with Penny's return and Alex finishing his degree and beginning to work in London from our home, family life had at last settled. Alex and I commuted to London at various times and Penny started her A Level studies at Chelmsford College, finding new friends and interests in the neighbourhood.

Within a few months, however, a strange bouleversement took place; John Potter accepted a Cathedral Canonry at Derby and who should be appointed to be our vicar but Peter Mason, the very competent senior curate of my time in Belhus! So I became an assistant curate to my own former curate, a relationship that required a degree of re-working – though in practice it only involved taking services at Writtle or Highwood and assisting with some parish training courses. It was 'all change' too on the WPF front as the entire outfit moved from Westminster to the ample space of the Maria Assumpta College in Kensington Square. Our 1978 Graduation ceremonies took place there on June 30th, September 4th saw its opening as a counselling centre and on September 25th training courses began. Under my new contract, ten clients were seen and the first supervision group met each week. At Writtle I had about half a dozen clients, a supervision group, and two training courses – also a Clinical Theology group, one-off talks and the meetings required for harmonious administration.

During 1978/9 I saw ten women clients and nineteen males, most of whom required six to nine months' work, and several came for over a year. They included a distinguished athlete; a Catholic priest; a junior social worker and a senior one nearing retirement; three clergymen with very different presenting problems; a 'small' farmer; a fascinating working class teenager; a lively RC monk, a senior civil servant and his wife; a gifted young musician; a businessman in late middle-age, unjustly treated by his firm, who courageously overcame depression and some paranoia to fight back and win a future for himself; a young engineer for whom all human relationships had gone dead; a nurse, and several so-called working class men and women – whose capacity for creative self awareness and change convinced me that counselling was not just a middle-class nostrum. One of the most challenging clients had a stammer that threatened his promotion but managed to overcome it in about a year, and another a young man who, though intelligent and well-motivated, had such crippling obsessions that he made very slow progress under an analytic approach so I searched around for an alternative method. I had read of a Dr Wijesinghe's work with such patients, so went to see him at Claybury Hospital (where I'd done a little RF training) and was inspired to try his contract-making method. Both my client and I were astonished when it worked. Slowly the destructive compulsions were broken; later he told me that for him the December day when I came to his flat and we systematically tackled each obsession, was 'like BC and AD in my life.' Mercifully when I left WPF he was able to find a woman counsellor with whom he achieved a high degree of freedom and completed the many years of therapy.

All this was backed by the settled happiness of life at Writtle, in our home, in morning meditation with Peter and others at church, in Sunday celebration of the Christian mysteries, and in nourishing exchange with colleagues in Kensington and the Chelmsford area. But often I felt very tired and despaired of effectively helping this man or that woman, or wondered how long it would be wise to follow this programme. In London I was wonderfully sustained again by sleeping at the ever-welcoming home of Alan and Joyce, and by recourse to music at the Festival Hall and elsewhere. However, one saving grace and resource was built into the programme. Whenever intensive counselling induced exhaustion, the wholly different experience of teaching would rejuvenate me. Drained by a day of five sessions I would be stimulated by the evening diploma course and somehow be renewed; or having shared the work of four or five student counsellors in an hour and a half of supervision I would feel that they had fed me with new hope in the process we were engaged in, and turn to the next sessions with fresh eyes.

One disappointment had to be faced and accepted. Wynn and I had hoped that we might have a child, and, in spite of the age gap, Tim might benefit from the companionship of a brother or sister: but intermittent discomfort and pain began to dog Wynn's physical health and towards the end of 1979 it appeared that only a hysterectomy would restore her well-being. This took place in November and by the new year, having coped well with the after-effects, she was feeling more herself. Looking into the possibility of adoption we experienced more discouragement on account of age from the agencies we consulted. However, it clarified the future of our family, and, as will become clear, the older children provided a happy alternative within a few years.

Another blow fell upon us not many weeks after Wynn's operation. On January 16th 1980 Bill Kyle suffered a massive stroke. David Black (then Counselling Co-ordinator) and the new Training Co-ordinator Paul Keeble had both felt that Bill was 'quietly tired' – a very uncharacteristic impression, and he had spoken to a close friend in terms of 'setting his lands in order' because he was going. Significantly he had in the previous year set up an Executive who were beginning to replace the charismatic leadership by a clearer structure of responsibility and decision. On January 28th Bill died. He was only fifty-four. For me the third in the line of leadership figures (father Eric, bishop John) to have died comparatively young: but the collective grief at Kensington and the genuine friendship of so many staff and students carried me through. I felt thankful for all that Bill had made free to me and yet glad that I had my feet also in another world, the local church. Benita asked me to speak at a Memorial Service for Bill but I regretfully declined: in this case I wished to be simply a mourner.

At this time Queen's College offered me a living in the Isle of Wight, but I declined it; the job would have meant abandoning the WPF altogether and it was too soon to leave Writtle.

In the 1980 summer we woke up to the approach of my priesthood's Silver Jubilee and resolved to celebrate it. On September 27th Bishop Falkner Allison, who had ordained me, came from retirement to preside, Bishop Derek Bond of Bradwell led intercessions of great sensitivity, the choir of Writtle church offered a musical canopy of immense beauty – I shall not forget young Richard Sayles's crystal clear tones in Vaughan Williams' 'O Taste and See' – and friends from all the years came to feast on Wynn's good food. These included John Bodger from New Guinea, Bill and Eileen from Belhus, Gill's brother John Deby and Alan and Joyce to name but a few: Hatfield Heath, WPF and, of course, the family were well presented.

The party was a happy backcloth to a more solemn undertaking. That weekend was the occasion of the Michaelmas Ordination, and Bishop John had asked me to conduct the Ordinands' Retreat and to deliver the ordination sermon. The bishop was unable to come to the party because he was interviewing future deacons and priests. I joined him at Pleshey and at once experienced a re-run of my own fraught ordination retreat of 1954. It was a painful experience and I confided in the Bishop's Chaplain, Wesley Carr (now Dean of Westminster Abbey) just how shattering it had been. Luckily the retreat addresses survived and the candidates actually asked for copies. In the ordination sermon I spoke about the minister as 'enabler of the laity', helping them to discover and practice their own vocations, rather than as officer in charge of the troops and parish jack-of-all-trades.

Term had begun again at Writtle with an increased cohort of students and about fourteen clients to be seen each week: the horizon appeared to be busy and interestingly peopled, the family in good heart and few clouds on the horizon.

CHAPTER XV

'IN SICKNESS AND IN HEALTH'

The 1980 Jubilee party crowned the two years after leaving The Heath and brought family and friends pleasantly together. In the family, Penny had completed her A level course and was working with Mothercare in Chelmsford, actively involved too, in local church and community. At College she had found a close friend in Adrian Shepherd. Alex had completed his degree and was trying out the life of an accountant. At a friend's wedding he had also met his future fiancee, Alexandra West. Timothy had settled into the Writtle community and school but was not getting the help he needed with the dyslexia, and when we asked for the diagnosis made by Great Ormond Street two years earlier to be taken seriously, the County Education Service did nothing except to suggest that we were middle-class parents who wanted something special for their son. Officially dyslexia did not exist.

A breakthrough came when we heard that the wife of the new Headmaster of Brentwood School was a qualified teacher for dyslexic non-literates and the Junior School Headmaster agreed to accept Tim as a day boy. In 1982 he began the combined programme of lessons in a small class and frequent individual dyslexic teaching, which led in 1984 to his being offered a coveted day place in the main school. However by then the County had been outflanked by one of its own staff. Brentwood School had brought in an LEA Educational Psychologist. In her assessments she came across Tim and immediately recommended that he change to a school with an experienced dyslexic unit. A new Education Act now provided funds for this under the heading 'Special Educational Needs'. Although my views about the impropriety of private schooling had already been breached through four years' frustration in the public sector, it was a lot more difficult to swallow my determination that no child of mine should be subjected to boarding education. There was no local school qualified to give SEN provision so if we accepted the county recommendation he would have to leave home.

We talked it through with Tim, who at twelve was perhaps better able to face the trials of boarding than the usual eight-year old neophyte, and decided that he should be duly 'statemented', but himself help us choose the school he would attend. In this we were enormously supported by recent new friends, Jack Dodd, a former headmaster and Secretary of the Preparatory Schools Association and his wife Irene, at whose home I had begun to spend the WPF night in London. Timothy took seriously his brief as co-decider, and after strongly rejecting at least one of the options we visited, plumped quite positively for Bethany School in Kent. In due course his reading, writing and general attitudes were quite transformed.

Meantime, Wynn had also decided to 'go to a new school.' She applied to join the First Year counselling course at Writtle and was accepted. She was also getting to know local people, helping in the Sunday School, being my receptionist and partner in the counselling at No. 27 The Green, and becoming fond of her new home, in spite of anxiety about beetles and the tiles vanishing in a high wind.

However a new cloud appeared on the horizon. Although generally sound in mind and limb, especially on the two hip joints now five years old, sometimes at the end of the two day stint in London I would get chest pain. I put it down to indigestion, but our GP insisted on a hospital appointment. On October 3rd 1980, angina was diagnosed and the consultant slapped me on to beta blockers and TNT. The cure was worse than the condition: I now felt as though kicked by a horse in the belly and could hardly walk upstairs. The GP eventually agreed that beta blockers were not essential to my well-being and referred me to a London consultant via St Luke's Hospital for the Clergy. In March 1981 he had me in for catheterization and kept a regular check over the next year or so. He recommended a lighter programme, but I could hardly suspend the WPF Diploma Course, the Writtle lectures or the supervision groups without virtually losing my income. However, Wynn and I began to take more time off, especially in short breaks away from 'the shop' – more easily done after Tim began to board. Better fallback plans were put in place for crisis calls. Gradually the angina pain disappeared and I have had none since.

Looking back I recall the occasional end-of-day dismay that more clients were due, or a sudden dread that my next lecture was woefully wanting, not to mention incredulity that my supervisory skills could possibly do justice to the needs of my supervisees' many clients.

David Black writes: 'It is worth remembering how much anxiety supervisors habitually carry, often in a group of three trainees (or staff counsellors) having to hold responsibility for work with 15-18 clients. The strain of this responsibility is a hidden but central factor in all the tensions of these years.'[33]

Through staff shortages at both WPF and Writtle I often had four counsellors in each of three separate groups. Each counsellor saw a minimum of two clients and the more experienced saw three or four. That could mean being *au fait* with thirty to forty cases. This continued throughout 1982-84 and was combined with my own casework, which I tried to reduce to an average of twelve. Teaching three separate courses gave a rejuvenating fillip, but also involved taking an appropriate interest in about sixty students.

All this coincided with a far from happy development in Pat's family life. Earlier she had, like me, had her hip joints replaced; that was a success, but in the spring of 1981, thanks largely to her initiative, her husband Sam was found to have a malignant growth in his left lung which was immediately removed; but the surgery left him in considerable pain from damaged nerves in the shoulder. He continued with radiation treatment for some months and returned to work. A year later he collapsed one evening, but his Basel hospital could find no cause. He continued to run high temperatures, so took himself to another hospital where eventually an abscess in the lung cavity was found and a drainage pipe installed.

In September continuing discomfort determined him to resign as President of Ciba-Geigy. Luckily he had put in place a detailed plan for his resignation in 1985. Pat was increasingly taken up with the World Wildlife Fund, but when she accompanied Sam on a Ciba-Geigy visit to Saudi Arabia, herself to see to the reintroduction of Arabian oryx gazelles, her heart gave serious trouble and she had to cancel a visit to the research laboratories at the Azir National Park. On her return to Switzerland a near heart attack was shown up on ECG and she was advised to rest. So throughout 1981 she and Sam had worrying ill-health to contend with.

The Westminster Pastoral Foundation was beginning to recover from the shock of Bill's death. David Black had been appointed Chairman of a Team who managed the WPF while searching for a new Director. Within a year they had appointed Canon Derek Blows and under his 'co-ordinating' rather

---

[33] Black *Op. cit.* p 33

than 'charismatic' style of leadership, the WPF began to gain a confident and more mature identity. Its tenth birthday was celebrated in May 1981 with Sir George Young, representing the government, speaking with real appreciation of our achievements, especially in relation to the NHS psychiatric service. The other main speaker, Ed Thornton, Professor of Psychology and Religion at Louisville, USA told us: 'The future is yours . . . the morning has gone. The era of the Founding Fathers is over. Midday has come. The era of the sons and daughters has begun.' The era too of proliferating Affiliates had also come. The Writtle Pastoral Foundation found larger premises and increased clients and trainees. It looked as though we were on course for steady growth.

Early in 1981 I was staggered to receive an invitation from the diocese of Lichfield. In previous years I had undertaken training events there and with other dioceses, notably Salisbury and Canterbury, but was wholly unprepared for the summons to be a resident Adviser in Counselling, with a small parish and responsibility for the care of clergy and their families. This attractively brought together the church and counselling arenas in a clear and manageable contract (unusual in the Church of England!) which pioneered in what I felt to be a critical area as yet ignored by the Church generally. But had the door been opened too soon?

I went to meet the Suffragan Bishop, the Archdeacon and the Churchwardens and thought them charming. Bishop John Waller had very clear and practical ideas of how the work could be conducted: but how could I face leaving my first house and new working centre after only two years? Wynn joined me for the second visit to Lichfield and though she liked the house and garden I now felt uncertain. At the foot of the longish garden the dark waters of the river Tame flowed on the way to the Trent. Near the opposite bank rattled overhead buckets travelling to a nearby quarry. The effect was mildly sinister. I stalled my decision, promising to give an answer soon, but this proved more than I could deliver. For a month or so I dithered, their lordships of Lichfield being remarkably patient, then 'took myself in hand' and wrote accepting. That night exploded in a terrifying dream. The quarry buckets had gone mad and Timothy had drowned in the river. I signalled my withdrawal as early as I could decently ring the diocese, and lapsed into several weeks of apathy, working on automatic pilot, probably a trial to my family, though they took it very gently. One good thing came from the debacle: during the uncertainty I had more and more felt that our friend, Peter Graham, who was thinking of seeking a final appointment before retiring, with his long association with Clinical Theology and pastoral counselling, was better suited than I to do the Lichfield job. I was immensely thankful when eventually their lordships agreed with me, became delighted with his ministry, and Peter served a highly successful stint before retiring to Dorset. 'All things work together for good . . .' even bad dreams?

It was a relief to move on to 1982 and watch the older children carving new lives for themselves. Adrian was reading Geology at Cardiff University, so Penny took the train quite often to see him. Alex had decided against accountancy and was drawn to teaching. In 1981 he began at Brighton Teacher Training College, and shortly before qualifying found a reasonably interesting temporary appointment in biology at a Comprehensive School in Reading; two and a half years later he was head of the biology department. His fiancee Alexandra was also a teacher (of music). Alexandra's home was in the same parish as Wynn's mother and brother, so their wedding took place in the same church as Wynn's marriage to her first husband and they moved to Reading. Penny and Adrian planned a September wedding at Writtle church with a reception at No. 27. Thereafter they lived in Nottingham while Adrian studied for his doctorate. Following the cheerful celebrations in our garden we settled down to being a threesome: Tim could take over the Eagle's Eyrie on the top floor. Having trained thoroughly in cross-country running, he went on to win a number of trophies at Brentwood before achieving similar sporting success at Bethany.

My own health was improving, so WPF asked me to take a novel additional supervision group consisting of two medics, one a GP and the other a psychiatrist, both venturing into the field of counselling and psychotherapy. It was quite a testing and enlightening experience to see our work through the eyes of mature practitioners in medicine, and had its humorous moments. One of them was presenting a case when she interposed, 'At this point our concentration was interrupted by mutual borborygmoi'. The GP and I sat up and looked at one another, wondering what exotic phenomenon had intervened . . . to discover that this was the medical term for what I call 'colly-wobbles': both counsellor and patient had the embarrassment of rumbling stomachs. Such unscheduled happenings did have a curious effect on the work, for instance the room where I'd started in the Central Hall was equipped with a wash basin, and the plumbing would gurgle unexpectedly. Sometimes a client would be opening up a particularly sensitive revelation when the plug-hole would emit a series of rather vulgar comments. My efforts to prevent it were in vain and, after some anxiety about the effects, I was pleased to get a new room at Kensington.

An entirely different challenge was presented between 1981 and 1983 in the persons of two clients with epileptic symptoms, one a lad of fourteen and the other a male adult of about thirty. The boy had suffered from grand mal since infancy; the man had had less clearly definable seizures since adolescence. In both cases it was thought that personal relationships past and present might have contributed to the syndrome and counselling could be combined with the medical treatment already prescribed. With regard to the adult our WPF psychiatrist, Sasha Duddington, confirmed this hope and a straightforward psychodynamic approach unearthed powerful anger about unjust family treatment complicated by personality problems. We worked together for about three years with a steady reduction in incidence and by 1985 the seizures had virtually disappeared.

With the lad, individual interviews were useful, but change came about chiefly through family work. I would go to his home, meeting with the parents and three other siblings, to engage in a method called 'sculpting'. Each member of the family placed the others in a sort of tableau, which for them expressed how they were experiencing family life. I was astonished how much they and I learnt, at a more sensitive level than the merely cognitive. It quite deeply affected their understanding of their own feelings and the interaction with the other family members. The boy reported helpful changes within the set-up and the seizures decreased. One of the parents came for counselling. However we ran up against an old problem for counsellors: the boy had a new doctor. He disapproved of such therapy and so after a while the boy's sessions ceased. Nonetheless improvement in negative interaction had taken place and family stress reduced. The end of our therapy obliged the doctor to look more closely at the medical aspects of the lad's condition. Later on, as a result, scarring of the brain tissue was detected and eventually removed by surgery. As an adult, he is entirely free of seizures.

The well-being of this lad's family had been my concern for many years, because, although living in another parish some miles away, they used in the 1970s to bring him to our Services of Prayer and Healing at Hatfield Heath. Right from Belhus times such services had been a low-profile component in our everyday pastoral care. At WPF Bill Kyle introduced them in early days and they took place regularly and open to all in the chapel at the Maria

Assumpta Convent. I used to assist.

This may raise the question: is it sound practice to combine overt spiritual or religious treatment of illness with psychotherapy? Nothing of course can prevent the sick from seeking alternative therapies; but those undergoing psychotherapy should be expected to examine carefully with their counsellor why they are thinking of doing so. Choosing overt spiritual treatment may be an unconscious attempt to avoid painful issues which really need to be addressed. This must be honestly faced. Equally counsellors must acknowledge any desire on their part to evangelize – in the case of clergy it will rightly be assumed to be a part of their vocation, but not to be engaged in during therapy, any more than Christian GPs or surgeons will use their professional relationships to convert their patients. Psychotherapy is a strict discipline to do with a person's mental and emotional health.

Nonetheless the spirituality of clients is a real and dynamic part of themselves. The WPF deliberately states that our counsellors respect and work with this component in clients' makeup, in contrast to the Colchester psychiatrist who stated publicly that if a patient of his had a religion he usually set out to destroy it as dangerously neurotic. However we took care to leave the initiative to the clients. If they substantially referred to religion then that became appropriate material for the therapy. Sometimes too it was evident that there had been or was an acknowledged spiritual component in their views or experience of life, so it was appropriate to encourage them to explore whether this was a resource they could draw on for their healing, or a hindrance to it.

David Holt was the first supervisor to recognize that 'in their work with clients our students were invoking resources which I, as supervisor, judged to be authentic in themselves and fitting the empirical situation of the client, but which I, as analyst, did not explicitly work with in my own practice. These resources are best identified by the words prayer, grace, spirit. I began asking myself whether in my own practice I was implicitly drawing on the same resources as my students, but perhaps calling them by different names. The answer that came was "Yes", which in its turn generated a whole series of questions as to how prayer, grace, spirit, were translated into psychological language. I realised how important it was for me, both as a professional and as a person to be able to translate the language of spirit into the language of psyche and vice versa.'[34]

---

[34] Black *op. cit.* p 62

David Black writes: 'David Holt refused to go along with the tacit blurring or rejection of religious beliefs which so often accompanied the move towards psychodynamics.'

A few counsellors had experience of what is called 'prayer counselling'. This involves the presence of a third person in the counselling session whose job is to pray silently throughout. Most of us felt that this disturbed the twosome dynamics of the session and the mystery person apparently on the side of religion might be felt as bringing pressure to bear on vulnerable and often suggestible people; so it came to be discouraged or converted into 'invisible' prayer outside the counselling room. Clearly, clients' mobilization of their spiritual resources must be a free process deriving from the persons themselves. In practice I was struck by the frequency with which even apparently non-religious people undertook an inner journey to find either spiritual meaning or to recover earlier insights of a spiritual character.

I wrote up a striking experience of this in the 1970s, in what I called 'Summary of a Counselling Partnership.' Here is an abbreviated form of it.

A young man aged about twenty-five to whom I will give the name Daniel had worked extremely hard to reach a university where he could read Philosophy. He came to counselling with anxieties about relations with women, his girlfriend and mother in particular. He had had a difficult start in life – his parents' marriage was already on the rocks, his mother a Christian, in his first year remarried a Moslem and brought him up as his stepfather's son. When the truth emerged Daniel was very angry and couldn't forgive his mother for deceiving him. In our early sessions he discovered just how fully he had internalized her ambivalence about him (probably arising from pregnancy while she was changing husbands). 'I realize now that my mother's message has been, "You should not have been born." I have always felt a "nobody".' It affected his attitude to his physical body and had probably contributed to his intellectualism. Sometime in this stage I remarked that maturity often began when we consciously chose the parents we had been given willy-nilly' but he replied, 'How can I choose a mother who has not chosen me?'

Just then the man with whom he shared digs was killed by a gas explosion in the bathroom of a hotel where he was on holiday. 'He had the same birthday as mine.' Daniel brought a poignant poem about this violent bereavement, and found himself in touch with his suicidal feelings. He feared deeply that he might follow his natural father's mother who had killed herself: 'The shock waves are still reverberating in my head.' He fell into a period of despair.

When I sent this summary to him in order to obtain his permission to publish, I received a reply and here are parts of it:

My recollection of the period of despair is remarkably in accord with yours. I remember it as about six months. It was a period in which the extent of pain and despair put me in a state where every living breath had the heaviness of potential suicide. I remember coming to a session and having in myself to gather the courage to ask you how long this state would last? As I said it I wrestled with feeling stupid; how could you know? It also exposed the extent of this desperate damage and the frailty of being human in such a storm. Life was not necessarily infinitely bearable.

Your reply, in this impossible situation helped me. You said. 'Ask me another', with a humour that wasn't about being funny. It both held me and complemented the terror of not knowing whether I could come through this. You then added that you had worked with a number of people and from what you knew of me it would change. You also touched my arm and held me with your eyes as I walked out of the room at the end of the session. In that distant half-lit emotional state, your response kept me anchored to the world and nourished the bit of me that was grasping for hope. If the text book response would have been solely to listen, in its fullest sense, I feel I would have slipped through the therapeutic cradle. You responded by giving something essential to me.

My summary continues:

During this despair we were led into very strong feelings of violence and death partly associated with sexuality. About the twelfth session, however, Daniel decided that his problems stemmed more from pre-oedipal issues of being and identity. He told me how his natural father, with whom he was trying to get more closely in touch, had climbed a hill to a sundial while battling with the question, 'To be or not to be'. Daniel had dreamt he was flying between the Sun as male Life symbol and mother Earth, and stretched out his arms so that he presented a living cross; but a storm burst and lightning struck him to the ground so that he bowed himself over like a Moslem at prayer. To me this sounded like a symbolic recollection of the parental problem but to him it had a religious significance which he expressed like this. 'The Islamic attitude of prayer is more like the foetal position. I think worship begins from a sense of Being; not from Christian ideas of sacrifice and redemption.'

These words seemed to echo my experience with other clients; namely their need to find themselves as valid beings, as 'meant to be' before they can give themselves away freely. (Too many children are in my view, asked to make sacrifices or to conform to parental ideals of 'unselfishness' before they know their own authentic self.) Daniel said, 'It's not what I am that people want; but what I achieve for them.' An upbringing that too early asks for self-sacrifice may produce a False Self, a mask to gain acceptance, or it may require the development of a reactive personality to defend the inner being from severe intrusion or occlusion (absorption). But the person tends to experience failure or sin in terms of total self-condemnation. The possibility of redemption only becomes an option when this False Self has been recognized and an attempt begun to dismantle it. The true self can then be rediscovered in a relationship of trust and increasing honesty.

It now happened that Daniel suddenly bought a puppy. It had to be inoculated and the restrictions drove both dog and master mad. 'His every whine precipitated acute anxiety in me: I felt I was cracking up in the attempt to look after him.' Together we looked at this symbolic 'finding' and 'trying to look after' his own inner child. He had to give away the puppy because he was working far too hard to find time for it; but the episode enabled him to begin to forgive his mother. 'I think I went through an anxiety condition like this at my birth. Thank God the anger has gone; I abandoned the dog just as she abandoned me. I actually felt she could have done no other; now I can set her free.' Daniel shared this with her and she responded: 'I was in such a bad way I couldn't give you what you needed; so I put you in a nursery.' She had not told him this before: but where did that leave him? 'Can I make up for my mother not giving herself to me or do I just accept that I am irreparably damaged?' (16th session).

This essentially ontological and spiritual question now became the focus of our work, and began with doubt whether Daniel could ever give himself any value. 'I can undo the confusion in myself, but what if there are no roots in me?' He was very frightened that his initial being had been so denied and crushed there might be nothing there to grow from. I asked if he thought the essence or 'seed' of a person's being is destructible and can't grow again. He said that belief in its indestructible nature was a matter of faith and he had to find that for himself.

This was followed by a remarkable trance-like dream in which he was in a large open room with nothing in it except himself facing a screen of something like perspex. 'I became aware that from my navel a cord stretched across into the screen to where a foetus was developing. As the foetus was ready to be born the ceiling evaporated as brilliant rays from a rising sun shone through with almost blinding force. It was like seeing myself born again, with a calm and awed observation; a bit like the end of the film 2001.' He had seen the foetus move and then come out, actively alive. In his letter to me he states: 'Quite literally after this dream life has been different.'

Daniel still had to dismantle the habit of substituting work and academic success for his authentic self. A few months later he looked different, saying: 'At last I feel it is good to be me.' Later still, '. . . I used to feel I had to do all the giving . . . now I am receiving and it feels good. I am now content to be myself. I've accepted the horrible sad, depressed part . . . I didn't want the pain cut out as a surgeon would because then I would have become a zombie . . . You made a better way possible by listening and then helping me strike through the rubbish to let myself out. I couldn't see it happening down below but you brought out the self, the emerging me that's worth something and I can care for.' Usually he hated his birthdays: he actually enjoyed his twenty-seventh and said, 'I feel at one with my body and feel my true age.' In the 52nd session he said, 'I have found faith as the way of valuing myself . . . I am excited by the discovery that faith is a necessary foundation for all thought, scientific or otherwise.'

The letter he wrote, twenty-five years later, permitting me to refer to these sessions, is so precious to me that, although its hyperbole arises in part from the powerful projections of transference, and to print them is close to boasting,

I want his words to be known as a rare and moving testimony, for which I am deeply grateful. He writes:

> My sessions with you finished, as I recall about a year or so before my final examinations. As I approached my finals and was needing to work as intensively as possible, I found I couldn't concentrate, felt very low and daunted by the demands. A close friend suggested I get back in touch with you, but I felt I had to do it alone. I think it was just before Easter that you wrote to me wishing me luck and also saying that if I wanted I could contact you. I saw you for one session, I can't remember what was said, I doubt if it mattered. With a magic that needs no wand all my intellectual and concentration powers returned. I did pass with honours. The follow-up of yours has been crucial for me, not just for that time but long term. It gave me a rich experience of being caught. And to be caught you have to be seen. To be seen without being there, is to feel valued in life itself. When I said you are with me, this may begin to convey what I mean – the man with an extraordinary gift for healing and spiritual travel.

As this work was ending a parish priest from the far north of England approached me. He had been severely damaged by almost unbelievable childhood horrors and the consequences were seriously undermining both his work and his family life with G, his wife, and five children. I forget how he had got hold of my name, but at the time I felt unready to take on another client and obscurely felt that he might need more than I could give. I tried to persuade him to see someone nearer home. Weekly travel to London would be immensely tiring and costly. He applied to his bishop who must have had a high opinion of him for the relatively impoverished diocese took on all the costs for a year. I could hardly say, No! As I'd expected, the work was extremely testing for us both, but he became deeply engaged in it: he sent me what he called an 'Afterthought' following each session and a 'Report' after what he called a 'term', roughly every four months. Here is one of these Reports, written in Eastertide 1984, into which I have inserted one bit and he another, from earlier Afterthoughts. I should add that his wife strongly backed him – with perceptive comment. Between January 1983 and December 1984 he was seen forty-four times. He writes:

Uncertainty over the financing of the venture coupled with the demands of the counselling combined to give a poor start to the term. A strong sense of vulnerability, isolation and frustration prevailed, precipitating moments of pain and hostility that appeared to render the whole exercise futile. This crisis of confidence, the origins of which could be seen in the latter weeks of the first term, and which was simmering over the Christmas recess, came to the boil in the second session, during the course of which R enabled me to grasp for the first time how the present moment, when flooded with the hurts of the past, triggers my anger against myself and the offender. This proved with hindsight to be a turning point in the progress of the counselling, the significance of which was marked by the fact that we both laughed together for the first time and I forgot to send my Afterthoughts.

I insert his account of the 'laugh' from an earlier Afterthought.

It comes to me that Ronald and I made a joke out of my predicament. The coffee machine had refused to deliver a cup for him just before our session. At the end of it, I asked jokingly whether he was going to try again. 'Certainly not! It's failed me once so I'm going to wipe it completely out of my life.'

He adds to this Afterthought.

Two things to work on: seek the children's forgiveness for yesterday: and G's too for punishing her and excluding her. If I can't do either this week, then be patient and gentle with myself until I can. [Significant resolve from a compulsive self-punisher].

He continues the Report:

A further development occurred in the fourth session, the crucial nature of which only dawned on me later in the term, when I was compelled to accept for the first time both the existence of my subconscious, the dark side of me, and its influence upon my waking life. At the same time, an area was discussed which precipitated deep depression and despondence culminating in a decision, agreed with

R to terminate the course at Easter unless subsequent sessions gave grounds to decide otherwise, which in the event they did. The demands of the course had reached a point of personal cost which I felt outweighed any benefits to be derived from it. This whole enterprise demands passivity, to be held there enduring. Subsequently, for reasons not entirely clear to me even now, I decided to do the hardest thing and hang on in. Possibly this commitment prepared the ground for arguably the most significant breakthrough of the year best described in the words of my session Afterthought:

Months of frustration and pain, despair and cynicism about me, R, and this whole process, fell into place last week. The best parallel I can find is that of micro-surgery. I cannot see the damage but R (the surgeon) can, and, using developed techniques, he is helping the reconnection of infinitely fine and delicate threads in order to reconcile that which has become separated so that, through the re-grafting, healing and wholeness can occur. At first I could not accept that R really knew what he was doing. I could not accept that the whole process had an agenda of inner healing. Somehow the crisis of rejection and the decision to continue has contributed to this sudden insight.

This breakthrough, and the acceptance of *I am the agenda*, has given the subsequent sessions a new kind of momentum and purpose. For the first time in this course, I have begun to sense in myself inner growth and healing for which hitherto, I have had to take the word of R and G. It is of note that dreams are taking an increasingly significant part in the counselling.

By the end of term, I had recognized the false correlation I had made between the end of the funding and the end of the course. The need for a second year of counselling had begun to emerge as both desirable and appropriate. After due discussion, R and I agreed that, provided the requisite funds become available, we would undertake a second year.

As it happens I was not able to complete the next year with him because of our move. The pain of enforced separation and the hazard of violent counter-rejection were negotiated together, and amazingly he eventually agreed to transfer and continue with a WPF colleague until he became strong enough to switch to an entirely new job in a chaplaincy.

I have chosen to mention two male clients because, for no obvious reason, nearly three quarters of my clients have been men. Work with women was equally varied and probably there was about the same fairly small percentage of each who appeared not to gain much from the therapy. Apart from my ineffectiveness the main reasons for apparent failure were premature termination by the client and resistance to making any changes. I write 'apparent' because some who left too soon or who had achieved little at first, actually returned to counselling later. But profoundly depressed people find it hard to use their insights and others tend to go round in circles repeating behaviour patterns because they cannot accept the implications of what they are beginning to perceive. More often than not, medication is required and that can be an uncertain factor in the therapy too though I tried to work closely with any medics involved.

Audrey, a Christian, began to recognize the powerful anger at the heart of her depression and was very frightened by the strength of such 'unchristian' feeling; but she could see good reasons for her anger and became more accepting of her insights into its origin. Gradually with her psychiatrist she was able to reduce her dependence on medication and, freed from its zombie-effect, could show an attractive mischievous side to her nature. I was reminded of work with a young nun, traumatized by conflict within her Order, who had remained almost speechless for a month or so until I took a risk and pointed to the impishness of the smile she very occasionally allowed to light up her face. Accepting its significance she went on to rediscover her humanity, her own spirit untrammelled by the institution that had wounded her: she eventually returned to the Order but as a maturer person. Too easily I expected of Audrey a similar recovery of herself; but forgot that I'd noticed the danger point in depressive illness is quite often when the sufferer is beginning to surface.

She had a harsh disagreement with her husband and phoned one Sunday evening asking to be seen at once. I was very tired and pointed out that she was booked in to see me the next day: could she please wait? – refreshed I would be of more use to her. She rang off – and I never saw her again. Early the following morning she took her life. The anger had been finally vented on husband, therapist and God. Few impulses are more powerful in damaged people than the desire to have the last word and no more effective way than suicide. Sadly it has to be accepted.

Later her husband came and as he also was a Christian we were able to pray together: this was some heartease to both of us (and we felt a link with her in doing so) but I have never lost my sense of failure in this case. It has joined the memory of other occasions when the urgent need of a parishioner, as much as a client, has been more than I could wholly and effectively respond to.

Looking at the pain of failure in this field, I became aware that after this particular blow strangely I became more accepting of my limitations – not condoning or playing down a professional lapse, nor ceasing to feel sad about its effects: but, having a more realistic perception of my skill, recognizing that blindness or lacunae were inevitable, and my work remained of reasonable value. I could release the long tendency to shame when I was not all that I myself and others expected, and in Christ's forgiveness and loving enablement could take into the future a truer attitude to myself.

CHAPTER XVI

SUFFOLK – UNDER ST MARGARET'S PATRONAGE

In the middle of 1984 the Bishop of Edmundsbury and Ipswich, John Waine, invited me to look at a cluster of four small country parishes near Hadleigh (north of the Constable Country) headed up by St Margaret's, Whatfield. Care of the parishes could be combined with co-directing a small WPF Affiliate in partnership with Canon Chris Gane, Vicar of St Margaret's Ipswich, who, in addition to a large town parish and flourishing church, was responsible for several areas of diocesan work. I could hardly ignore a second opportunity to bring together the parochial and counselling arenas! A brief visit one afternoon to the villages of Nedging, Naughton, Semer and Whatfield in high summer was an enchanting experience. The rolling countryside, brilliant gold with early harvest; smiling blue skies, radiant foliage and singing birds, presented a rural paradise after a relatively urban Essex and London backcloth. Wynn came over to see why I was drawn and fell in love with the Rectory – a no-nonsense 1930s spacious home on top of a small hill with all main rooms facing south, recently renovated and with no ancient roof or beetles to worry about: she also felt more ready to manage a parochial life. Tim now had an independent (if not personally attractive) existence at boarding school where the dyslexia was really yielding to special methods of teaching. The older children would be able to bring grandchildren to country holidays. This time I knew it was right, at least to agree to meet the churchwardens.

One of these was not happy about the counselling link; I sensed the others rather agreed with him but they had been without a rector for over a year, and seemed prepared to work out a *modus vivendi*. Gainsborough House, opposite St Margaret's Church, Ipswich, was the home of the counselling service which had been set up by the Ipswich churches under their collective organization, called 'Concern'. It was, therefore, known as the Concern Counselling Centre and housed by arrangement with St Margaret's Church and School, and with

215

diocesan approval, in this elegant, if mildly dilapidated, seventeenth century mansion some twelve miles from Whatfield.

The first time I approached St Margaret's, the evening sun had converted its stones into a shining temple with a dark sky beyond: there was something quite thrilling, even melodramatic, about the challenge it offered. I entered the gloomy hall of Gainsborough House and passed through to the narrow high-ceilinged office: then mounting the stairs discovered a beautifully proportioned room with medallioned plaster ceiling and full-length sash windows. The summer evening light cast a benign and tranquil aura. I could imagine one-to-one exchanges and thoughtful seminars here – there was enough room for a dozen students. That room was asking to be loved and used, with a promise of hidden gifts. Later on our diocesan landlords let us use all that side of the house, both floors, and eventually a grant enabled us to re-order the entire interior and refurbish the exterior, a programme that cost us a lot more than we could really afford, but in time gifts and loans met the deficit, and the new Gainsborough House won the Ipswich Award for the best restored building in the town.

After a few months Chris Gane was glad to relinquish his co-directorship. He had built up a team of five counsellors who were competent and devoted but mostly with other commitments too, so the actual availability for counselling was limited. Together we set out to extend the service and to draw in potential trainee counsellors. This brought an immediate response and by September classes began with ten trainees in the morning (including two clergy and two medics) and another ten in the evening, (including social workers, teachers and occupational therapists). In Whatfield a former County Intake Worker lived next to St Margaret's Church – so Connie Russell soon took over the assessment of an increasing number of applicants for counselling. Chris had bequeathed a very pleasant secretary, Rosina, and several church people, including Jean the wife of the Bishop of Dunwich, came to help with reception. The Bishop himself enlisted me in a group searching out ways to support clergy and their families under stress.

Astonishingly the father of an early client was none other than the hero of my youth (page 20) reminding me that life can be remarkably like an Anthony Powell novel. By then I had an outstanding colleague. Dr Joyce Board as well as exceptional supervisors in Don Smith and Martin Bevan and outstanding tutors in Jill Hawes and Sylvia Cullum together with Richard Fryer the centre's devoted Treasurer from the start, Laurie Wood a lovable

Administrator and Audrey Cullingford, an especially competent Secretary, I had a backup team to envy.

The Advisory Council led by the town-centre church's vicar, Keith Jones (now Dean of Exeter Cathedral) was an invaluable support and resource. The professionals received standard fees but many worked voluntarily, our receptionists being particularly generous with their time, and one of them later making a very substantial anonymous bequest to the Centre. A prominent churchwoman gave a very large sum when our debts threatened to swamp us. Inevitably finance tended to be rather a hand-to-mouth affair with uncertain annual grants, donations and loans from charities including the diocese. Clients gave what they could afford – often no more than a pound or two: we turned no one away and lived by faith!

The next year Bishop John Waine appointed me Diocesan Adviser in Pastoral Care and Counselling, to visit groups of local clergy, to present the value of listening skills in their pastoral work, and to be available for requests for personal counselling or to discuss special problems in their parishes. His successor, John Dennis, was one of the first bishops to recognize that priests and their spouses need an independent resource for support, other than built-in 'line managers'. Like many carers, clergy too easily feel that they are failures if they themselves need help, and fear that to confess this need to their bishop or archdeacon will condemn them professionally. Since they cannot turn to their parishioners who are liable to demand 'perfection' anyway, and their family life is no less exposed to stress than every one else's today, they are particularly vulnerable and even isolated when trouble strikes. Private therapy is expensive: so John Dennis arranged that clergy could make confidential arrangements with me and he would foot the bill.

Soon he found that clergy accepted his recommendation to come for counselling because it was known that interviews were completely sealed. When on exceptional occasions a report on the therapy was required it was prepared only in joint consultation with the client's permission. By the early nineteen nineties I had seen over thirty parish priests. Most required regular interviews over several months, some for a lot longer; three had been obliged to give up their jobs altogether and though they made progress, needed continuing support while settling back into work. Several clergy spouses had used the service and appreciated seeing one of the experienced women counsellors at the Concern Centre. Any of the clergy and their families could come to the rectory at Whatfield instead of to Ipswich. By 1986 we had ten staff seeing people weekly, and professionals to supervise the counsellors.

However, at the start not all was easy. The local Rural Dean, who had helped us to settle in and had tried to assuage parochial anxieties about the addition of the counselling centre – suddenly died at the age of fifty-nine. Simultaneously I had a very distressed sister Pat on the telephone from Basel to say that her husband Sam (also fifty-nine) had contracted pneumonia and was sinking rapidly. I advised her to contact the Anglican Chaplain, who turned out to be a great strength. Pat and Sam received communion together and he died on January 25th. That was a fortnight after we'd landed at Whatfield so I could not get to Switzerland until early February, but then fortunately in time to help Pat with voluminous correspondence and business. She reminded me that I too was fifty-nine! We met again in London when she returned to England to attend to her Gloucestershire property, and there at Miserden Church we held a Memorial Service for Sam on Easter Monday.

Pat thoughtfully came to Whatfield for my sixtieth birthday, but not only was her situation profoundly sad, it was also life-threatening in that shortly afterwards she was diagnosed as suffering from hypertrophic obstructive cardiomyopathy (a blocked ventricle) and had only a few months to live unless she underwent open heart surgery and a bypass. This particular operation had been once performed successfully, two years earlier. Determined that her girls should not, if possible, be deprived of both parents in one year, Pat prepared at once to enter St Thomas's Hospital, London. Operated on in 'deep freeze' at 10 a.m. one day she surfaced at 2 a.m. the next with the ventricle completely cleared and rejoiced to find she had not required the expected life-support system. Eight days later she insisted on walking to the X-ray and ECG departments and back, and persuaded the staff to let her return home. In the New year she had to cope with an acutely painful embolism, but emerged into far better health during the following months, making memorable visits to Spain (a concert in the Alhambra in aid of Mexico's Earthquake Fund) and the 25th Anniversary meeting of the WWF in Assisi. This launched a new initiative in conservation dialogue between five of the world's major religions. Buddhist, Christian, Hindu, Islamic and Judaistic pilgrims converged on the Franciscan basilica for the concluding pledge to protect the world's resources, and Peter Scott, a close friend of Pat's, was awarded the WWF Gold Medal.

Behind the bright tapestry was, however, the sharp pain of having to sell the Swiss house and garden that she and Sam had made together. She wrote later: 'I had planted 150 trees round the house and they had come to their glory, with maples and red oak, tulip trees flowering, walnuts loaded with nuts, the fruit trees bearing wonderful crops.' It must have been heartrending; but eventually she settled in her Gloucestershire home, surrounded once again by friends and her animals, and ready for several years of fascinating and action-packed tours abroad, many on behalf of WWF.

Wynn and I were gradually acclimatizing to the smiling face of a county where time moved more slowly and human habitation had the feel of permanence, with hundreds of years behind it. In the middle ages the area was known as Seilig Suffolk; 'seilig' has been translated 'silly', but the Anglo-Saxon really means 'happy' and, indeed, as I biked and drove through winding lanes from one village to another, invariably escorted by flocks of little birds singing loudly, quite a new feeling of well-being slowly enveloped me. From the time we had begun to come over from Writtle on days off to redecorate the rectory, the sun always shone (or so it seemed), and, though rather daunted by the garden with a quarter-mile of hedge to be controlled and heavy clay to be turned, Wynn felt at home and vowed that it was the best house she had ever had. It was surrounded by fields and rich meadows with woods: walks were varied and manageable, down the hill to the rapid meandering of the river Brett and its ford, or over the fields to Kersey, one of Suffolk's gems. A brief car ride would bring us to a footpath, incredibly clear, our farmers being more generous than their Essex counterparts about leaving a few feet between the edge and the plough. Of course the ramblers might have to contend with a broken bridge or the occasional wipe-out of the path, a forlorn sign pointing across substantial growing crops, but that was a challenge to ingenuity and Samantha was game for anything.

Samantha was our border terrier. She loved the great open space of our new parishes, having grown up in the limited confines of Hylands Park and the fields by Writtle Agricultural College. She came to us as a puppy in 1979 and soon became the next best thing to a daughter. An affectionate, alert and wayward nature made her 'a character' in the sense of someone to be reckoned with. She had a pleasing instinct with people. I had had mixed feelings about her arrival and, after the initial fuss in the sitting room, I withdrew to my desk in the study. With some surprise I felt a small body clambering on to my feet and lying very still for a few minutes, the first act in a long partnership accompanying me on therapy sessions or visiting parishioners, when she would offer an appropriate brief greeting, stretch herself quietly on the floor and convey a sense of relaxed calm.

The two cats had moved with us and become slightly more tolerant of one another. When moles attacked our new lawn they figured out the mole run and stationed themselves at either end, effectively discouraging the invasion. Once again Tiger attached himself to a neighbour with whom he remained for the rest of his life, greatly appreciating her warm conservatory. Reflecting on Tiger's habit of adopting our next door neighbour, I realized that, as a kitten, he had been born in the house next to Hatfield Heath Vicarage and given to me by its owner. Ponto made yet another move, and reached the distinguished age of twenty-two before departing the world he had enjoyed so briskly.

Timothy found the countryside rather uninteresting during the holidays, but supplemented his funds by realizing the assets of the orchard, selling daffodils in the spring and apples in the autumn. When he left for Newcastle University we would have disappointed customers at the door asking, 'Isn't he doing it this year?' One of the miracles of this period was Tim's emergence from the dyslexic jungle of the previous ten years to gain a university place on a degree course in Pure Mathematics.

Wynn discovered that the country Rector's wife was expected instantly to take over the Mothers' Union and had to face a daunting deputation wishing to argue with her refusal. Reluctantly they had recourse to a neighbouring retired clergyman's wife with impeccable MU qualifications. Wynn hoped they would be pleased when she consented to judge the Fancy Dress competition at the fete, but having made her choice was told, 'You can't possibly have him: he won it last year.' However, these were but blips in otherwise cheerful and businesslike relationships, from which arose friendships that are still intact. Wynn could do little in the counselling service at first because she was still completing her supervised casework at Writtle but by the autumn started taking Ipswich cases. As I was engaged most Sundays the exeat trips to Bethany fell mainly to her but she worked alongside Hilary Preston in the Sunday School when she could.

Hilary's husband, Alan, manager of an engineering firm in Hadleigh, was an invaluable colleague. He was a parish Elder, an office or 'order' introduced by Bishop Leslie Brown for laity to work alongside the ordained ministers after only minimum training. They were chosen by the incumbent and the church council in unanimous agreement, and licenced at a diocesan service.

An Elder did not administer sacraments or preach, but could lead worship and undertake pastoral and admin. tasks. Alan was a natural helper with a gift for leading services and useful practical skills. Later he was joined by Ann, whose gift was in caring for the older village families, especially the aged she had known for years; and Clare who, as a young nurse, was admirable with the new families moving into the village. Ann was sure that a bad stammer would prevent her from taking services but grasping her faith and courage did so, and found that the speech impediment simply didn't raise its head when she officiated! As all four parishes expected a Eucharist *and* a non-Eucharistic service most Sundays, even with these helpers, we should not have mounted them all but for our Reader, Jim Schofield, a former Headteacher, who had undertaken the three years' training and had a licence to preach. He was an effective and often amusing speaker, whose roots were in the neighbourhood: Joan his wife often played the organ at whichever church was lacking a musician. If we were short of the required function, our various skills had to be shared out: I would play the organ while an Elder conducted Matins, and then leap up to preach. The parishes resisted any re-planning of the services – the last rector did it all so why shouldn't I? Behind this was a chronic difficulty over accepting that I had other jobs beside the care of the benefice.

By the grace of God and the willing support of parishioners, the pastoral work of visiting the sick at home and in hospitals was not neglected and newcomers were welcomed. In time, with the churchwardens' and organists' staunch help, Family Services were set up in three parishes and in one attendance increased to about half the village population (i.e. about eighty), this very largely because the farmer-warden went round or telephoned to remind them! At Whatfield Church School I was invited to teach once a week (and to play for assembly) and for a time was Chairman of the Governors. But the shower of new directives from the Department of Education with admin. and syllabus changes became so indigestible that I thankfully handed over to a more competent neighbour.

Teaching adults was on the whole a more attractive way of exercising an educational ministry, and in addition to undertaking nearly all the seminars (at first) at the Counselling Centre I received stimulating outside invitations. The Warden of Pleshey, John Tyerman, invited me to speak to a very interesting group of spiritual directors, about twenty in all, I think. He wrote afterwards in terms I specially valued:

Thank you very much for spending yesterday with us. It was a most useful day. Sometimes the best things in life are the unexpected, it so happens that the exercise which you asked us to do in our small groups came just at the right moment in the development of those groups, and will enable their further growth.

But there was much else. You gave us many things to be thinking about. I was particularly grateful that *in your own self you integrate the psycho-dynamic approach with a full Christian experience.* (my italics)

At Ipswich we were creating our own new generation of teachers, who gradually took over from me as the numbers grew. Our July 1987 report reads: 'The 1986/87 training courses ended with thirty-two students, mainly professionals with medical, social work and church backgrounds: the new academic year has begun with forty-six (and a waiting list). Counselling hours increased to over a thousand in '86 and this year look like topping 1200 – with eighteen counsellors, all under weekly supervision. Local interest is growing and we may look for larger premises during 1988.' For a time local GPs provided extra room but in the end, as already mentioned, we took a financial risk and embraced the radical solution of enlarging the premises. The staff in all departments were increasing – by 1990 there were over forty, and counsellors were seeing about eighty clients a week. Could I manage this rate of expansion and continue to do two other jobs?

The bishop, John Dennis, thought not, and considerately proposed a change. I should now leave the parishes after a five year stint since I became pensionable in 1990, and also receive payment from the diocese for the work of Counselling Adviser and from the Centre for my teaching, supervision and counselling. This would produce a living income; but we would lose our bright and spacious rectory; another move, another home was not an attractive prospect. Previously, however, since leaving Writtle, and eventually managing to sell the house on The Green, we had had surplus cash to put into property, perhaps an eventual retirement home. Wynn had seen a number of properties in the area we chose, namely a ten mile coastal strip running from Felixstowe to Lowestoft. The main object was to be within about an hour's journey from Whatfield, to have a *pied-à-terre* for days off and short breaks. I had never seriously imagined we would end up living on the coast, least of all by so charming a town as Southwold, (In 1932 my father had rented a house on the North Parade, Southwold, for a fortnight; so memories of a sunny beach holiday were resurrected.) However, in 1987 in nearby Reydon, distinguished by a pub called The Randolph (prime recommendation to an Oxford man) and beautiful fourteenth century church dedicated (of course) to St Margaret, Wynn had discovered a bungalow we could afford. With no thought of making this a permanent home, we had bought it and enjoyed days off and short breaks (one after a prostate operation which happily yielded nothing malignant) and so did the family.

John Dennis's proposal, of course, gave the bungalow new significance: to move there was practicable if it could be enlarged to give Timothy a permanent room for the vacations (and possibly from which to go to work or await employment). I also needed a study with room for counselling interviews. To purchase another house with these additional features would be beyond our resources: but our bungalow had a garden larger than we wanted; why not fill some of it with extra rooms? Early '89 was part-given to making plans with a sympathetic architect from Lowestoft and his really admirable friend, a small builder who had his own working team. The living room opened straight on to the drive: why not build a porch from which a hall-corridor could be carved out of that room, making it a sizeable study? A new room for Timothy could fill the gap between a free-standing garage and the house. An extra shower, basin and loo could lie alongside a brand-new guest room, and, happiest concept of all, a large sitting room could jut out surrounded by garden, with a patio and big picture window. Behold, almost as much space as at Whatfield! The work was begun and finished in the four months left to us before moving in September 1989. Our kindly parishioners contributed a generous leaving present, so the next year we enlarged the 'eating recess' in the kitchen to make a respectable dining area and accommodate the growing grandchildren at table during their visits. The bungalow had doubled in size quite economically.

The Ipswich Concern Centre was about forty-five minutes away by road: not a difficult journey, but the distance introduced a sense of semi-detachment and encouraged staff to be less dependent on us. In our new 'village' (population about 3000) the vicar Harry Edwards and his congregation welcomed us (he had been amongst our first students at the Centre) and the GP friend Andrew with whom he had attended became our doctor. Soon I was happily celebrating the eucharist, preaching a bit and starting up a bible study group. A year later Wynn was rather alarmed to be elected a churchwarden.

That was about the time when Andrew, our GP, asked whether his practice might refer patients to the small group of us ICCC counsellors living in the neighbourhood. He went on to persuade his partners to agree to our using their surgeries on certain days. Luckily an experienced Relate Supervisor Margaret (yes! Margaret) Child, who later received an MBE for her services to counselling, also lived in Reydon and agreed to supervise.

Shortly afterwards a group of workers in statutory and voluntary services, and Lowestoft College itself, aware that we were running accredited WPF courses in Ipswich, asked if we could set up local classes. The College offered accommodation and so did the County Adult Education Department at the Benjamin Britten School. Again this was too good a chance to overlook, though it required prolonged negotiation. Here were the seeds of a new WPF Affiliate, whose name eventually came to be the Waveney Counselling Service.

This was particularly interesting because, unlike Writtle and Ipswich it was in no way a church initiative and had no overt link with any ecclesiastical body. To me this was a strong recommendation as it would be clear that the secular world was taking seriously, and asking for, a contribution offered by a more or less Christian movement – through WPF the Church was refreshing the life of society, providing a service that the secular community wanted instead of seeming chiefly to be a minority activity within that society. Some Christians might question whether it was being done explicitly 'in the name of Christ', especially when a minority of workers were not overtly Christian; but how much missionary hospital and education work is done with a large Christian label? Such organizations also employ competent specialists who do not wish to publish their religious allegiance. Christ's authority for such an approach is perhaps implied in the parable of the Sheep and the Goats (Matthew 25:37–40) To me what mattered was whether staff were really competent counsellors within the WPF model, which gave due weight to the spiritual aspect of personality and spiritual resources for healing. In practice the majority – without any test of religious allegiance – had a positive view of the Judaeo-Christian tradition. Some have been profoundly committed to a denomination; none have jibbed at the spiritual commitment and most have been ready to attend the religious services that have arisen in the life of counselling centres. But orthodoxy of a religious character can never be a substitute for thorough-going competence and integrity in the art and science of counselling.[35]

---

[35] Anthony Storr *The Art of Psychotherapy*, (Secker and Warburg, 1979)

It would be otiose to describe yet again the process by which another WPF affiliate came into being. It was not all beer and skittles, nor even sweetness and light. In 1991 a public meeting in Lowestoft attended by about forty, produced valuable support including a Methodist Minister (seemingly appropriate after Bill Kyle's lead) who agreed to chair a Steering Committee. He and a very pleasant probation officer joined the existing group of pioneers (at first I wished only to act as a consultant) and it looked as though the small counselling and training octopus would have a head. But sadly Minister and Probation Officer got cold feet – I think the financial problems were frightening – and after resigning at a Committee meeting were heard to say, 'Well we've pulled the plug on that.' The other volunteers were made of sterner stuff and declared that the Committee continued to exist in spite of the Chairman's resignation. They went on to co-opt fresh members including myself, and together we decided to link up formally to the Ipswich Concern Centre as a 'branch' and come in under their umbrella charity status, financial know-how and staff resources. The ICCC Management accepted us as bona fide partners – mercifully solvent because our twenty prospective trainees had trustingly paid in advance for their first term! Soon my wife Wynn joined the staff as Co-ordinator of intake and Louise Donovan as Training Co-ordinator.

In 1993 I was delighted and honoured to be made a Canon of Bury St Edmunds Cathedral. As I had been in the diocese for only eight years it was not for long service, so I felt there was genuine recognition of the value to the church of what I was doing. The ICCC thought so too and gave me the means to purchase an original Simon Palmer painting to celebrate my elevation.[36]

My canonical stall was dedicated to Eorfwald, the first Christian king of East Anglia. I was amused to learn that he was a belt and braces man. To make sure of a favourable reception in the next world he built his church at Rendelsham with two altars, one to the Christian God and the other to the pagan pantheon.

As so often with the earlier developments of our affiliates I felt that the new centre was more an act of providence than of my initiative, indeed set up by a will and provision quite beyond my expectation or planning. The County's and Lowestoft College's willingness to provide rooms for training was a major gift; the CAB in the middle of Lowestoft followed by offering four

---

[36] Artist – great nephew of Samuel Palmer. I find his country scenes fascinating.

rooms for evening counselling. But the most striking example of providence followed. What we most needed was a headquarters and administrative home. It seemed logical to go and see the local Housing Officer, though I expected no more than a useful contact which might yield a later bonus. Johnny Johnson heard me out patiently and then said in a matter of fact way:

'Would you like a shop?'

Slightly thrown I replied, 'Well yes, but we haven't the money needed to convert it.'

'We would do that for you,' he responded, 'and charge you a peppercorn rent.'

'That is an extremely attractive prospect,' I said, 'but can it be done in the near future and won't it be competing with local housing needs?'

He answered, 'The Council has a surplus of estate shops on small parades: we cannot let them easily. We shall be glad to have one looked after by you and you will be benefiting the people on the estate.'

He was as good as his word and less than a year later, in September 1994 the shop front had been made into a fine room for therapy, group work, seminars and other meetings, and large enough to take a class of 12 – 16. At the back, with a separate entrance, was an office with a sink and cupboards and ample electric points: and next to it a small, quiet room for counselling, opposite a loo equipped for the disabled too. The shop had problems arising from its position – good for access but exposed to shoppers and inviting football practice against its front and the attention of intrusive youngsters. We tried engagement with them and with the District Council's support an evening club was set up; but older children molested the younger so it was closed down. Really the counselling and training functions did not mix well with youth work. Later the Council offered us the flat above, which has its own front door, a lot more space – and no high jinks.

So we had to take the rough with the smooth, the hardest being the loss of our colleagues. When the training began, an Ipswich student, Ros Dalrymple, had transferred to Waveney because she lived in Lowestoft. She soon became a competent counsellor and took increasing interest in the way the Service was run. In 1996 she accepted our invitation to become Manager and Simon, our Deputy Director later wrote: 'Most of us have at least one memory of the caring manner in which Ros always responded to queries and crises, whether coming from receptionists or counsellors (or externally). Few, however, will realize just how much energy she expended on developing the systems which keep the WCS afloat.' And this energy was being seriously undermined by cancer. When it first struck she had made a good recovery after chemotherapy, but slowly it reappeared and I could see her gradual loss of power in 1997. It was agonizingly difficult to know whether I should relieve her of work or, as she continually insisted, let her shoulder the whole burden because 'it made her feel good'. When it came to preparing for our application to become a WPF Affiliate it was obvious that the plethora of statements and all that was needed for the visit of the Appraisers could not be handled by one person, so we worked together – to the triumphant presentation of March 1997 and the award of Affiliate status (two years sooner than usual) that May. But as so often with the relatively young, the illness took rapid hold thereafter and I was with her in hospital the day she died: it was as though I was at Gill's bedside again. The whole Counselling Service grieved.

We had a few links with local churches. I had spoken to the Deanery Synod and other groups. From these we found some more staff, Joan Watson being a specially competent and gentle receptionist. Her vicar, John Eyre had qualified as a psychotherapist and offered to help as a reserve counsellor and then became Chairman of our Advisory Council: big in size and in personality, be brought calm and authority to our proceedings. Yet the Lord who gave, also took away: Joan suffered sudden terminal heart failure and a year or so later John returned from his usual jogging work-out and suffered the same. Perhaps it was salutary that we should not be protected from the trauma that we ministered to in other people. Certainly a parish priest who has suffered can be more empathic with his parishioners' pain. A different pain was the experience of defection when those who had urged us forward in the early days withdrew their practical encouragement. Nonetheless further encouragement came for good cheer as when the Lowestoft High Street GP Practice opened their surgery to us and Dr Simon Prince became a powerful advocate, eventually helping us to benefit from the new Primary Care Groups.

In 1996 to 1997 Wynn and I had also suffered family losses. Throughout the '90s we had regularly travelled to be with her mother Joan and my sister Pat for short spells. Both were failing, Joan with decreasing mobility and loss of weight, Pat with severe haemorrhages, which her home staff were adept at staunching even in the middle of the night, but which usually led to a period in a local hospital. I cannot speak too highly of her wonderful team of helpers, Paddy, Betty, Anne and Michael. She had a particularly bad time after Christmas '95 and we went down to be with her: it was touching how much she appreciated a little spiritual ministration, and I felt much closer to her again. Soon afterwards she had to be readmitted to hospital and on February 27th 1996, sitting out beside her bed, she asked for a cup of tea. When it was brought she had already died. After so much pain and so many agonizing crises this was a blessed end. Her daughters, Monica and Lucy, and her household prepared a memorable and meaningful service in Miserden Church attended by a vast number of friends.

Rightly, I am sure, Monica went ahead with her planned wedding to Mathis Buttiker in July that year – also at St Andrew's Miserden. She and Lucy continued to work in London, but when Lucy also married a Swiss, not surprisingly they began to reorientate their lives to Basel. In January 1999 Pat's first natural grandchild Max was born (she had been a fond grandmother to Sam's grandchildren by his first marriage). Happily we could enjoy the girls' lively and stimulating company from time to time.

On April 8th 1997 Wynn's mother Joan, also died peacefully. She had seen her great grandchildren increase to fourteen. Her eightieth birthday had been a very cheerful celebration with each of the twelve grandchildren making a speech. Timothy, as a student of Pure Mathematics, congratulated her on her mathematical originality: when asking for another glass of her evening tipple she always said, 'I'll have the second *half*': so $1 + 1 = 1$.

In 1995 I had retired from the Ipswich Directorship, and in 1996 from the Diocesan Advisership, remaining only as the Director and the Counselling Co-ordinator of Waveney. I was keen to lose at least one of these jobs and the WPF appraisers had urged that they should be divided, but no replacements were forthcoming. So at the end of 1996 I gave a year's notice. I had admirable back up from Simon Raven, the Deputy Director, but he was surprised by my declining to take the chair at the first committee in 1998. To be honest I had almost forgotten my 'resignation', such was the grip of habit and the force of everyone else's expectations, but a break had to be made. He proved a really admirable successor and initiated new Service Agreements with big firms, notably Shell.

Meantime I had to soldier on as head of counselling, until with happy synchronicity in the spring Ruth McCabe moved to a nearby village, and, having worked for the Writtle Affiliate, sought us out. The Counselling Co-ordinatorship was slightly more than she had bargained for and we could not offer a full professional 'going rate', but in partnership with me she gradually learnt the job until she took over at the end of 1998. For me the new year brought a heady sense of freedom as I retained no more than a seat on the Advisory Council, a general consultancy and a few private cases.

In ten years the WCS had trained well over a hundred students (fifty-one in 1992 alone), and had about eighty clients in counselling at any one time, two thirds referred by GPs, about a quarter from hospitals and Social Services, and the rest (an increasing category) referring themselves. Usually about a fifth have been in counselling for over a year (with severe depression or personality problems) and another fifth for six months and over. Now more are being seen through service agreements with large organizations, including youngsters from schools. It is exciting to see these developments, but I am glad to be without client responsibilities, though I miss the teaching and rejoiced when the local churches asked me to train a group of sixteen parishioners in listening skills and bereavement visiting – with the help of an experienced WCS counsellor. Long term financial security and admin. efficiency are probably the main issues to address at present; again, I am thankful to be only an observer and occasional adviser.

However, my former colleagues, the other Diocesan Advisers, chose me to be the secretary of their professional organization which we set up in October 1998. Back in 1986 the doyen of church counselling training, Michael Jacobs, invited the English bishops to send their pastoral care and counselling advisers to consult at Launde Abbey. Only a few had earlier made such appointments; but now twenty-five bishops responded, sending representatives whose skills ranged from the experienced to the virtually untrained: but a mutually supportive and instructive ambience was realized and biennial consultations followed – nearly forty attended in 2000, showing that the hierarchy are beginning to take seriously the contribution that professional counselling can make to the effectiveness of the church.

Partly as a result of the consultations at Launde, Advisers have gained a deepened understanding of their work, faced pastoral issues before they became general (like concerns arising from women's ordination and same sex relationships) and also looked at such general but often overlooked issues as the handling of anger, of boundaries, of fear of 'failure', and of confidentiality, in the church. A booklet on Standards of Practice was produced, widely circulated (though not widely observed as yet): and a crucial section of this has appeared in the church's report 'A Time to Heal'. The booklet also set out a comprehensive job description for Advisers in the belief that the church should recognize that properly qualified people (lay or clerical) need to be appointed to monitor the quality of pastoral care, to see to the provision of counselling and training for counselling or listening skills, to network amongst carers and disseminate information about sources of support and referral, to promote greater respect for confidentiality in this field, to encourage professional supervision of carers and, in particular to look after the pastoral needs of the clergy and their families.

In 1994 Bishop Peter Selby began to take an interest in these ideas and gradually increased his support until he has become an official link between Advisers and the House of Bishops. Others of the hierarchy have attended or spoken at Launde, so it became evident that a professional association of all who were acting in the role of Adviser could give more drive and focus to our aims. Accordingly the 1998 Consultation formally inaugurated the Association of Anglican Advisers in Pastoral Care and Counselling and adopted a constitution which I had been given the responsibility to formulate. Needless to say, all this has led to interesting and quite absorbing work, as the Association begins to learn how to address live and sometimes urgent pastoral issues as they arise, to speak on behalf of its members, and to encourage the church not to duck the implications of its pastoral calling.

Is this 'retirement' or is the daimon of compulsive cause-promotion still in the driving seat? In practice each day has its leisurely visit to beach or gorse-adorned common with the new border terrier, reading and writing mainly for pleasure (but inevitably some business): leading and participating in groups for bible study and for meditation, for the enjoyment of music and theatre, or simply for human exchange; delighting in the heavenly, yet thoroughly earthy group of our church neighbours either as fellow communicant or celebrating priest in the inexpressible wonder of the eucharist, all accompanied by the amazing gifts of wife, family and friends.

Looking back, as I travel into the future, I know certain prime causes will always capture my concern and commitment (at present the appalling increase of world poverty, amongst children here and amongst all ages globally, and the dangerous power of multinational business). There will always be prime people either with me already or appearing on the horizon to command attention, perhaps to the uttermost: but more and more the agenda will be to live in a provisional Present without anxiety – where the total uncertainty of each day is held in the utter reliability of God's Eternity: to 'kiss the joy as it flies' or embrace each cross as it is offered, in the hope that I shall do so lovingly and through Christ be ready for 'eternity's sunrise'.

After viewing my life over the rolling contours of a three quarters century I back a little less blindly into a brief future enlightened by some vision of Christ the True Word in the Jesus of history, trusting that every sparrow will fall into the everlasting arms and 'death is not extinguishing the light, but putting out the lamp because the dawn has come.'[37]

[37] Rabindranath Tagore